FLICKER

— AND —

SPARK

FLICKER AND SPARK:

A CONTEMPORARY QUEER ANTHOLOGY OF SPOKEN WORD AND POETRY

CO-EDITORS

REGIE CABICO & BRITTANY FONTE

Lowbrow
Press

Dear Reader,

I was an NYU graduate with a musical theater degree, and I quickly got tired of playing Chino from *West Side Story*. American theater had no place for me. I was not "Asian" enough for what was out there. While I considered going to law school or becoming a massage therapist, the multicultural publishing boom of the 1990s was in full throttle. Poet and AIDS activist Essex Hemphill published his collected poetry and essays, *Ceremonies,* and at a City University of New York reading, I was blown away by his bravura and political passion. I was a closeted actor and, as I wrote my poems, I knew that I could not hide my sexuality on the page. Coming out before a crowd of strangers at The Nuyorican Poets Cafe in 1993 was a big deal. Many poets remained closeted. This was before *Will & Grace*. At that time, once you were out of the closet, you couldn't go back.

My very first time at the open mic, I stepped on the Nuyorican Poets Cafe soap box and received a standing ovation. I couldn't believe or understand how and why numbers were held up after each poet read his or her work, like the Olympics. When I found out that this was a poetry slam and that there were at least two other cities doing this work, and that there was a National Slam Champion, I was hooked. The poetry slam kept me on stage. I could be me. I did not have to be a certain height or have a particular look. From The Lollapalooza stages with The Beastie Boys and George Clinton and off-stage with Courtney Love, I wrote the role for myself and performed it myself. The audience embraced my sexuality.

This was almost 20 years ago, and over the last two decades, I have seen the proliferation of openly gay poets who were bringing other shades of sexual identity to the open mics and in publishing. Bisexual, Trans, Gender-Queer, Queer, and 2 Spirit poets have pushed our ideas of sexual identity. I missed the 1990s when the annual Out Write Conference sponsored a Poetry Slam in Boston and queer poets from all over the country slammed their poetry and found new audiences and literary camaraderie and inspiration.

Starting Capturing Fire: A Queer National Spoken Word Slam & Summit with Natalie E. Illum would jump start a spoken word renaissance in Washington, DC . Some of the poets that we invited were Tara Hardy, Kit Yan, Sonya Renee Taylor, an emerging poet from San Francisco, Baruch Porras-Hernandez who began co-hosting The Legendary Queer Open Mic in San Francisco, & Chris August (our 1st Capturing Fire Slam Champion), and we opened it to other queer poets. Since then, Sarah D. Lawson has led The Beltway Slam Team, which has consistently nurtured international champions and teams in the top 5 nationally. Danielle Evennou and I host *Sparkle: A Queer Open Mic for Everybody* at Busboys & Poets to combat the homophobia and misogyny that exists in the present day spoken word art scene.

What you have before you are some of the poets who have made the first two Capturing Fires in 2010 and 2012 a pivotal underground success. Brittany Fonte's vision to bring contemporary living queer poets who are not traditionally associated with the poetry slam into the same volume with page poets, and our similar mission to make Washington, DC an international literary spoken word art capital, led to

Flicker & Spark. Sophia Walker was the first representative of Scotland to perform after signing up at The Sparkle Open Mic a few months before. Walker opened the doors to the array of inspiring poets from The United Kingdom that grace this collection. I owe a lot to Sheri-D Wilson, The Mama of Dada and Director of The Calgary Spoken Word Festival for making international connections of the spoken word in Canada, and introducing me to some of the most passionate gay poets in North America through The Banff Arts Center and her Spoken Word program that she initiated and designed.

As Brittany Fonte and I discussed the parameters of this anthology, we realized that Internet technology made queer poetry accessible, and this volume could be a passport for queer writers to share their work, to make new underground platforms across the Atlantic, and give each other voice and courage to be audacious and to be ourselves. We also knew that spoken word history was not archived. There have been poets pushing the envelope and giving back to the community. Some of these poets include Nathaniel Siegel, John Giorno, Tara Hardy, Bill Kushner, Gerry Potter and bill bisset. And we also felt it was important to highlight the younger poets who burst with queer genius: Jo Bee, Danez Smith, Max Wallis & Andre Prefontaine, to name a few, inspire me to shed my bitterness and recapture my fearlessness and edge.

I was deprived of elder queer mentors when I started to write poetry. I sometimes wonder what would have happened if the AIDS crisis did not exist. I imagine what my literary career would be like if Essex Hemphill were alive performing with us at Capturing Fire or Sparkle or The Beltway Slam. *Flicker & Spark* is an earthly call for writers to move and nurture on an intergenerational level, to share the heartbreak and celebratory and sometimes humorous and soulful moments of our lives. These sections are meant to give insight and hope to the stages and complexities of queer experience. We hope that, somehow, we can spark our way through the dark with sheer language and moxie.

Love,

Regie Cabico
Co-Editor

Dear Reader,

This collection is the product of a Capturing Fire (National Queer Spoken Word Summit and Slam, D.C.) epiphany. As I sat and watched passionate, talented queer poets read and slam one evening, I knew that there was a whole world missing on bookshelves everywhere. As a university professor, I knew many page poets, even queer ones, and taught them, though I lamented I couldn't buy their work from local bookstores. What I didn't know was the vast world of queer spoken word and slam poets who, truly, bring as much to the literary table as page poets with less tangible proof. Regie Cabico invited me into this slam world through the Capturing Fire slam and various open mic nights in D.C. Today, I believe that there needs to be a cohesion of all queer poetic artists; there needs to be a way to bind these people together in solidarity, to uplift one another and call attention to this art throughout the globe. What we do, we do because our hearts won't let us do anything else; our hearts should not be in competition, but in working towards a common goal of introducing our work to a new generation.

And so the journey began. Regie and I made lists upon lists of artists we knew we couldn't create an anthology without. We called and emailed these poets and asked them to be a part of our brainchild. The responses we got were beautiful and grateful; this was a collective vision. We quickly collected over a hundred cutting-edge poets and performers from the United States, the U.K., and Canada. Reading through the submissions made my heart soar! We needed this conversation with the world; in the face of anti-marriage legislation, we needed our stories of love. In the wake of anti-trans policies, we needed to show readers that people are people, and we love and break and live in families that don't always work, just as everyone else does. We needed to hear immigrant voices of our own community to see what is at stake for our bi-national families without protection. And, most importantly, we needed to bear our souls naked and flash our gifts without embarrassment.

So, I hope as you travel through this collection of verse you remember the necessity of diversity in our world, and note the diversity in age and geography of our queer poets, here, to teach harmony and empathy. We are in the midst of a life-changing queer tidal wave of politics and social interactions in 2013; we have seen huge changes before, and we can track our movement in our community's mind through artists like Bill Bissett, Eileen Myles, Gerry Potter, then Carol Guess, Ching-In Chen, and Jericho Brown. Finally, we can see our forming beliefs and struggles in perfect focus with our youngest poets: Dan Lau, Sam Sax, and Sophia Walker. Our queer history has challenged our laws, our ideas of morality and compassion, as war and sit-ins and crimes against humanity have in the past. This is a call to compassion and international goodwill, despite your orientation, or color, or physical ability.

In Peace,

Brittany Fonte, MFA
Co-Editor
Author of *Buddha in My Belly* and *Fighting Gravity*

TABLE OF CONTENTS

SECTION ONE: PRE-STONEWALL POETS (PRE-1970)

SECTION TWO:
STONEWALL-FIRST DIAGNOSIS OF AIDS POETS (1970-1981)

SECTION THREE:
AIDS DIAGNOSIS- BRANDON TEENA'S DEATH POETS (1982-1993)

PRE-STONEWALL

(PRE-1970)

JOEL ALLEGRETTI (U.S.A., B. 1955)

The River Styx Reconsidered as a Brook Flowing Through the Backyard of a Six-Bedroom
Home in the Suburbs

Over tea on the patio
One Thursday morning at ten,
Elise Brookshire thinks about the photo
Of her daughter Margot's old boyfriend
That she found in her husband's wallet.

Bin-Bin the Dog-Faced Boy

July Something-or-other, 1930.
Someplace in Ohio, maybe Indiana.

"Good morning," Bin-Bin greeted the fellow in the little wall mirror.
He combed his forehead, ears, cheeks and neck.
"Give the people what they pay for. A bark here, a growl and a howl there.
That's showbiz. I'm worth a hard-earned dime."

They pull in the crowds. Bin-Bin and What Is It?
and Francis-Frances the Extraordinary He + She
and The Countess Ludmilla, all 560 pounds of her,
and her husband, the Human Skeleton,
and the Human Octopus
and the Cyclops of Ceylon
and all the other Boys …
Artie the Alligator Boy
Phillip the Fish-Skin Boy
Cyril the Snake Boy.

In a couple of hours, the rural hordes will tramp the midway to the tent of curiosities,
those peanut-crunching, licorice-chewing, cola-guzzling, jawbreaker-sucking pigeons,
come to stare, gawk, gape, gaze, point, joke, wince, cringe, recoil and generally look aghast
39 years before Tiny Tim and Miss Vicki
exchanged vows on *The Tonight Show*,
67 years before "My Boyfriend is a Girl"
aired on Jerry Springer's talk show
and 80 years before Snooki
inked the contract for her book deal.

The Bob Crane Poem

A single hit TV series that's older
than the Beatles' breakup,
a bit part on Dick Van Dyke's show,
a supporting role on Donna Reed's,
a one-star Disney movie.

You, Bob, were footnote bound,
but sex and murder kept you in the text.
You were luckier than most, though.
You rated a bio-pic, and let's be honest.
Greg Kinnear is better looking.

DAVID BATEMAN (CANADA, B. 1956)

Blood Simile- Like a Buffalo

the first person he ever loved
was a Canadian expatriate
living in Buffalo
and working at a Ford Motor plant - shift work
transferred from Brantford Ontario
in the early 1960's

one wife, two daughters
his wife had a twin sister
it was a perfect transnational
border-crossing life
shot through with the conflict
of being a gay man trapped in a straight man's body

like wallpaper in a pup tent
like pillows in a rock garden
like swag lamps hung from cliffs
like diamonds in the mud
like caterpillar soup
like rust on a crinoline

like children in a smoky room
like cigarette butts in a piece of half-eaten birthday cake
like clowns at a funeral
like promiscuity at a wedding
like chastity at an orgy
like sex in a chapel

like nuns in a speakeasy
like sequins in the war
like boas in the rain
like mink stoles at the zoo
like monkeys in a rage
like ferrets in a huff

like lemmings gone astray
like fire and hay
like a stack of bibles holding open doors
like a party girl in a room full of bores
like crystal bulls in china shops
like vegetarian matadors
like a postcard of a buffalo
with words printed on the back

claiming that the word buffalo was a mispronunciation
by aboriginals when the French settlers
looked at the Niagara River and said "beau fleuve"
and natives thought they had said buffalo

a city borne of something that it isn't
a marriage born of something that it couldn't be
a beautiful river that drops suddenly
into the butt end of an overflowing escarpment
like his mother's twin sister
married to the first man he ever loved

a Canadian expatriate - a beautiful river of misidentified love...

like a white buffalo

Why did you have to Go Through a Car Wash on the Way to our Mother's Funeral?

why did you have to go through a car wash
on the way to our mother's funeral?
I have tried to love you for such a long time
and have succeeded at every turn
but this really takes the cake
I may not be able to get through this one
without serious long-term therapy

It was like being encased in a single soapy teardrop
with your only living relative
from your immediate family
sitting beside you & listening to the radio
inside that teardrop

like a simile wrapping itself around you
without a scrap of mercy
just pulling you carelessly
through an aisle of chemically disenchanted
cleaning products

hoses and brushes like giant tentacles
ripping away grimy manes of protective veneer
laced with gloom and greyness
I didn't spend all those years cultivating melancholia
a clear and present sadness
gripping my body like emotional barnacles of doom
just to have them threatened
by an over-mechanized
shower for automobiles!

and then we came out of the goddamn car wash
and you had to pull over to the side
of the parking lot
spending twenty minutes vacuuming
the interior of the car

I asked you to back over me first
I would gladly lie down on the asphalt and die
if you would only answer my single prayer
"get me out of here!!!"

but you couldn't hear me over the hummmmmm of the
other car wash patrons' gentle roar, not to mention the
whirrrr of the vacuum cleaner you wielded in every living
surface nook and cranny
of your filthy jalopy

but did I say a thing? did I complain?
no, I just sat there silently, listening to the radio,
suppressing tears, cursing conception
and the rise of brotherly love

I love you a lot
but I love pretentious cafés more
overpriced appetizers
outlandishly small entrees served in the middle of a pristine
white plate
smeared elegantly with pureed broccoli
sour apple martinis with a slice of
green apple on the rim
and people who know enough not to take me with them
to the car wash
on the way to my mother's funeral

I know that she was your mother too
for four years longer than she was mine
and that she went a lot of places with you
and that you might have resented my moving in
to your old womb

windowless, reddish walls, veiny and damp
only four years after you had left
but let me tell you, it was no picnic!
and I know that you took her to the last movie she ever saw,
The Titanic

and I refused to go because I knew how it ended
and I hate re-makes
and computer generated romance
but I do not think that anything I have ever done
warrants your unspoken
perhaps unconscious belief
that I would ever have any desire whatsoever
to accompany you
to the car wash
on the way to our mother's funeral

and then, when that spurt of murky water shot
through a tiny crack
in the passenger's front seat window
and laced my secondhand tuxedo jacket
with a delicate spattering of tarnished droplets

I saw a tiny bubbly rainbow
laughing in the rear view mirror
and it peeked its arched prismatic head
through the little crack in the window, and said
"Cheer up, old friend
a car wash is good for the soul"

and then it spit in my face and disappeared
in a flood of Ark like proportions
I think I even saw pairs of animals of every kind
flee from the car wash at that moment

it was a terrible and needless urban apocalypse
and I did not appreciate being a part of it
but I did hear the most beautiful version of
My Bonny Lies Over the Ocean
on the radio during that car wash
and sang it softly to myself for days after
as comfort against the piercing sadness
over our mother's death
a sadness that at times I felt
I would never pass through
in one piece or even alive
but I did, and I both blame and applaud you for that

you stripped me clean
brandished unconscious mechanized love
all around me that day
like a tattered war-torn filthy flag
being waved and flung mindlessly
in a wet & terrible storm

When you took me
in your usual vehicle
to the car wash
on a day full of tears
on the way to our mother's funeral
drenched with remorse
at the end of the world

BILL BISSETT (CANADA, B. 1939)

what brings abt th suddn quiet manfred

what brings abt th suddn quiet in th middul uv morn
ing tai chi
waking up waking up   all th voices klanging wanting
ovr
  whelmd with multi tasking hi shrieking what did
religyun
      dew did it uplidt us destroy us all th mewsik
    in
th worlds our soddn teknolojeez n allegianses ahh
th
    towr uv babell why cant peopul love all th diffren
ses
  reelee love all th diffrenses n leev evreewun alone
    th
glans on th clock towr th lites going on n off on th
        keybord th realitee bord thru transmittrs rock   closures   cud i find yu in all ths
xciting disharmon
ee
  or th disturbing agreementz   we ar now byond
  content byond byond in
        denial uv denial
      byond in fakt wher
    th tremorings reveels all th
    lettrs writtn at midnite
        out on th palace wall
    i saw yu rushing 2 th
    northern libraree 2
        meet sumwun
  2 tell sumwun a secret abt sum
    wun politiks n fakts hyperbolee
      n th last matadora sighing as
  if th upside down lake reflekting
      upon all uv us   wer enuff

speeking uv environmental issews

i dont think its fair uv peopul trying 2 stop
fish from farming dew yu why ar peopul

sew mad at say salmon farming isint that
gud 4 th salmon all th xercise in th work n

opn air wunt farming make salmon stronger
mor agile mor full uv nutrients 4 us 2
benefit if peopul dont want 2 farm themselvs
aneemor why not let salmon dew th farming

why stop th salmon from farming isint that
theyr decisyun 2 make n wudint it b gud 4 all
konsernd

tho it cud b sd how cud salmon farm on
theyr fins 2 push th ploughs etsetera can
they bcum primates n if not can they reelee
farm on theyr backs as sum claim can yu

imagine salmon floundring as sew manee
peopul have farmd on theyr backs or was
that farming

sout refuge in an abandond car

outside uv waa waa   hitch hiking in a blinding   snow
            storm our hands frozn 2gethr ser wer our lips whn
they found us n hosed us down we made a run 4 it well
            b4 spring brek up inishulee tho we wer   on xhibit
as th best ice skulptur uv th yeer th first time 2 men
            wer shown kissing in ice in wa wa n thn in kenora
wher we wer also displayd that town another hell 4
            hitch hikrs b4 we meltid n cud breeth agen
th full moon in april a huge hole in th sky th world
                                        cud fall thru

nites undr th silvr pier

chattring voices frm th next
door ovr   a template thru th hot
nite   tree houses and whethr we have
relee   choises ovr our opsyuns
n can we know all our opsyuns   yes
n theyr results   n yes   n hello

does what happns   happn bcoz we
want it 2   duz it   if it happns   is all
redee happning   in the works   n we
obsess   pointlesslee   abt the narrativ
interpretaysyuns   regardless uv our
lost   n doomd   intensyunaliteez

whil he wuz wundring these qwestyuns
abt haunting   or plesurabul raiment ovr
still sturdee n not yet brittul bones   n
romanse   loving th almost militaree
monagameez   n puritanisms   n xcesses
n spiritual   omms   n our cumming 2gethr
again   yr beautiful bodee in my wundring arms

undr th silvr pier wher othrs as well cum
thru th watr   n sun   n ocean drenchd beems
sighing   hooking up   moons in our eyes
strong   n swaying   all th multiplisiteez
evreewher   grass mountin medow   desert
lake   rivr   n see front   flying   flying   thru
sew manee time   zones   ice floes

bombs wer falling all around   n th elites
wer holding us all up   th elite has veree
big guns   can onlee b witness

JEFFERY CONWAY (U.S.A., B. 1964)

Teen Angel

(Season 3, Episode 64, Airdate February 28, 1979)

A knuckle hit my thigh. *"Charlie's Angels* is gay," my brother sneered—
his attempt to start a battle with a younger male over finite TV territory.
My three older sisters, zigzagging between two worlds, threatened all-out war
amid the orange shag and fake wood-grain paneling of our TV room.
The channel stayed put and four of us (at least) weaved ourselves
back into the power of female figures onscreen:

Patty Cantwell has been strangled—murdered!—at Blackmoor College.
The Angels are deployed. Kris Monroe goes undercover as a new student;
Kelly and Sabrina join the faculty. Meanwhile, in the horse barn
at the edge of campus, diabolical Donna distributes bottles of booze,
"happy pills" & downers to her "salesgirls."

I was starved for that all-girl world. At Los Altos Junior High,
I'd planted myself in the middle of my school's female alphas,
where Jackie Pruter (staggering feathered hair, stuffed bra)
reigned supreme, gave orders to her minions:
Heather Persons, Julie, Sheri, Beth, Barbie, Lori, and Lynette Laffoon.
The snobs. The cheerleaders. There was nothing like being
that close to Jackie, breathing in the scent of her
Lip Smackers (watermelon, strawberry), nothing like an invitation
to her house, a plush one-story with pool in Rancho Thomás.
Envied by all the guys, I posed happily at her side for trophy photos
for the 1979 Trojan yearbook.

My brother pinched my forearm, determined to sever
my connection with the Angels.

Kris, Kelly, and Sabrina try to break Donna's grip
on Cissy and Bo, her fembot pushers/SS-like fashion guards.
Bo is caught cheating in Miss Garrett's English class, while
Kris discovers that Cissy is a kleptomaniac.

At school, Jackie Pruter felt the heat: Our principal got
a call from a concerned mom—charges of drinking and
pot smoking, of coercion, intimidation.
One of Jackie's pack (Heather) had let it slip
to her lone smack (read: bookish) friend Lisa Casey
what was going on at Jackie's after-school swim parties.
It was the talk of the halls for weeks. Poor Lisa (wire-rimmed
glasses, stringy hair) could kiss any hope of a future good-bye.

I sang along to the Jordache Jeans jingle as my sisters acted out
strutting across a disco floor, just like the girl in the commercial.

"You're such a fag," my brother said matter-of-factly.
After the break, Miss Duncan asks Kris to model
for the other students in art class, so she sits
on a stool and poses. But Donna doesn't like the angle,
says she needs to adjust Kris's position, slinks toward her, slyly
twists and yanks a clump of the youngest Angel's long blonde hair.
Donna sketches an unflattering drawing of Kris.
"Looks like the Creature from the Black Lagoon!" laments super-pissed
Kris, hell-bent on an arrest.

Jackie Pruter, suspended for a week, simmered at home
in a hot tub of hatred while Lisa Casey underwent a make-over:
contacts, curling iron, white three-quarter-length sundress, bronze tan.
Heather Persons repelled Jackie's subjugation, became Lisa's best friend:
radiating the power of a conquering emperor, draped in jaguar skins
(cowl-neck sweater, tweed blazer, and high-heeled pink Candie's),
she swapped locker combos with the band geek turned teen angel.
Desperate to secure a place in the new school order (and a much-needed
cover), I asked Lisa Casey to go steady.

Donna locks the Angels in the barn, tries to burn them alive
but Sabrina figures a way out, of course, and leads the interrogation
of demonized predators Cissy and Bo, who claim they were
routinely blackmailed by Donna, a daredevil who delighted in sadism.
Accomplices to attempted murder? "*That* was all Donna!"
Their defiant, now defunct leader keeps her up-turned nose high,
reveals the true identity of the killer. Turns out it's Victor
the maintenance man who strangled Patty Cantwell with
pantyhose (apparently just for kicks—sick) and at this moment
he's taking Kelly hostage, peeling away from campus in a jeep.
Brie hops on a motorcycle (with Kris in sidecar), in hot pursuit.
Victor rolls the jeep; Kris leaps with pistol drawn, tackles him:
"Guess what Victor, you just flunked out of Blackmoor."

"That's so fake," my brother yelled.
"Shut up!" my sisters hollered.
"Yeah, cram it," I added, emboldened.
He kicked me: "You're a big girl. And anyway,
the Angels can't really do all that stuff.
Those are just big bull-dyke stunt doubles in wigs."

Jackie Pruter returned to Los Altos, quickly gained weight and was
haunted by a rumor she had to see a child psychologist once a week.

Back at the Townsend Agency, Charlie, over intercom, coos,
"Good work, Angels." The girls and Bosley open gifts from the president
of Blackmoor—graduation caps, declaring them honorary graduates.
"It's not my style," quips Kelly; "Yeah, it's kind of *square*," Kris smirks.
"Graduate of a girls' school?" asks a befuddled Bosley, shooing the tassel
out of his eyes. "How am I going to tell *that* to the guys in the locker room?"

Dead Poet

You wrote in a poem something
I often think about—countless encounters
with men and that with each you felt
"a kind of love." Wish I never
read that—truth hurts, love hurts—
and here's my idea of death,
which *isn't* a cliché, or at least
I haven't heard it (though as you
know, in this day, chances are someone's
already said it), but here goes anyway:
The dead know everything, or have the option to.
You sit up there and watch a kind of big screen
TV with billions of channels—one for each of us
bores here on earth. I'm sure you haven't
tuned into my station, but if you had
a few months ago, there I was
minding my own on a nude beach
under the harshest sun when he crossed my path
wrapped in a pink (I know) towel.
He sat down and I moved closer.
The rest, dear dead poet, is Jeffery history.
One afternoon spent naked on the highest dune,
drenched in Skin-So-Soft (horrible flies),
with a man so beautiful and kind
that even *I* had to wonder
if we'd really been there at all.
But the next day, there was his number
on a piece of scrap paper and the memory of him
placing it in my hand: "Just in case," he'd said.

Two months later: He's standing in front of me
(because I called)—his eyes so blue even
in the dark—asking "Why now?"
One can't whisper, "Because I felt
'a kind of love.'" But you know that
because you're dead, and you see clearly
how we mortals fill our lives with work, and bills
(even though we work), and daily gum care,
and the gym, and our parents who despise
everything we do, and relationships
with really good people, with marginal types,
with losers, with alternate side of the street parking,
laundry, the food shopping,
and the freakin' dishes day in and day out,
the mail, e-mail, with reading for classes
we don't like but "have to" take, reading
to stay smart, or get smart—oh yeah,
keeping up with whatever is on TV so we
don't feel out-of-it, or old, like with music,
which we love, but can't help feel pressure
from the board of directors in our head
to know and form an opinion about the video.

There I was, standing a few inches
from his confused face with nothing
to say because I'm realizing
our "kind of love" was never meant to be
expressed in person, with words, down here

on earth where we buy the truth with our lives.

Sestina to a Tattooed Boy

We were talking. He said, "Excuse me," and asked the bartender for a glass
of red wine. This seemed strange for a boy
like him: ripped jeans, shaved head, and a tattoo of an angel on his perfect ass—
something I discovered later, after I'd lit three candles in my dark
bedroom. He stripped by flickering light and removed the safety-
pin from his right ear; his skin glowed like milk.

I offered him a drink. He whispered, "I'm dying for some milk."
I was drunk; my liver ached. In the kitchen I poured myself a glass
of aloe vera juice—it helped the pain inside. To be safe,
I drank two that night, hoping I wouldn't vomit booze all over the boy
in my bed. Shaking, I carried the quart of milk down the dark
hallway, opened the door to my room, and sat my ass

down on the futon. He rolled over and we kissed. There was a loud crash: "You ass-
hole!" My roommate, Michael, was screaming. I jumped, knocking the milk
carton to the floor, then fumbled my way through the dark
apartment and pushed open his door. "Heart of Glass"—
a warped tape—was playing. William, Michael's ex-boy-
friend, had picked the front door lock like a thief cracking a safe.

He'd taken his clothes off outside. "Let's fuck," he screamed, "unsafe
sex only, baby—no rubbers, let's get some ass—
everyone gets a piece—I can smell my boy's
ass anywhere!" I punched him in the nose, blood splattered like the milk
on my bedroom floor. Michael yelled, "Get out!" and threw a glass
vase containing a dead, dark

red rose. Someone was hiding in the dark
under the covers in bed. Michael ordered, "Stay there till it's safe."
I shoved William towards the door. He cut his foot on broken glass,
turned on me screaming, "Come on, I'll kick your ass!"
His blood on my hand felt like warm milk.
He took a step. "Hey Michael," he hissed, "does that boy

in bed with you know you've got AIDS?" The boy
beneath the blanket didn't move. Everyone was silent in the dark
bedroom. I threw William into the street. Rain poured like milk
from the drain pipe, drenching his pile of clothes. I slammed the door. Safe
inside my bedroom, I found the boy with the tattooed ass
up and dressed. "Don't go," I begged. "The milk—let me pour you a glass."

I ran to the kitchen, rinsed the aloe vera from my glass. When I returned, the boy
was gone. Still drunk on my ass, I fell to the bed and passed out in the dark.

The next morning I found the boy's safety-pin on the floor, in a pool of spilled milk.

GUILLERMO FILICE CASTRO (U.S.A., B. 1962)

Argentine Music

I cannot rival this piano I hear
the little twisters plunging
into dark dark chords and then up & up again so fast
    to reach
               a clearing
before this:
            If I could only suspend myself on a single violin note
like this one,
           travel to Buenos Aires with my hunger
and the rumble of a piano in my stomach.

Oh if I could only play anything like this,
a bandoneón that slits through the creamy scream of strings
the tenderest knife!
that violin again   a skater cutting figures in solitude
and underneath the piano
                  a
             single phrase
        four notes   bloom
          repeatedly

I think of you, Papá.
You loathe Piazzolla and yet resemble him.
He wrote this piece for the passing of his own father.
You're well and alone, 70 years old,
               in that new house,
and it rains with the fury
of tango steps.
A bottle of wine on your table.
The ghost of dogs and a tool shack
with instruments I wouldn't know
how to use.

The main theme is back—
Piazzolla and his bandoneón unfurl
            breath in and   out
out and extended, a bridge.
          Papá,
a son of your traditions,
you combed your hair in the reflection
of fag-cleared streets.
        I want you to feel it,

please really listen
      the lick of Piazzolla's fingers
      on the bandoneón's slick buttons
                      and now
         the urgency
            the emergency
a rupture in the structure of the bridge
a near collapse,
               his entire band an exquisite machinery
  carrying out melancholy's orders:
     Get drunk on this!
                    Maybe we're bound for disaster, Papá,
maybe we'll never understand

Ode to Lindsay Wagner as 'The Bionic Woman'

Lindsay
because your slow-
motioned sprints
Seasons 1 to 3
made me happy
I used to do something
involving
tongue
and the back
of my throat
to approximate
the odd clicking noise
accompanying those
leaps and bending of iron
Julio said
I sounded like
a dolphin using echolocation
and I said
Finally
you got
your chance
to use a big word
anyhow Lindsay I loved
your grimace
lips bracing tight
against teeth
in a show
of strain
despite
all the aid
from your costly
fictional
limbs
yet
what was hard-
er to copy
how
your whole body
winched upward with each
short stride
as though yanked
by parachute strings
which now makes sense
you might say
female
agents
are never
truly free

oh the irony to what Julio
sneered
Meh
you run
like a
girl
and I lisped
You punch
like one
letting him
come
after me
with the zeal of an Español-
dubbed fembot
who still falls down all that power
notwithstanding
oh Lindsay
you might agree
back then
the self
seemed greedy for a good
wreck
because some-
one
was always
there
to fix it
as they fixed you
or so we thought
under clouds
greying fast
like the cast
on Julio's
arm

You Wake Up

You wake up	an amnesiac
You wake up	to the sounds of construction
You wake up	in a crane with LULL painted on either side
You wake up	in the middle of the night when the engine of the mind cranks its chainsaw
You wake up	in the acid reflux of Jesus
You wake up	past your stop
You wake up	near the blocked exit door
You wake up	after sticking your hands in a minor's pants
You wake up	on the train to Dismal Boulevard
You wake up	Sleeping Beauty with a bitch slap which she promptly returns
You wake up	cadavers
You wake up	encased in ice
You wake up	as a homophobic youth in the 1950's and again in present times
You wake up	as a butterfly inside Walt Whitman's freshly fingered beard
You wake up	when Hades barks only the ugliest of people are the most ill-mannered
You wake up	and reach for the gun your old man used on himself
You wake up	in the shower with your formerly graceful self reflected on the spouts
You wake up	and release frantic bubbles in the sobering places where you drown
You wake up	bang
You wake up	caught in a rain of ashen fedoras
You wake up	under the terrible gaze of cancer
You wake up	like the cod fish amongst the meats on your boss's grill
You wake up	equal in worth and weight to Third World currency
You wake up	there's a burglar fiddling with your lock
You wake up	wrapped in scarves that unfold like the largest foreskin this side of Brazil
You wake up	on an L-shaped red sofa with vomit snared in your chest hair
You wake up	and float in the timorous light coming from the moon
You wake up	a drone in flight
You wake up	amid untold dead
You wake up	keenly aware a member of Al Qaeda's slipping inside your garage
You wake up	the Marines
You wake up	but they remind you of all the men who refused you a kiss
You wake up	L-shaped a red bitch with bangs
You wake up	in America
You wake up	terrible gaze freshly fingered
You wake up	Beauty's crane beard
You wake up	America
You wake up	timorous icy moon vomit
You wake up	bang and LULL
You wake up	America
You wake up	the mind and the gun
You wake up	and forget
You wake up	America
You wake up	the gun the gun the gun

THERESA DAVIS (U.S.A., B. 1965)

Because She Thinks She is Going to Hell

honey,

you are not being judged
because your bones decided
maybe in a moment unplanned
to rest near my bones
passion has no punishment
except the ones
we place upon our own hearts
we were runaway trains that night
and I was wearing my voice
just the right decibel
you never stood a chance
besides, I understand those urges
that make you question things
like sexuality and I want to know
what this feels like
regret doesn't live in my heart
it simply can't afford the rent
and I am no test dummy
no one takes advantage of me
without my permission
if your tongue is tied
my prayer is that your thoughts are not

I am drawn to all things beautiful
and like it or not you were
you are beautiful
but,
we were a head on collision that night
and I never saw you coming
well,

until I did

Like-Like

When she touches me the way she touches me.

I like it. I tell her, I like it. I say I'd like-like more, please.
"Like-Like?" her smile is a question.

So I explain to her as it was explained to me by my
twelve year old son sees there are two kinds of like.
There is like and there is like-like. Like is, "I like you."
Like-like is, "Yeah, I LIKE you."
He is explaining the phenomenon of "like" to me
because he like-likes a girl at school. He tells me how
pretty she is, how they sat together at lunch
and had a conversation. She is so smart and,
she is so nice. I like-like her.

My heart swells, crashes partly because he is more like me
than I imagined, and mostly because he is more like me
than he knows. I am also a sucker for a pretty,
smart girl who eats food and can have a conversation.
I also sweep up the shatter that is my heart
every time a girl breaks it. My son will have his heart broken a lot.
He is just like his mother.

I want to warn him. Explain what the hopeless
in hopeless romantic really means, but I don't really
believe that shit. I refuse to believe that romance,
in love or like-like, is hopeless. I love the way his face
breaks open when he talks about sharing ideas
with this girl he like-likes. The way he wants to give her art.
I don't care that he uses all of my paint. He wants to give her art.
He is just like his mother. He gives her art, and he + art
is his heart and she will break it.

When it happens we will snuggle on the couch,
eat comfort food as we commiserate. I will have ice cream
he will eat those Cheetos that bear no resemblance
to any color on the wheel. We will hold each other up.
The way he held me up when heartbreak just looked like
mom is sad.

The day he comes home and tells me the girl refused his gift.
He calls his hard work, his consideration, and his art junk.
He tells me he is stupid and that he wishes he could have
known somehow that she didn't like-like him the way
he like-liked her. I ask if I can have his heart.
His art. I tell him I like-like him just fine. I wonder if this will jade him.
Before I can get too lost in that thought he tells me about the girl
who sits next to him in science. "She's pretty mom. I like her."
He will like-like her soon, because he is so full of hope.
He is just like your mother.

After the story, my girl whispers in my ear,
tells me she like-likes me, a giggle on her tongue.
I know she will break my heart, but I have hope.

I am just like my son. I simply smile back. Tell her
I like-like her too and I'd like-like more, please.

RON DRUMMOND (U.S.A., B. 1955)

Why I Kick at Night

I kick in my sleep because I haven't yet figured out how to sing in my sleep.
If they're high kicks, I'm auditioning for the Rockettes or the June Taylor Dancers.
If they're side to side with a lot of running in between, I'm making up for all the time
    I spent benched in junior high school soccer.
I have strong calves and I sit in a chair most of the day. And I'm mad about
    the chair part.
Actually, I'm lazy and I kick because I don't have to leave the bed to do it.
My twin brother Rob and I first communicated in the womb with our feet.
    I'm the older twin. Rob claims he kicked me out.
I used to kick more often when I ate chocolate and drank coffee and alcohol.
    I could kick myself for giving them up.
Sandi says I kick to annoy Terry, says I'm acting out some kind of hostility.
Michael says I kick to annoy Sandi.
Terry knows when I first started kicking. He says it's my HIV medication.
I say I kick because Michael's heart is troubling him and Bruce has lost an eye and
    I've lost too many friends, and because the two times I've been called a faggot
        I've also been punched in the face and twice in one life is enough, thank you.
Kicking warms my bony feet. I envy the meaty padding on Terry's insteps and heels,
    the cushiony undersides of his toes.
Maybe I'm too quiet during the day or I don't write enough, or lie when I do.
Did you know that old people kick a lot in their sleep?
I worry that the kicks mean something is wrong with my nervous system.
My parents smoked when I was little. But that's too easy.
I kick in my sleep because I've learned that if you kick a desk when you're awake,
    you can break a toe.
I kick because I don't want to be asleep. There's a party outside my bedroom
    and there's singing at the piano and I hear my older brothers and sisters laughing.
Stay trim! Kick! Like that diet that says all you have to do is drink this miracle liquid
    five hours before bedtime and eat nothing till morning.
I'm kicking bad habits, kicking up a fuss, kicking the devil in the teeth
    and Richard Nixon when he's down.
I'm kicking my Stingray's kickstand to set a land speed record.
I must get a kick out of it, kicking.
Sometimes I kick to wake Ter up so we can stick our tongues down each other's throats
    and I can feel his legs wrap around me and we can coast without pedals downhill.
Or because I have to take a piss. I can wake myself up if I kick hard enough.
Or because I have shrunken my world to a world of symptoms
    and my feet are saying: *Break out!*
I kick in my sleep because so far death seems to be able to take the subtle hint,
    although Terry reminds me: *Honey, everything's not about dying.*
        And when people say you're looking good, they really mean it.
Paul tells me my kicks are prayers not put into words, unuttered groanings
    that can't be heard. It's all a gift. Amen to Paul.
Kick because you can, I say.

DAPHNE GOTTLIEB (U.S.A., B. 1968)

in praise of weeds

I wish I did not know your name, Paige Clay,
CeCe McDonald, Brandy Martell,
and Brandon, to have yours fade
like things do in the rain. Or to find all the names, all
of them lost to sharp things, things that bang
and things that hit. The other things used against you:
Your hands. Your head. Your brilliance. Their laws.

Hate goes between the legs first. When it finds what it wants,
it rips. Hate does not like surprises. When there's no gash,
it rips its own. With bullets. With razors. With the pink
and blue blankets. With the doctor. The police.
The body bag. With the image the image amen.

CeCe, if the scissors were theirs,
we would have known where to look
for the cut.

Krissy Bates, Tyra Trent, Marcal Camero Tye,
Miss Nate Nate, Lashai McLean, Camila Guzman,
Norma Hurtado, I wish I did not know your names.
Hate builds things with such hard edges,
says either, says or, says asphalt, says concrete,
says everything so hard it is a bullet, it is a gun:

I wish I did not know
your names, Toni Alston, Faith Iman: shot in the head,
Taysia Elzy, Foxy Ivy: shot in the head.
Brian McGlothin, Adolphus Simmons:
Tell me your real names/shot in the head
Patricia Murphy, Stacy Brown,
Ashley Sweeney: shot in the head.
Lawrence King, Simmie Williams Jr.,
Oscar Mosqueda, Christopher Jermaine Scott:
no, your real names/shot in the head
Victoria Carmen White,
Duanna Johnson, Lateisha Green,
Ebony Whitaker, Nakhia Williams: shot in the head

Hate builds things with such hard edges,
either/or, but there is the slash in between,
and that is how grass breaks the sidewalk,
the soft ripple of skin or the new tremble of hair,
to choose who to love and how to mean the body

in the shadow of the valley,
so that even now, in the name of Angie Zapata
and her fractured skull, of Dee Green,
bleeding famous to death in the street,
of Faith Iman, stabbed and burned

into the headlines, the click of heels
on the sidewalk, the sidewalk
cracked by grass, by sheer love
of the sun and the audacity
to reach for it, the click of your heels
is your name, your laughter at night
is your name, on the streets,
in sensible shoes, on the make,
in the suburbs and on the trains
that murmur your name
that belongs to a body
that belongs to a woman
who belongs above ground,
the grass under her feet,
both of them reaching for the sun
in some better world
where we don't live.

goodbye summer

There is no summer
this year. The weather

is metaphor. If you aren't
saying something. That's all

you need to say. Keep your tongue
in your mouth. Too much summer

on your tongue can turn you. There is no
summer this year. You are all hello

but I am not making lemonade. I am not oiling myself
up. You vacation at the Cape. You send a postcard.

It says. Not much. It says. Having a time.
You were all hello on me. I drop it in a puddle.

Hello from the Cape. Hello from the Coast.
Hello from the Cake. Hello from the Cunt.

Hello. Hello.
I wish I wished you were here

to break my bed with your lure and line.
But I will not blow up my beach ball

and there is no pollen. The lake is cold
and no one is swimming. I don't care how

hello you are because it is not
summer. I have moved on. Sown and reaped. Built

a fire. Cleaned my house.
There is no summer.

I buried armloads of tomatoes and zucchini
into shallow, sordid graves.

Burned my bathing suit and danced
it into ashes under my flip-flops.

Forked the raft to shreds.

poem for the woman who read a haiku at an open mic about homeless people having sex that ended "if the shopping cart's a rocking, don't come knocking."

1.   You were a teenager.
              You had one
              condom and nowhere
              to go. This
              is nothing like that.

              Homelessness is transmitted
              through body fluids. Through sharing
              works. Through kissing, public toilets,
              through thought, through seeing.
              Don't see it. Don't touch.

              Sex is a luxury the way
              the moon is a luxury, meaning that it is
              always there but it needs time and space
              to be yours and the incontinent man
              in a wheelchair. The woman with scabies or lice
              whose pants don't close has no space.
              The two men collecting cans
              before dawn, arms caked with
              garbage cans. The immaculate
              woman working two jobs
              and sitting up all night
              in a drop-in. The man
              talking to himself,
              to the moon,
              to God.

              God is too busy
              to have genitals. God is just
              trying to survive. Desire
              has no home. The homeless
              have bodies. Is there love
              during wartime and is this anything
              else?

2.   Nothing was rocking.
              There was no door to knock. The woman
              was raped. The police report and so what.
              Move the body from the center
              to the side. Now move the body
              farther.

              Move it harder. Move the body across
              the city in bare feet, move it into
              the shadows, move it in police
              citations, move it into shelters
              or still in the streets
              hands together—the body
              stays warmer if it moves,

move it under blankets,
hand in hand, it's warmer,
stay close.

The raped woman is so hot
she's burning up.

Start again. That is about violence.
Not sex. Not love.
Not the moon, the silver coin
in night's palm, a hand
that can hold and kiss
and in doorways
and alleys
and parks
and anywhere else
people will fuck.
there is desire
and sometimes love

3.   Nothing was rocking.
If you got it on you.
The body stays warmer.
Move it into the streets.
Don't come knocking.
Burn it down.

JOHN GIORNO (U.S.A., B. 1936)

God Viracocha and the Stone Giants

God Viracocha is one of many gods
who created this world,
God Viracocha is good looking,
suntanned, medium height,
almost beardless, rosy cheeks,
strong brow, and an incredibly beautiful face,
his eyes are a hook
with a shining kindness,
radiating a wonderful sexual warmth,
his voice has a deep attractive resonance,
he is wearing white cloth
tied around the waist with braided gold,
and a red mantle on his left shoulder,
he can be fiercely wrathful and a nightmare,
shy and deeply loving,
his mind is the most incredibly brilliant
being with a great pleasure,
we are on the middle floor of the three-storied
palace called the Copper Colored Mountain,
I am visiting him
and we sit together on cushions
covered with colorful, finely woven textiles
of flowers, plants and vegetables,
in a square room with stone walls
made with a special technique by the architects and builders,
who use a thick acid paste
to soften and melt the rock surfaces,
fitting the stones together seamlessly,
which harden, remaining separate,
perfectly joined,
the walls are covered with sheets of delicately embossed gold,
in high niches are bundles of treasures,
ceramics of feathered anthropomorphic shapes,
soundless repetitive reed flutes
and voiceless wisdom.

God Viracocha tells me a story
that happened a very long time ago,
before our history began,
God Viracocha came to earth,
which was a very beautiful place,
and he was enjoying himself
surrounded by his retinue,
when he saw that nobody lived here,
there were no people,
God Viracocha had a great idea,
make people,
create people from stone,
inspired by the soaring, majestic mountains,
he made stone giants,
fifty feet tall, some sixty feet,
their legs were black basalt

from the oceanic ridges of tectonic plates,
pelvises of bluestone oozing rust,
torsos of grey granite with sheens of quartz crystals,
arms of wrinkled sedimentary rock ribboned with color,
their heads were boulders
that had rolled around since the Ice Age,
their teeth were pointed peaks sharp as knives,
eyes of sapphire with diamond pupils,
God Viracocha breathed into the stones,
and they came to life,
when they walked the ground trembled
when they made love the earth shook,
God Viracocha, after all the work
and a job well done,
was tired and exhausted,
and departed for one of his glorious heaven worlds
to relax, take it easy, and have substanceless bliss,
preoccupied with divine activities,
he occasionally fondly remembered the stone giants on earth,
sent them blessings,
sometimes in the form of gold
and business opportunities,
sometimes in gusts of celestial wind filled with useless good things,
but basically forgot about them.

About five hundred years later,
God Viracocha went back to earth
curious to see what was happening with the stone giants,
it was a disaster,
the giant stone people were always fighting,
had invented all sorts of weapons
and were continuously at war with each other,
sling shots hurling boulders,
throwing spears made of fifty-foot oak trees,
rocks tied to ropes swung in circles over their heads
released as multi-projectiles,
huge bow and arrow missiles,
spiked wood clubs,
axes called neck-breakers made of stone and tipped with copper,
horrendous, mindless,
violence and cruelty,
surfing lava flowed from the volcanoes,
the stone giants crawled around on broken limbs
screaming with pain,
the earth was scorched and scarred with craters,
a wasteland,

God Viracocha was very depressed,
and started crying,
sat down on the ground
cried and cried and cried
weeping big fat tears,
the worst had happened,
he had made a big mistake,
he had given them emotions,
but forgot to give them
souls,
forgot to put love, wisdom and compassion
in their consciousnesses.

God Viracocha stood up,
put on the gold crown with the red feather headdress,
and got furious,
he raised his arm with gold star-headed spear,
and his mantle sewn with feathers burst into flames
and surrounded him with fire,
strikes of lighting and thunder,
earthquakes set off
volcanic eruptions and nuclear explosions
melting the eternal snow and ice in the Highlands,
torrential rain poured down relentlessly,
the salt sea swelled up from the ocean,
a great flood rose and covered the mountaintops,
and destroyed the stone giants,
annihilated them completely,
triumphs and disasters,
still today, you can see the remnants of the disembodied giants
broken rock thighs protruding from mountainsides,
cracked torsos embedded in hills,
stone bellies laying in valleys.

God Viracocha can see the future,
as well as the past and present,
and interned in the mountains along with the broken stone giants
are the dead from the massacres of the Conquistadors,
the army and the terrorism of the Shining Path,
executions and epidemics, car bombs and death squads,
six million people killed then and seventy thousand people killed now,
the Quechua language lost
and culture destroyed,
it was very depressing,
the very worst was true,
God Viracocha departed earth
heartbroken,
disappointed
and disgusted,
and went to one of his highest heavens
the Palace of the Union of Great Bliss,
to forget about it
and he forgot about it,
but every once and awhile for a fleeting moment,
he remembers the horror of the stone giants
and the hell he made.

God Viracocha is telling me this story,
I am visiting him in the Palace of the Copper Colored Mountain,
we are drinking,
smoking cigars and joints,
and have coca leaves in our cheeks,
talking to him is touching him,
hearing him is the warm tenderness of his embrace,
put your arms
around me, baby
hold me tight
put your arms around me, baby
hold me tight,
put your arms around me, baby, hold me tight,
warm naked skin,
huge hugs
deep kisses
feel really good,
happy
thank you
more please
happy
thank you more please
happy thank you more please
happy thank you more please,
dicks, tongues, tits and assholes
kissing in our heart minds,
substanceless amyl nitrate,
pulling free in full glory,
in one taste,
without concepts, without substance,
formless and emptiness,
cumming
makes your life longer,
a long-life blessing as a bonus,
catch
the afterglow,
an eternity in bed doing nothing,
resting in perfection.

I can feel in the mind of God Viracocha
a subtle residue
of sadness,
almost imperceptible,
the trace of something unresolved,
sure enough, shortly after,
in a spontaneous burst of curiosity,
he puts on the headdress and crown,
mounts the shoulders of his golden-winged hummingbird
and goes back to earth
to see what is happening,
he is very surprised,
it has become beautiful again,
green trees cover the mountains,
forests of flowers,
rivers of crystal clear water,
he starts laughing

laughs and laughs and laughs,
it is totally wonderful,
an earthly paradise,
but there is nobody here,
no people.

God Viracocha is an artist,
besides liking to work with stone,
he also likes sculpting with mud,
he was taught by his father Padma Sambhava,
he sat down by the lake
and started playing with the soft, wet clay,
working it quickly,
making little figures
creating small people,
splashing them with water,
working the clay with his fingers,
making men and women
in different color clays,
some skinny, some plump,
some tall, some short,
shaped their cheekbones, eyes and lips,
he painted on each the clothes they wear,
God Viracocha lovingly made
the Quechua people,
God Viracocha lovingly created
the ethnic diversity of the Quechua people,
he held them in his hands,
laughed and laughed and laughed,
and put each in their own unique place of origin,
and blew his breath into them,
wind of light went into each
becoming blood and bones
muscle and skin,
created consciousnesses,
from his heart center
radiating beams of blue light
he made their minds into a mirror
of his own primordial, empty, wisdom mind.

God Vircocha then went through the labor-intensive job
of inventing their different languages
and the qualities that suited each,
he showed them which plants to eat and which were poisonous,
and named the plants,
taught them to sing, make music and poems,
he explained how to recognize
their local gods and spirits,
build houses for them called sacred places,
and how to invite the gods and spirits
to come and enjoy themselves,
and being pragmatic
how to appease them with blood sacrifice,

God Viracocha is inherent in everything,
he comes sometimes when needed
as a shaman,
appearing as a crazy man in poor clothes
and gives them teachings,
creating chaos
when there is too much complacency
making peace
when there is too much disorder,
creating chaos
when there is too much
complacency
making peace when there is too much
disorder,
creating chaos when there is too much complacency
making peace when there is too much disorder,
trying to show them the empty, true nature of mind,
God Viracocha was very happy,
this time, he had done it perfectly,
and departed in the western direction
for the Palace of the Copper Colored Mountain.

A short time after, which is a long time in god world time,
God Viracocha had a strong feeling
about making beings from stone,
he was an artist, and liked working with stone,
he went back to the lake
and made new stone giants
with all the magnificence of the old stone giants,
making them more beautiful,
awesome taut strength in granite carved by glaciers,
bluestone draped with moss and mottled with lichen,
he gave them all the qualities of the humans,
but refined their intellectual capabilities,
gave them a relaxed enjoyment of all phenomena,
and high degrees of realization
of the empty nature of mind,
God Viracocha also knew, fortunately,
that humans and the new stone giants
could not successfully
inhabit the same world,
it was trouble,
God Viracocha magically transported the new stone giants
to an underground world of caves and crystal springs,
an underworld realm
where they stay, today
hibernating safely
as hidden treasures
waiting their turn,

when the time and conditions are right
the new stone giants will come back into this world,
when they have been properly invited,
have places to stay,
and the auspicious circumstances created,
according to recent oracles,
forecasts and the feelings of other gods,
the time is right now,
the new stone giants are coming.

The glorious God Viracocha has visited earth
many times in many forms,
when he comes here today,
it is very upsetting for him,
distressful and depressing,
he could annihilate the old stone giants,
but with great compassion
he cannot destroy the human race,
now, when you see an old woman
sitting alone in the street,
an old woman in poor clothes
waiting in a bus station, any public place,
a desolate woman
weeping tears
for the suffering created,
it is God Viracocha

visiting us.

CAROL GUESS (U.S.A., B.1968)

You sell everything you own. Force the five fingers of your only hand into your palm, fist the stone you skipped as a girl. You were a boy then. The secret of skipping was never wanting a ring. Water was home, if only inside you. The places it took you required departures, skirt after skirt, dirt under the wheels of your truck. Stuck in a ditch past Lincoln you left that, too, shirt on your back sweet as the last girl's head thrown back, bed of your truck, sky as water, blue above both of you, her legs always opening, light changing green to Walk All Ways With Walk. You wade past the logjam into the sea. *Anna, Susanna, Matilda, Marie.* What comes next? No one knows--not the red-winged blackbird, not the preacher. You enter a solitude you will never escape. A million televisions blame someone else as your beautiful country erupts into Empire. You cover your ankles and your waist with water. *Aretha, Denira, Tamika, Louise.*

We watched the girl through her open window. 45th Street was hot but she was on fire. We were thinking we should fuck her as she undressed in front of a face or a mirror. I said look at her hair, soft. You said look at her lips, bloom. We'd prepared our room: dog in her cage, silk over skylights because of the heat. You said she's sweet. I said three's sweeter. And after we'd take notes on who was better. Seattle had never been hotter. You had a bottle and I had a bottle. A building caught fire, rows of condos attached at the hip. Fire trucks slipped on glossy pavement. Water filled the moonlit basement. A man flew from a balcony into the air. Ash stained our hair and the whorls of our dresses. Water caressed us, the thick blue knife slicing away burnt boards and glass. We lit cigarettes off the burning grass and breathed smoke until the streets were clean, the dog lay dreaming, and you were mine again. Breezes fanned the trees and the tinderbox lawn. Both the window and the girl were gone.

In Nebraska the sun is a terrible lion which will chase you down the road you live on. In Nebraska you must cover your mouth when you speak of God. In Nebraska work is always hard and the temperature consults with the leaves before falling. In Nebraska words cost more than bread. In Nebraska people still listen to records, bright stacks of vinyl for weddings and funerals. Tall grasses sway like water, glint more beautifully than any river. Nebraska doesn't give a shit about New York or L.A. Nebraska has corn, wheat, and cattle. Nebraska has cakes slathered in icing so thick bakers drown at birthdays. Nebraska has an annual March for Jesus and a March for Cheeses that is not the same thing. You have learned many Nebraska lessons. You know how to cover your nose with a cloth to drown out the smell of the stockyards. You know how to bow your head before dinner, how to close the curtains before you have sex. You know how not to get killed in Nebraska. How to drive in whiteout as if parting the sea.

When you first begin thinking of leaving Nebraska the sky splits open, drowning the prairie in rain. Flat brown dirt turns to soupy mud. Your shoes sink and stick. You fall to your knees. Nebraska says, "Is this really what you want?" Nebraska says, "If you leave you can't come back." You listen carefully for some hint of grief, but Nebraska is matter-of-fact. You are packing your bags. Nebraska can take it. You whisper goodbye and Nebraska is gone.

Your new home is the highway. You roll the windows down and the music up. On the interstate food comes wrapped in plastic. You must eat with one hand, one hand on the wheel. Sometimes at night you miss Nebraska. You scrunch your pillow into a giant mouth and kiss it, saying, "Oh darling Nebraska, you big hairy bison," and other things you are ashamed to repeat in daylight. Your friends tell you not to be silly. "There are lots of cute states. Try something with hills." But you remember oceans of razor-sharp grasses. Long, flat stretches of nothing but brown. You remember the slur of stones beneath bare feet as you searched the riverbed for fossils. You remember the harvest moon staining your skin blood red.

Revival of Rosemaling

1. The Ruined Garden

Everyone lost someone in the avalanche that year. Nights, we held dances in
the ruined garden. Wolves wove the trail but stopped short of the fireline. The
mountain refused to name what it knew. When a dog, child, or mitten went missing
we wore miner's headlamps, bright sieves for thick dark. Everyone waltzed, but not
everyone tangoed. Hard-packed snow tumbled, gathering speed, eating ice farmers,
sentries, and skis. We shouted questions, but our questions stirred rocks. We had
to learn not to talk--to move mutely, we of the valley--and to bury the bodies when
spring thawed ice walls. Our dead came down perfect, red in their cheeks, palms
flexed as if resisting the pyre.

2. Marietta

No one knew about the cabin. People thought I lived in town in a wooden house
with a bright red door. No one had ever seen the house because the house wasn't
real. I lived in a cabin on the outskirts of town. I had to haul my garbage to the
dump. When someone got hurt, the ambulance came from somewhere else. No one
could see the cabin from the road, although I could see the road and the bay. No
one could see what I was doing or who I was with. All winter snow kept the shape
of snow, sirens muffled, Amtrak derailed. Llamas stumbled into the field and slept
standing up, manes brittle with frost. Once a hawk flew into the window. Once you
dressed me up as a boy. Once you came home in a stranger's coat and shook strange
snow onto the concrete floor.

3. Crown Hill

Stairs spiraled up to an attic filled with salt. We slept thin as tripwire, taut among
pillows. One night strangers stared down through the skylight. Glass divided stage
from audience. What we wanted was applause. We showed them everything, and
when it rained they never went home again. Our hands signed the story of what it
meant to be warm.

4. Field

We fled the city at night. I was distracted by your body. My suitcase chipped at
the bone in my thigh. Thieves stole doorways and sold them to trees, scrubby
oaks that grew up on the street. Beyond the factory we slept in a field littered with
swansdown, beer husks, and bees. We fed a fire to blister coyotes. We strung death
along on thinness alone.

5. Museum

The house that lived beside us is gone, replaced by concrete for a three-car garage. At the estate sale, dealers priced Norwegian dolls. We saved a squirrel from a tangle of chard. Maybe *charm* got confused with *harm* by someone like me or maybe by me. We chipped ice from boot prints to brew into tea. What did we know of strangeness? What might've saved us lived somewhere else. We hung aces from trees axed for newfangled holidays. We knit shadows from snow, leading wolves to false prey.

TARA HARDY (U.S.A., B. ?)

The Femme Alphabet

A is for the ally or asshole that it's all of our choice to pick between.
Because everyone, including me, is programmed to hate femininity.

B is for Breast...pocket, where I keep my list of assholes. Sometimes,
if they do their homework, I cross them off the list.

C is for choice and the cup of holy good luck that I came out like this,
swishy. And it stuck, despite my mother trying to beat what she mistook

for frivolity out of me. D is for Detroit, from where I learned to not hide
my sores, that everything is covered in a coat of pain, and, despite it, I was

full of music, dance music. E is for Elvis, my first crush on a femme drag
king. Unfortunately, he taught me that no matter how hot your snot,

you shouldn't go stealing other people's good shit to make yourself famous,
especially without paying a toll and givin' credit. But, oh, his girly hands,

strong jaw, and long eyelashes. F. You know what F is for and if you don't
it's 'cause I told you to stop sniffing around my back door. G is for that

spot. In the garage where I learned I liked the smell of gasoline and dirty,
dirty jeans. H is for Hornet, which is to say my tongue stinging its way out

of my overactive mouth. I is for infinity, because what some call a limiting label
is what I call the universe tied together with a loose and ever expanding string,

inside which everything, and I mean everything, is possible. J is for Joke,

my lips and tits and hems and heels have been the butt of a slew of 'em,

not to mention the target for a whole lotta exoticization. Even though, secretly,

femmes know that at the center of the gay rights tootsie pop is none other than

femininity. L is for lick. Whoops, out of order, but no worry, we femmes know

how to back track, how to rescue what's been chucked by the truly liberated

into the trash and fashion it into a functional flashy, post-modern gender fuck.

What for some is leftover, is my liberation. You see, we working class girls

get by like that, been callin' it hand-me-down way before polite society

invented the word recycle. So, officially, to back track, K is for Karl Marx who said,

"Anyone who knows anything of history knows that great social changes

are impossible without feminine upheaval." Translation: derision or disgust

for my bobbles and bells will simply convert into fuel for the revolution

that the fairer sex is destined lead. But by fair, I don't mean pale, I, M, mean

justice. Fairness. Both might mean spending as much time on the obvious link

between, say, immigrant rights and gay marriage as we do on fighting

over who's gonna throw the best party at this year's Pride Parade.

Are you kidding me? N is for numbskull. Because while we're off throwing pity

parties and suing each other over who legally owns the word "Pride"

we should be ashamed of ourselves for not even knowing where the front

line is. It's gonna go like this: immigrants, the poor, perverts. Two stones throw

and we're criminals living in a Police State, running around saying stupid shit

like, "How did they end up at my front door, I thought they were just gonna
put up that nice privacy wall at the base of our country tastefully blended

with Southwestern earth tones, and next thing I know they're arresting me for
what…possession of an implement of sodomy? But oh, what would I know

about that? O is for Of course my corset doesn't obscure my view of the obvious
fact that the right to express my gender is directly related to retaining ownership

of not only what I'm allowed to, by law, to orgasm over, but also P Profit from.
Now, it may seem like I'm off track, so let's go back to C is for Choice,

and how we oughta have the right to Choose what we do with our bodies.
Like who & how to fuck, whether or not to tuck, to keep or chuck

the contents of our uteri. Also, what to do with our tits, like glue 'em on,
stuff 'em in, push 'em up, buckle down or get rid of 'em all together.

Much like whether to have leg hair, big hair, no hair, blue hair.
Y'all get how these are about to how you own your body, and you have a right

to do what you want with it, right? Okay, so here's why it's threatening.
If we O own our bodies, then we O own labor, as well as its resulting corporate

profit. Own body, own labor, own profit. Meaning it is a brilliant oppressive design
to interrupt that formula at its outset—to fuck with body. Which is why we all

gotta knock off asshole and pick up ally, for our own damn good. Because P
is also for the pure fact that any compliance with femme bashing

is supporting the industrial enslavement of the worker. Do you need me to R
Review for that? Okay, for the last time: Pushing up my tits is my very resistance
to the corporate machine that would otherwise own me. Got it? I hope so

because I'm S, Sick of saying it. Even though, let's face it, I would be T
Terribly bored if I didn't get the opportunity to mention that the U

Underclass has always been more radical than we good liberals
have been programmed to perceive. Why? Because obscuring the V

view of the fact that femmes have been paying the price for everyone's
femininity means we don't have to sit with the fact that we are all dirty.

Translation: W Walking machines of desire who have S.E.X.X.X.
Femmes know we make people nervous because we don't apologize

for our fuckability. So, if you really want to be a femme ally, then commit
to not hide your own femininity. And repeat after me: I am fuckable.

Femmes are not to blame for this, are not responsible for the fact that we have
holes. (No, we're just the ones who are not ashamed of them.) So, maybe

the next time a girl with a swish like Elvis, looking like she might
have a hornet for a tongue, a list in her breast pocket, and a cup of holy good

luck to be the gasoline on the fire of Marxist resistance crosses your path,
you can skip the joke, forgo the exoticization, and instead go ahead and profit

from her commanding example, and loosen the ever expanding string
around your own infinity. Which is to say you can un-Z zip it!

Advice to a Young Femme

This is for any woman who's ever run a razor up her shin and not come out the other side, "Like stupid, like duped, like responsible for the oppression of women, okay?"

This is advice to a young femme dyke:

1. Your knees are not the enemy. Showing them does not mean you're stupid. Neither do hairspray nor under-wires. However, I'll advise against the nude pantyhose, especially with shorts or any shoe involving a toe thong. Also, before injuring anyone, you may want to consult a *Femme's Guide to the Universe* for how to fuck safely in fingernails.

2. People will accuse you of trying to act as straight. You look 'em right in the eye and say, "Who's stupid now? Because femmes have been carrying the cause longer than you been spelling womyn with a 'y.'" Remind them that the last time they were harassed you put your body, your pumps, your eyelashes, and the "o" of your mouth between them and danger. I once procured medicine we could not afford for my butch lover by leaning a little farther over the emergency room counter. I'd say that's selling myself for the cause. I hereby declare that I have and will put my breasts in front of whoever it takes to keep someone I love alive!

3. I, too, tried to drive like a dyke, walk like a dyke, spit like a dyke, and play softball. What I ended up with was the driving posture I'll call the "single-handed-raised-pinky," the ever seductive swagger…SWISH!, the oops-I did-it-again cleavage loogie, and cleats that sit in my closet and are simply impossible to build an outfit around.

4. Inevitably someone will suggest that the time you waste in the bathroom could be better spent on curing cancer or the advancement of astrophysics. I suggest reminding them of the time they waste sorting their recycling, curing tofu, and having to reapply, and reapply, and reapply that natural deodorant, because let's face it, it does not work! Whoever sold us that shit? It's like the pet rock for dykes. I swear, they took one look at the rainbows flying out of our asses and read, "Suckers!" right across our faces.

5. You should know how many safety pins it takes to put on the Michigan Womyn's Music Festival. No one really knows, but guaranteed the femmes will have 'em. I once saved a camping excursion by repairing an otherwise useless tent with duct tape and barrettes. (True story.) The reason we carry purses is to save your asses. Any time you need a tissue, a Tylenol, a Tuck's, a tiny tool set, or a tampon, who do you ask? A femme.

6. Do not discount other femmes as dates. Have you looked around? We're tough, we're hot, we're prepared, and we've worked a helluva lot on our internalized sexism. We've had to in order to create our unfortunately undervalued by extraordinary selves. Plus, we're great in bed. By the way, two femmes in bed together are not just waiting for a butch to come along. We're plotting.

7. When you're asked for the 300th time whether or not you cultivate any hair on your body, you just smile and say that when the revolution does come, you, too, will be glad to be rid of compulsory misogynist hegemonic paradigm (giggle). But when it comes to it, who shaves and does not shave will have nothing to do with what we put in its place. So, let's cut through all this conform to the anti-conformity bullshit. Without all that misinformed superiority between us, you just might recognize this chip on my shoulder as what ought to be your own.

TREBOR HEALEY (U.S.A., B. 1962)

These are the Places Where I am Broken

A payphone in Yosemite Valley
where I called David to tell him
I was going to be a suicide
Because I had come here to the mountains
believing
that stone was my mother
and she had turned her shoulder
and all her rivers tears

These are the places where I am broken
The Psychiatric Clinic
he convinced me to check into
There are scabs on my wrists
"I know, I know" he said
"Just try the medication, if it doesn't work
you have my blessing—do it"

These are the places where I am broken
On a street in Vancouver, Canada, when I was only 11
where my father pointed out a man walking
and said, "Look at that fag
Look at that fuckin faggot"
And I knew, I knew

These are the places
And my bedroom 3 days later
where I woke up screaming
and my legs wouldn't move
and I told my mother I was a homosexual
and she said no, no *it's just nerves*
and never remembered afterward my words

My words
My words
These are the places

On Folsom Street
where he told me that I was a pig
a white middle-class pig
And then only 2 weeks later he was gone
And turned up an OD
at the Denver City Morgue
And I have never even been to Denver
It is a place I have been broken

And I keep seeing the 6-inch scars
running up both his arms
we shared that jewelry
I see his scars in my dreams
running like the dashed line highway
out across the salt flats

I would have gone with him

The kanji tattoo on his neck
like a stamp
by the county coroner
another casualty—didn't make it
finalized
That was my stamp you bastard
That was my heart
my heart
Those were his words

And these are the places
A hospice on Diamond Street
where hundreds of faggots have died
some of them my friends
Diamonds discarded
and not all of them died like Wayne
who went like the sun
and made us all jump like crickets or frogs
so powerful was his resurrection
was his shattering glass ending

These are the places
In a courtroom
when he threw a cup of coffee at me
And he tried to strangle me
in front of the judge
And as they dragged him away
"You haven't seen the last of me"
And the violence and the court orders and arrests that
followed
in front of the gate of my house
which has become a shack glued together by tears
I had loved this broken vase

These are the places where I am broken
On the school playground
where he bullied and kicked me
calling me a fag
in front of Douglas-fir
in front of cloud
in front of sky,
in front of sun
And now none of those things can ever come unglued from
sorrow
from that moment, which is a feeling, of humiliation and loss

These are the places where I am broken

And as I break
everything around me fuses
together
The places where I have broken are the places where I am
stuck
I am not talking about entropy
I am talking about the consummation of experience and
sorrow
I am talking about fucking
I am talking about Denver and Vancouver
I am talking about the playground and Folsom Street
I am talking about a hospice and my bedroom
I am talking about a mental hospital
And I am talking about the fact
that if you lived long enough you would meet sorrow
everywhere eventually
and you wouldn't be able to stand it
You'd be like a fly in amber
and you would beg to die
God Bless entropy
I am not talking about entropy
Or the decay of Vince's OD'd body
I am talking about Vince's tattoos
I am talking about his neck and his arms
I am talking about the finality and elegance of his 6-inch scars
These are the places
I am talking about the courtroom
and the wince on Colin's face as the police cuff his wrists
because he does not know how to love
I am talking about millions of eons that made the stone of
Yosemite
I am talking about reincarnation
and the habits of hell
I am talking about yesterday fucking today
and the deformed baby that is born tomorrow
I'm not talking about entropy
God Bless entropy
I am talking about glue
And as everything falls around me
like rain and mudslide
despair builds an edifice
like a tomb
to keep me contained
to give me a home
I could not find outside
And that tomb is the place I will finally break
These are the places
And if I am Wayne
If I am Wayne
God, nothing matters now but to be Wayne
Then it will be the breaking of the husk of a seed
It will be ground
it will be soil
It will be a final place
This is the final place…
And the breaking will be as bread

Busboy Sutra

Everything about him is long
The Indian nose
The long sling of his chin
cradling the infant soul
He's got spider legs
and monkey arms
and something constant
and stable as stone
in his eyes
of long ago
brown

Long are his lips
twin bridges
cataracts of teeth
The living river inside him
I'm all wet with it

To be with him
would be to be in mountains
a long way away
To travel the river
bending and turning
back
through the steeping stones
where everything changes
to waterfalls
and great swaths
of dizzying flashing brightness
of snow
to the precipitation of him:
Great tears,
beyond emotional correlations
a rain of sparks
from those same eyes
Are they brown and stone
of planets?
Is he the whole universe after all?
I am inside him then
forever
and he in me
Some young man
I've never touched
but seen
and seen beyond
and long back behind
all these pictures
kaleidoscoping this coffee,
this red brick shop, these cars, sycamore trees, voices,
suns and moons in infinitude, mirrors facing mirrors and the
long roads born of them

And so to sleep naked in his arms
would be as if to gather all the light of the sun
spread all over and bouncing about
It would be to record the memories
of all the stars
That's how improbable
the consummation of this love
How comic
when I've found—
traveling as I've done
the towering pine-treed forests within him
the length of their shadows
echoing his eyelashes
and the ever-changing horizon
mimicked by his mouth—
that we are one inside the other
forever
and inseparable
as the brown is within his eyes
as water and stone

The universe is love made
and making
So why do I lust for him
as if we don't share that already?

There is no need for introductions then
I set him free
for we are in love regardless
of what we may either believe
and all my longing draws
a big circle
like a comet orbiting
I'd love to see him again sometime too
in a hundred years, or a million
—or tomorrow even

For now,
I sing—
for him and for me
and for all who see what I see
—this song

Shooting Star

He came like any other
In a corner sipping tea
Eyeing me
"How you doin'?" I chanced
"Okay, dude," and he kicked the chair leg opposite him
An invitation to sit

We spoke of the rain
Which led to his truck and his horses
Mostly I was fascinated by his naïveté
"I got no gaydar, dude"
He was just back from Iraq
"I was there twice"
And the shrapnel scar he shows me on his knee

"I wasn't afraid," he said defiantly
Nor am I, I think to myself
As he told me how he came home to therapy and Zoloft
The foster homes as a child
"My parents never wanted me; I was a mistake.
I joined up because *what else was I gonna do?*"

"What's the worse thing you saw?" I asked
"Charred bodies—you could still see their penises, just burnt
black things.
–Oh, and the women and children ground into the pavement
like roadkill. You know, like black stains?"
And he said it without feeling
"Did you ever shoot anybody?"
"No, we just ran over people already shot a long time ago;
I was a radio man
I think it's the wrong war
But I'm Marine Corps"

I nodded.

He brings that up later as we move into sex
"I'm a top," he says, "this'll never work."
"I'm not about that," I tell him
I lick the shrapnel scar on his knee
"I don't know," he muses, "I can't imagine it. It's kinda like
what the Marines say:
I came to conquer, not to bow."

I think it sounds stupid, as stupid as war
But I will not judge him
I am a Buddhist
I came to bow not to conquer

He calls all the time for a while
Then he disappears
I am not so young to be a fool for love
I bow
I whisper
His name
Again and again

Then out of the blue: *He's been busy, how about next week?*
All day, lying about
I give him a tarot reading with no great news
He wants to learn, and so he fakes a reading for me
All about this new young man I've met
and how important it is for me to know him and become his
    friend

After all his talk of never being afraid, I come to pity him
He'll make me cry, I think to myself
Again and again
You'll be lucky the day he goes
He looks at me now in a way that makes me think he'll never
    leave
But also that he can't afford to look at anyone like that again
    or often

I'd do foolish things for him
Against my better judgment
His parents didn't want him
But the Marine Corps did
Shock and Awe
Tracers in the night sky

Those who care and those who don't

He vanished next time for good

Shooting star
Warrior
No honor among thieves
But the light's the same

Only brighter

SCOTT HIGHTOWER (U.S.A., B. 1952)

Idyll of the Seronegative

We roll the dice and, in the twinkling
Of an eye, the sharp blade of diagnosis
Separates us from the clean lambs

Of sacrifice. We await the next
Reported case of frenzied HIV cells
Ensconced in CD4 lymphocytes.

You describe for me what you sometimes
Come across in your journals, photographs
Taken through electron microscopes

Of T cells infected with HIV. You evoke
The close-up of a head of lettuce
Covered with bright, round blood ticks;

The curdled surface of a cauliflower
Riddled with a parasitic caviar;
A floret of broccoli enlarged to an exotic,

Satellite-grainy landscape freckled
With toxic poppies. The T cells and HIV
Are closely matched combatants

Like Enkidu and Gilgamesh, who made
The doorposts tremble and the walls shake;
Who, together, in the forest tore out

All of Humbaba's insides, beginnning
With his tongue. *Death is our shepherd.*
Like sheep, we shall be laid in the grave.

Wilde and Genet Bequeathed

a hemi-quadriga--
two--of whatever

they were . . . two-bit
peg boys; a slightly

more seasoned chicken
and his mate, artists who opted

to work in a house rather than
sail away and grub for blubber;

or two provincial boys
with an innate sense

of the parameters
of their ethereal voices

and the tender limits
of service or local

glamour, the charade,
the harshness of the trap

or team; two squeaky
boys by greatness

in the indelible posture
of Claire and Solange,

Blanche and Stanley,
George and Martha;

or one in the guise
of Cleopatra, Ophelia,
"Kitty Litter,"
"Thea Uther Bolyn,"

Irma, Violet, Delilah,
rhapsodic Salome.

Wash us Away

Someone consumed by hate
would like to see someone
else consumed by fire.

There is always someone
hate would like to wash away.

The Nazis, wanting to eradicate
art by representative "degenerate"
artists; they didn't care that a heart
beats in every piece of art. Brown
armband, yellow star, pink triangle.

Even before the 2005 Hurricane Katrina,
Randy Newman crooned,
"They want to wash us away."

La Calavera Catrina
opens her umbrella and smiles.

Piss Christ, a 1987 award-winning
photograph by Andres Serrano,
alongside the work of other gay
artists such as Robert Mapplethorpe,
became a target of derision
for divisive politicians.

What are we to do with Schiele's drawings,
Brancusi's birds, Duchamp's "Fountain,"
Preston's I Once Had a Master,
Duhamel's The Woman with Two Vaginas?

In 2010, politicians created a commotion
over "Hide/Seek: Difference and Desire
in American Portraiture,"
a Washington, D.C., art show.
The Smithsonian was exhibiting
a four-minute excerpt from a video
by David Wojnarowicz, who
among many others died of
an AIDS-related illness in 1992.
His 1987 piece, "A Fire
in My Belly," was a tribute
to the photographer Peter Hujar;
Wojnarowicz's partner who had
himself just died of AIDS complications.

The piece is a stream of images set to
the musical wailing of Diamanda Galás.
It is about 30 minutes long.

For eleven seconds of that meandering,
a crucifix appears on screen with ants
scurrying over it. It seems such an
inconsequential part of the total video
that neither I, nor anyone I've spoken to
who saw the work, ever remembered it at all.
Wojnarowic, inspired throughout the piece
by a broad set of Mexican images,
hoped the passage would speak
to the inevitable corruption of worldly flesh.

A sensitive reading of the piece
puts it smack in the middle of a great
and ancient tradition of showing
hideously grisly images of the body
of Jesus in an attempt to speak
to the ostracization of suffering.

*

I am sorry for those among us
who do not understand – and therefore
cannot be moved by [the mob
at the gates shouting "unclean"
"unclean"] the expressive
greatness of this most
sober, most sacred of pieces.

RACHEL JURY (U.K., B. 1968)

Porn Star

Waiting outside
Quiet chatter and gentle moaning
Some fooling from the resident clown
When the head of the girls' gang turns to me and asks
'Doesn't your boyfriend mind
You dying your hair bright red?'
I pause
'No, my girlfriend really likes it.'
Thirty faces stop and stare
Then crashing through the silence
'Really? Can I watch?' asks the clown

I laugh

It's the first and only time he's ever sincere
But she slaps him down
'Just ignore him!' she says and quickly changes the subject

Sharing a table
With paint-stained, beer bellied men
In a crowded pub after work
A little friendly banter ensues
The talkative one of the two
Thinks I look like her off the telly
I can't think who he means
Then he makes it plain
'She's like you'
She's got short hair
She's like you
She's gay.'
Rona Cameron?

I'm not sure if he's being insulting
But he smiles warmly
Asks if I've got a girlfriend
'Yes.' I say to put him off
'Good' he says. 'Can I watch?'
Beer explodes from my lips
But he persists

'Seriously.' he says
'Seriously?' I ask
He nods
'No' I say and turn my chair away
Surrounded by
Mini skirts and shirts worn out
I turn and swirl to the thump of the beat
Not giving a shit I'm not part of this

Taking a break from the heat
I leave my friend in the thick of it
To swig on my beer
He leans in close wants to buy me a drink
I decline but he wants to know my name
'It's Jane.' I say
Tell him I'm not interested, I'm gay
'I know.' he says
I laugh, it's that obvious
But he insists tells me I'm really attractive
Asks me back to his
'No.' I say 'I'm gay.'
'I know.' he says 'Your friend can come too?'
'No.' I say 'She's straight.'
'I know,' he says 'Can I watch?'
I shake my head turn back into the crowd
Glad to see when I look again he's not around

No bleach blond long curls have I
No crystal blue eyes
No supersized silicon breasts
Or cellulite-free thighs have I
But hey
I'm a porn star
In many straight men's sexual fantasies
Bounce away Samantha Fox
Dribble away Annie Sprinkle
Introducing Rachel River

We all do it

A blood curdling scream
Explodes out of the blackness
A moment of still
Then she emerges
Breasts heaving, lungs reaching
She's hot—she's very hot
She's just killed an alien
And with no need for words
Our bodies meet
It's gonna be dirty
It's gonna be sweet

A single droplet of sweat
Like a tear rolls down
Her forehead past her eye
Down her structured cheek
She's hot—she's very hot
'Vita' escapes my lips like a breath
As she pulls me down
Among the flower beds
And I know I'm going
To howl just like
A wolf

She closes the door
On the final flash light
Alone at last
Our eyes meet one intent
We're hot—we're very hot
The Wimbledon shield
Clatters to the ground
As we stumble towards
The steaming shower beams
Where we're gonna relieve
Some of that
Match point tension

Her husband's faded jalopy
Swings out of sight
I tuner the dinner sign to closed
She's banging plates
Making out like nothing's taking place
She's hot—she's very hot
She's tall and blond but there's
Nothing lang – uid about her right now
I fling open the kitchen door
And in one swift move
We're right up close
Writing on the kitchen counter
And I do not hesitate to reach down
And grasp hold of her
Crotch
Masturbation—we all do it.

COLLIN KELLEY (U.S.A., B. 1969)

Siege

California sunset, Ronnie's head to the west,
finally out of his ass, and Nancy's death's head
resting on the coffin, patting it
like she must have patted him
with her stranger's hands these last ten years,
his forgetfulness absolute.
You can't help but cry, the old bastard
finally dead, like a daddy who beat you
almost to death, but still there is that time
you cannot erase. Those years of silence
from the east, while the sound of blood boiling
in veins was deafening in the west.
Somehow it's fitting that they are burying him
here, in this decimated land he called home.
Where the sunset began for millions long before
he arrived draped in a flag, one he fashioned
into a noose, those old cowboy knots, and hung
over a high limb and let those California boys swing.
They brought disease on themselves, he knew
their kind from his Hollywood days, grab-assing
in the Warner Brothers' dressing rooms. Faggots.
Bad enough he had to dirty his mouth with the word
AIDS, but gay would never pass his lips,
as if his withholding the word banished them,
made their cries of *shame, shame, shame* outside
the White House nothing more than a collective
bad dream. He made it seven years without giving in
to those bleeding heart homos, liberals and whiny doctors.
He made a joke out of untying the purse strings,
while he was a rainmaker when it came to warheads,
arms trading, terrorist training and knocking down walls.
He ended the Cold War while his own country turned to ice.
So they bury him as the day closes, the sky on fire
like the hell he'll have to talk himself out of if it exists.
Give the Devil an old song and dance, make promises,
barter with empty pockets, cast uncertain eyes skyward
at the screaming angels who lay siege to Heaven's Gate,
prepared to fall again before he's allowed to enter.
One lost kingdom is enough.

Fairy Tale Eating Disorders

No food is safe in a fairy tale,
a single bite enough to stop your heart,
or put you into a coma.
So who could blame the starving wolf
for wanting to eat Little Red,
suck the gristle off her skeletal frame,
hidden behind her Riding Hood,
the picnic basket a rouse,
so the girls won't notice at school,
her sharp shoulder blades and sallow skin
stretched over toothpick ribs.
And what about Snow White,
who already has texture issues,
she'll never eat fresh fruit again,
or comb her hair for that matter,
because the mirror is back talking,
making her paranoid about the Prince,
says he's got eyes for a skinny maid,
so she'll hide her dinner in napkins,
or discreetly vomit in a chamber pot,
the comfort she once took in apples
now gone to rot.
Pity the witch in her candy house,
luring chubby children into her oven,
having them build their own pyre,
she's too weak to even cut them up,
hopes their flesh will fall off the bone
into her swollen mouth, even a crone
isn't safe these days from poison,
and processed foods.
And Cinderella, slenderizing for the ball,
working her fingers to the bone, blaming
the stepsisters, so she can fit in a size zero,
ride a garish coach, not be the pumpkin
she sees in the mirror, that whispers to her
at night, calls her Two Ton Tessie,
says she'll be alone if her foot cracks
the dainty glass slipper, no one likes
a fat Princess.

At Southlake Mall

My parents made up while I was in Spencer's Gifts
examining fart in a can and hopping cocks,
waiting for other boys to finish flipping through
posters of half-naked women and sports cars.
Greasy fingerprints all over Daisy Duke's cleavage
on sale for 1.99 rolled and bagged, long and stiff.

They sat on a bench by a gurgling fountain, holding hands,
making googly eyes and sipping from the same slushie.
Even then, I wondered what she had promised.
What would erase the image of her naked legs
wrapped around another?
The lover sent running with clothes in hand
to his oversexed Camaro, face bloodied, while my father
slapped my mother repeatedly in the bathroom,
so she could see his cuckold departing in dirty mirror.

With unsigned divorce papers on the dining room table,
my parents devolved back to earlier selves,
teenagers in love, giddy with necking, third base diddling.
They couldn't wait to get home, made me eat my giant pretzel
in the backseat, her hand on his thigh as the Ford shuddered
in excess speed.

While they fucked their way back to middle class malaise,
I shot my wad all over Daisy's mid-section, would never
hang her in my room, just roll her wet and sticky under the bed
for future abuse, the same place I kept a shoplifted *People*,
Christopher Atkins bulging from his *Blue Lagoon* loincloth,
his face and abs wrinkled from my salty spray.

BILL KUSHNER (U.S.A., B. 1932)

An America for Matthew Shepard

I'm a kid in America, you go straight
up your ass & turn left. I am a nut
in America, sir. I am a gone out of
mind in America, ma'am. I am a not
what I am. I am a kiss on that pretty butt
of you, Miss America. I am nut what you
tinkle I yam. You say I am there I am
here. You say I am queer I am queer.
I am Superfly on the Calvin Klein jeans
of corporate America. Here I cum to
save the day, yum. For I mmm The Shadow.
Now you see me. Now you don't. Now
I am in your wet hot dreams, don't you turn
over, don't. For I mmm The Whistler, beware.
I Whistler put my two lips together, you
better run quick. I, he stepped belly up to
the Cheers bar, somewhere in you, America!
Am I not a man & a brother? Am I not a
woman & a sister? Am I not thirsty, just
like you, my America, & oh are we trembling,
as we look around us, thirsty for love?

Moon

I do like the word. Moon. "Moon," I croon,
and as I say it I see it, oh my beauty, just as day
light fades into moon, a tilted moon, I see you,
oh moon, see me. I'm not myself tonight, but
soon oh moon do see me as I walk alone along
your very cusp in this evening's hush, and was I
dreaming? am I so lost again somewhere in a
dream? and am I always babe naked? and babbling
crazily to no one, a curious loon? There's always
a crazy guy like me walking slowly along the
ever darkening street, just an ordinary guy like,
say, me, and trying to hide his fear by whistling.
But who am I frightened of? No, not you, moon.
But yes, I thought I saw a shadow on the moon,
was just the shadow of a man, that's who, and that's
all it was, he was just walking along, whistling in
the dark, the dark of the moon, just walking along.

Wings

I'd never felt a man's lips on mine!
We climbed his stairs, my heart going wild!
"You're mine, boy" he uttered, his deep voice
In my ear, "So sweet," slap slap, "so sweet!"
He opened his door and felt me: "Yes!" and
He pushed me inside. "But where's the light?"
"Are you my little angel?" What a dumb question!
"But why don't I run?" I wondered, but no answer came.
I woke naked in the night to his heavy breathing.
Was he still inside me? Was it almost morning?
Had I spent the whole night with a total stranger?
"And how's my little angel this morning?" he hummed.
"With dirty wings, sir," I answered. "Dirty wings!"

ELEANOR LERMAN (U.S.A., B.1952)

The body, which used to

The body, which used to
float down the boulevards, wraithlike,
radiating attraction, topped by
a face like a knife with a baby pout

now refuses to get out of bed.
Why? Ask it. Go on, anyone,
see what it has to say.
Are you sick? Are you tired?

The poor body shudders under its
thin sheet, each flat year laundered,
faded, gone, gone, gone.
What can it do but pull the lever

that operates a moan while the body
plunges back into sleep, into its
one dream of finding its way home
to queer street in the diamond days

when it was as brave as a boy,
as young as it would ever be, and
driving a stake into its own heart
was only a trick

Homage to the Commune

Having spent "the formative years"
in front of the blond wood television,
watching the Martians invade Maple Street,
aim their death rays at our hapless cities
and flap off to their spaceships, dragging
with them our most buxom girls

has unexpectedly enriched my thinking,
especially now that I am in my decline.
That I haven't much to do except sit around
the house all day in my Yankee cap and
Tibetan hiking boots (which is a good costume:
homage to my father, homage to the days
of the commune), encouraging myself
to think that "anything is possible."
That in fact, "you can never tell"

So when the letter arrives—as I
always knew it would—announcing that
The Committee in its wisdom has decreed,
I will have no doubt that indeed, somewhere,
people are stamping papers and drafting legislation
aimed at global capitulation, or at least
the Final Solution for my little town

What I will do then is get the others, the believers
The ones who spent their lives, like me,
spoiling for a fight. We'll call the Martians
(You didn't know they've been our friends
since we all tripped together in the 60s?)
We'll get our dads. And we'll go rocking
down the highway like we used to,
demanding justice and freedom and
whatever else those people who think
they're now in power think they can spare

That Sure is My Little Dog

Yes, indeed, that is my house that I am carrying around
on my back like a bullet-proof shell and yes, that sure is
my little dog walking a hard road in hard boots. And
just wait until you see my girl, chomping on the chains
of fate with her mouth full of jagged steel. She's damn
ready and so am I. What else did you expect from the
brainiacs of my generation? The survivors, the nonbelievers,
the oddball-outs with the Cuban Missile Crisis still
sizzling in our blood? Don't tell me that you bought
our act, just because our worried parents (and believe me,
we're nothing like them) taught us how to dress for work
and to speak as if we cared about our education. And
I guess the music fooled you; you thought we'd keep
the party going even to the edge of the abyss. Well,
too bad. It's all yours now. Good luck on the ramparts.
What you want to watch for is when the sky shakes
itself free of kites and flies away. Have a nice day.

R. ZAMORA LINMARK (U.S.A., B. 1968)

Psst

Means hey it's just me thinking of you
as usual about us in this crowded train
where I know just about everyone is whispering
I'm your heart's biggest yesterday's hit and
your world's worst blind spot right now
they can read my face today's tragic news you
haven't been waking up on our side of the world
it won't be long now before you leave me
just like that Billie Holiday song say it isn't so
so I'm going home try and not cry especially
the part where Billie half-sings half-wails
that everything is still okay because you're
still my every still even when the door
is growing tired of my hurt my only

Channeling Lady Sarashina

I am sitting at the bar of Artsy-Fartsy in Shinjuku nichome, buzzing from sake and three-month-old culture shock, when the salaryman of my dreams appears from a cloud of cigarette smoke, smiling to reveal a surprising set of perfectly straight white teeth. With an accent borrowed from British alcoholics teaching at the Nova Language Institute, he introduces himself as Kenji.

Kenji: I'd like to buy you a drink.
Me: Shot of Patron tequila, onegaishimasu.
Kenji: America-jin?
Me: Hai.
Kenji: What do you do?
Me: Dream.
Kenji: Like Lady Sarashina?

My eyes light up like a pachinko machine. The mention of an 11th century diarist who preferred chivalric fantasies and dreams over Buddha and mommyhood tells me Kenji is not just another salt-and-pepper-haired salaryman in a Burberry suit who soaks his repression in sake. I smile; he smiles; I want to weep.

Kenji: What's your favorite season?
Me: Pollen-free.
Kenji: That leaves me with summer or winter to remember you by.
Me: You must be married.
Kenji: With children. And you?
Me: Divorced.

With a Mont Blanc pen, he writes on the back of his business card:

> My boss is golfing in Hawaii,
> Shall we moon-gaze?

I reply:

> Neglect the cattle,
> And I'll abandon the gods.

Kenji: No problem.
Me: I don't do motels.
Kenji: Me neither.

From the fiftieth-floor lobby of Park Hyatt, the moon wants to crash through the tinted window. I reach for the memo pad:

> Off to the monks, moon,
> Kenji's mine until wake-up call.

Complimenting the elegance of our super-sized deluxe suite are: Sade on repeat mode, peppermint Altoids, and this resignation:

> He is married to his boss;
> I to my poetics.

A slice of bathroom light guides his nakedness to my lips:

> Come, my prince.
> Undress me with your silence.

Minutes later, these lines come to me:

> Diamond life,
> I will not compete with your boss.

Sighing in sync, I ask a poem:

> Is this a dream?
> If so, do not wake me.

A recurring dream of a broken heart: Father De Leon: handsome sixty-something priest from my childhood province in the Philippines. So deep was my crush I signed up to be his four-thirty a.m. altar boy, from age six until my parents whisked me away to America at age nine. Thirty-three years later, Father De Leon returns with a lipsticked message on the gilt-edged mirror:

> Senseless love engenders
> Your future haikus.

I wake up, gasping for breath:

> Engenders?
> Endangers?

Morning arrives with several Kenji Post-It notes. On the nightstand table, right next to the Hello Kitty alarm clock:

> First kiss always bruises.
> Encore at eight?

On the counter, next to his ATM card:

> I love you in Burberry.
> PIN: rain69

At the Internet café, I compose an e-poem to Lisa:

> Count me out for Kris Kringle.
> How homophonic: Kenji, genji.

For dinner: Blowfish roulette, then sex with sake.

Five-and-a-half days later, a Yahoo chat with Lisa:

Aries69: Is it winter
                    Or did the snow forget to fall?

Fishing4Lisa: His boss has him on speed-dial mode.
              You still have his ATM?

Aries69: He changed the password.

Fishing4Lisa: When?

Aries69: Night of the blowfish.

Fishing4Lisa: He came with the smoke.

Aries69: He vanished with the smoke.

Fishing4Lisa: Treat it like a one-night stand.
                    Extended to five.

Aries69: Easy, if not for the Burberry
                    And the nightly facial.

PAUL LISICKY (U.S.A., B. 1959)

Bulldog

The bulldog kept the woman alive, but the woman didn't know that. She had other problems on her mind, such as where did she put her keys, and what was her car doing in Florida when she'd parked it in Tennessee?

The bulldog got very still when the woman started shoving her fingers into bowls. He figured he could make the earth spin a little slower if he were sitting on its axis, so he'd quiet his panting. He'd look straight ahead, neither left nor right. The woman would trip on him, wince at him for being in her way, then lean down and palm the top of his head, thus assuring him they were in their correct positions to one another, and they'd get through one more day.

After she loaded the dishes in the dishwasher, the woman headed to her recliner every night. It was always a bit of a production. First the blanket went over the legs, then the cushion went behind her neck, and once she settled in, the bulldog commenced his stunning leap and landed in her lap. The woman always told herself she was watching her favorite program, but she was inevitably sound asleep before the first commercial. And inside the warm nest of the lap, the bulldog began his work, which was to calm the woman while the woman dreamt of lost things. It took great work to be her purifying organ, but he always felt better when he did so. It gave him the illusion of aliveness even if it made him tremble, even if he had to play dumb and weak in order to get the tenderness he craved.

What was the woman thinking when she looked at him as if he were an intruder? Her eyes went wild that day; her hands flew up. But there was a quiet in her too that took away any desire he had to speak. He didn't go out to pee as he usually did but let go right there on the rug, by the umbrella stand. And when he tried to leap on the woman's lap, his nails snagged in her afghan. Gone was her old face of curiosity and concern. In its place was something more remote. Her face might have been made of granite, which wouldn't have been so bad if granite hadn't smiled.

When the woman could no longer tell the difference between the phone and the channel changer, the woman faced the front door. She stood there a few minutes more before she was guided by two strangers to a car outside. How new she looked to the bulldog. Though she could barely put one foot in front of the next, she might have been walking into the world for the very first time, learning to make it through a day all over again. And in taking that in, the bulldog's face went completely white in an instant, as if someone had taken a match to it.

He never saw the woman's face again. The apartment grew dirty, he took to whatever was left in the cabinets: raisins, mice, the bristles of an old brush. It might have been years, it might have been days. And when he grew tired of living the life of the saint, he squeaked out through a crack of light beside the door, and lived longer than he'd ever predicted.

Monster

1.

Because he could picture himself curled up on the shelf of the refrigerator between the bread and the light.

2.

Because he stared up at the sprinkler attachment and thought of it as a metal flower.

3.

Because he'd get right up again after he was told to stand up straight, like a soldier.

4.

Because his brother knocked and knocked on the other side of the locked door.

5.

Because he wouldn't scream for his life when the mother invited Monster to stay with him.

6.

Because the mother seemed to think it all right to have Monster's sister stay with them.

9.

Because Monster's family had a statue of a quiet saint amid the bushes on the front yard.

10.

Because Monster came to him in the form of a pretty young girl.

11.

Because of the hush in the room and the pictures in their frames holding absolutely still.

12.

Because when he broke his promise to Monster, the word could no longer be contained, and the mother's voice got loud and angry.

13.

Because the mother's face went red, as if he'd been the one who had wanted those things.

14.

Because the father tossed off a joke about it down the hall one night, just out of sight.

15.

Because one brother was bad and one brother was good, and that meant one brother was inside the room and one brother was not.

16.

Because Monster pushed the boy onto his back with his wing.

17.

Because the boy did silence better than anyone: He was no slouch.

18.

Because the father stopped looking at the boy in the eye for years, as if he were afraid of him.

19.

Because the boy girded his arms and his legs, for he knew not how to stop the story that had been written on him.

20.

Because Monster said, I can eat whatever I want to eat.

21.

Because the boy went looking for that feeling everywhere.

22.

Because the blood of the weak goes down like tea.

23.

Because Monster appears again and again in the form of a man, in the form of a woman, and in the form of a dog who shits on the grass.

24.

Because a bath will warm you all the way to your lungs.

25.

Because he's not able to take no without feeling a piece of ceiling breaking inside him.

26.

Because when he says no he must shore up a mountain within himself.

27.

Because it is easier to cry for the woman on the porch who can't seem to find a way to cry for herself.

28.

Because he nods when he's told: The Devil's come here to help us.

29.

Because he knows it is his duty to find the bomb beneath the couch.

30.

Because he stops returning the calls of the friend who wants to make a lunch of him.

31.

Because he doesn't mind when his face is cut off in the photo.

32.

Because across the sea a man puts a leash around the neck of another man and screams at him to bark 77 times.

33.

Because he will look past the ash in his stocking to the one glittering thing.

34.

Because the woman thinks his brain is something she can sculpt.

35.

Because he could find the needles in the bag and not think the needles could be put to use.

36.

Because the deer leaps through a cut in the fence, plays out on the gravel for a time, and goes back in again.

CHIP LIVINGSTON (U.S.A., B. 1967)

Nocturnal Admission

I went to my mother's room at 13
past midnight, and told her I was dying.
I'd wet the bed, I'd had this crazy dream,
about a sexy neighbor I'd been spying
on. Well, I didn't tell her that, I mean,
the day before she asked who I was eyeing
when I didn't want to go outside
for ice cream. The truck was parked out front,
and she was buying, but I couldn't join
the other screaming kids –
not with Lance applying suntan lotion
to his muscled teenage skin.
Stretched out on a beach towel
in his front yard, his body mystified me,
while mine seemed happy to defy me.
My dick would tent my cut-offs
at the sight of him.
I wore two pair of underwear,
but even then I thought I'd burst
right through the seams.
So I didn't dare tell mother what I'd dreamed,
though she did think to ask me.
I'd have been a fool to tell her that.
She thought my blush was any boy's,
puzzling out his sexuality, but I swear it was
as much because the fantasies
were always other boys,
some from my baseball team,
some the roughnecks at school,
but usually Lance. He was flying
naked in the dream I had that night,
the one that made me think that God
was mad and killing me. I was lying
(also naked – and hard as cinder block)
on the beach towel I'd seen him lay
across the grass the day before.
I tried to understand the signs implying
I might turn into some kind of freaky thing.

But it would have been cruel to tell my mother that,
especially when she was already crying,
and trying not to laugh at the same time,
when I showed her what came out of me.
She apologized for throwing such a scene,
said I was growing up to be a man, that's all it meant,
said it was normal for a boy my age's thing
to start uprising like a metal beam.

She apologized again
that I didn't have my dad around to train
an 11-year-old boy in the ways of puberty.
I was as stupefied as I've ever been.
She never mentioned him.
And I have never turned a deeper red
than I did then, at 26 past midnight,
when my mother helped me change my sheets,
and said the next day she'd teach me to wash them.
And then she said she'd ask the man across the street
to talk to me. Would that be okay?
Or would I feel more comfortable

with someone younger, like his son?

Day One.   Go under water at the glow of morning. Face East. Dry by the sun's rays.
                      Where you hear the beloved whistle, steal his step. Hold his footprints in your hands and
                      whisper, *This is your name. These are your people.*

Day Two.   Wash your face and hands in river water at dawn. Face North. Find the
                      seed of a hardwood tree and hold it in your hands. Speak to it. *This is your name. These*
                      are your people.

Day Three.   Stand in still water at dusk. Wet your hair. Face West. Cup the water in
                      your hands and sing to it. *This is your name. These are your people.*
                      Use this water and the earth imprinted with the love's step to plant the seed in a container
                      that will fit beneath your bed. Let the seed germinate under good dreams.

Day Four.   Rise with the sun and drink four sips of water. Remove the container and raise it in your
                      hands. Face South. Tell it, *This is your name. These are your people.* Replace below
                      your bed.

Repeat this last morning's ritual daily, blessing water to keep the soil wet, reminding the lover his name, for approximately four weeks or until the seed displays visible roots. Transfer the seed outdoors on a new moon in early sunlight, returning these words in each direction:

This is your name. These are your people.

This is your name. These are your people.   +   *This is your name. These are your people.*

This is your name. These are your people.

ROSIE LUGOSI (U.K., B. 1960)

Queer Thanksgiving (with special thanks to William S. Burroughs)

Thank you for history.
For Queen Victoria and half of us wiped from existence.
Mary Whitehouse and jail-term blasphemy.
James Anderton and the swirling cesspits of our own making.

Thank you for religion.
For Christianity, Judaism, Islam,
Buddhism, Scientology, Mormons;
For all those who use their God's laws to hate.
Thank you for *Praise God for Aids* banners.
For *Gay Plague.*

Thank you for politicians.
Especially Margaret Thatcher and Section 28,
and all those who shied away from its repeal.
Thank you for Communism:
for we are bourgeois revisionist deviant scum.
Thank you for Fascism:
for we are pinko commie weirdo deviant scum.
Thank you for *scum.*

Thank you for psychology:
she must have been abused;
too close to his mother;
it's the parents' fault;
must have had a bad time with a man.
It's just not *natural.*
They shouldn't work with children.
They can choose.

Thank you for vocabulary:
For shirt lifter, fudge packer, shit stabber,
bull dyke, faggot, fruit, lezzie,
rug muncher, turd burglar,
bumboy, poufter, willy woofter,
pervert, predator, queer,
For *too ugly to get a man,*
what she needs is a real one,
unnatural, diesel, man-hater, deviant, paedo.
Thank you for giving us two choices:
camp queen or butch lezzer.

Thank you for *it's Adam and Eve, not Adam and Steve.*
For *Are You Arthur or Martha?*
Thank you for the obsession with what we do in bed.
For top shelf hot girl-on-girl action porn.

Thank you for telling us it would all be so much easier
if we just kept things quiet. Didn't scare the horses.
Stayed in the closet.

Thank you for burning us at the stake
Declaring us illegal, breaking us with hard labour.
Thank you for the Pink Triangle.
Thank you for beheading us in Saudi,
hanging us in Iran,
Forcing us into marriages we don't want
in Islamabad and Burnley.
For bombing our pubs,
knifing us on Clapham Common.
For grinding us into the tarmac
of the world's school playgrounds.

Thank you for trying to douse our pride.
For giving us crumbs, for making us grateful.
For persuading those of us who are white and rich
that the battles have all been won.
Thank you for never going away.
Thank you for making us strong.
Thank you for our history.
We are writing our own future.
Thank you for keeping us on our toes.

Dignity

Throwing up over the consultant
when he asks you how you're feeling.
Throwing up
so hard it comes out of your nose.
Acquiring the skill of throwing up accurately.

Farting.
Discovering that chemo farts are more powerful than semtex
and can clear a room just as effectively.

Saying, *I don't need a zimmer frame to get to the bathroom!*
Then falling into a chemical waste bin
and getting a two-inch scar on your forehead.

Getting out of bed and showing the whole ward
and their relatives your knickers
except you aren't wearing any.

Fainting.
Coming round on the bathroom floor
wringing wet, stark naked and stretched out
under the eyes of seven nurses who've had to kick the door down.

Tolerating strangers who whisper *you're so brave.*
Resisting the urge to deck them.

Going bald.
Watching your tits shrivel to the size of peanuts
and your arse go flat as a burst paper bag.

Remaining polite
when the close friend drops off the face of the earth
when you tell him your diagnosis.
Remaining polite
when the same close friend reappears when you are better
and acts like nothing's happened.
Remaining polite
when people cross a room
in case you talk to them about *it.*

Wearing long sleeves in June
To cover up the scarlet tracklines
chemotherapy has etched from wrist to elbow.
Rolling up those sleeves to show them off as battle scars.
Learning to stare back.
Wearing a feeding tube up your nose.
Learning to stare back.

Refusing to wear the prescription wig
that makes you look like you've got cancer.
Refusing to wear the cheerful floral scarf
that makes you look like you've got cancer.

Standing up, falling over.
Standing up, falling over.
Standing up, hanging onto the arm of the sofa, the edge of the table,
grabbing at furniture in a dot-to-dot of small stages.
Waddling to the kitchen on a toddler's unsteady legs.
Making a cup of tea unaided
for the first time in three months.

Standing up
and saying *I've got cancer*
without need, without self-pity.
Standing up
and saying *I'm clear.*

EILEEN MYLES (U.S.A., B. 1949)

I always put my pussy
in the middle of trees
like a waterfall
like a doorway to God
like a flock of birds
I always put my lover's cunt
on the crest
of a wave
like a flag
that I can
pledge my
allegiance
to. This is my
country. Here,
when we're alone
in public.
My lover's pussy
is a badge
is a night stick
is a helmet
is a deer's face
is a handful
of flowers
is a waterfall
is a river
of blood
is a bible
is a hurricane
is a soothsayer.
My lover's pussy
is a battle cry
is a prayer
is lunch
is wealthy
is happy
is on teevee
has a sense of humor
has a career
has a cup of coffee
goes to work
meditates
is always alone
knows my face
knows my tongue
knows my hands
is an alarmist
has lousy manners
knows her mind

I always put
my pussy in the middle
of trees
like a waterfall
a piece of jewelry
that I wear
on my chest
like a badge
in America
so my lover & I
can be safe.

Transportation

I bought a bigger
pinker dick
for you
but then I
didn't
call. It seemed necessary
you're tall
& I miss you all
the time.

I love missing
I guess
it's mostly
that. You pulled
yourself up
like a big cat
but shorn

Hate to see
you that way
so I'll just
stick
it in
the ground

I imagine you flying
around
like ancient art
all gold
don't be scared
when I call
I'll be new

I want to lie
with you
on mounds of sand
and the power of the
sun

I'm missing my boat
by the way
& all of the sudden
the voice
stops

Paint me a Penis

If the best thing the world discovered today is that at the inside
of the universe is a cat
I love your braids; I love your peaceful eating
I hate that the sum total effect of the schedule
was sadness. Do you read the schedule. Nope.
I'm jealous. If he used the same words
over and over in plays and movies and commencement
addresses is that wrong. Is it wrong. What if art is wrong.
Is there only one sun. Some planets have two.
When the rain was pouring I wanted to be in there
silent with you. In the dog's beady black gaze. In the room
with the sleeping dog. With you leaving the room.
I've stopped the rain, I've silenced you.
I think the story was that one woman had gotten
the painting from the other and they were dating
but she never paid for it and then she moved out.
The painting sat in the second floor window and the painter
saw it and demanded it back. No. So the painter wrote
Marie O'Shea give me back my painting and put
it in the window opposite. She's a mess. We call her
cunt face. Twat. When it blasted I asked you to put
your headphones on. The dog's wheezing. I think
smack in the middle of that time was a virus
and it gave itself to everyone freely. We learned that
everything was related to everything else. Just as everything
was getting more separate and no longer a simple bowl
of fruit everyone was dying of the same thing. Not everyone.
Later when they hit the buildings it was just like everyone
in the city felt it. Not the same. We felt the shake. The request
in the air was how are we all feeling it now. It wasn't the same.
It was like you kept breaking off another square of the
bar and tasting it. He came running back into the room.
He was *moaning*. And now he just stares. And the rain
starts up again. I've never been invited to one meeting.
Do they have them. I remember the time I was invited
and we went around the room saying how we came
to be here. I was invited and everyone
stared and they never let me know when they were
meeting again. She wore a yellow dress. Everyone's watching you. He stands
in the doorway watching you eat. It stopped.
I want the painting in the window. Yeah. And you can
really ask her questions when you get her alone. And you were reading all the
time. And you said it a lot, that you wanted one which
you don't remember. I guess I wanted one. Now some
people in that mysterious time there it goes again
decided to in a very dedicated way begin talking about it
because there wasn't enough of that. That part had waned. Otherwise
you could just take it off the walls, you could go to funerals
and get fucked. You could recite it so that all they saw
was you. Huge numbers of them banded together marching
slowly into the room. There's footage of us dancing. I wouldn't ask
the stars to be quiet but I'm closer to them now. She was so
smart. I'm serious. I bet she'd make a good one. Since I didn't grow

my own I'd like to see what she'd make me. If he demands that no
one tells theirs at the breakfast table I think he probably pulls
it out of his pajamas and slaps it on the table. Dreams to me are
always receding. It's the only perfection: it's vanishing, stoking my
appetite so I'm drawing it for you as it becomes less the experience
that just happens as I'm resurrecting it for you. I'm making it
for you. I'm asking her. Make it for me. I'd like that. I'm putting it
in real deep. Out there, where everyone is.

Pencil Poem #2

Is it wrong to think
you're getting excited
he pulls the window
down on the golden & brown
now I remember
when I began to speak
I began to speak
like him. I mime.

Pencil #4

A dog walks into barber
shop.
I'm not into gender
OK says the barber
so don't think of me
as a bitch
but just one of your regular
customers
who wants to do something
a little different
I'm okay with that
said the barber. Hot towels warm my
head, smelling of
mint. Warm lather
on my neck. Woof woof
You're a dog.
No I'm not.
And I bit him.

#5

Half asleep; generous
clatter of straws
a cup into a plastic bag.
Eyelids flutter
gulp of decent coffee
and back to nod
it's a strange gig
this body I'm riding
for 59 years.

6 in and out

cute 50 something top
will you bring you to life.
Butch bottom wants
tender master. At
the bottom of this
pencil is an eraser
something soft that takes
it away. I may have
had my "lovers"
my partners. That
was a waste. Here
I'm casting about
for my parts. Ingredients
for enjoyment. Anyone
can be beautiful
at 19 or 30. This
is life. Take a deep
look.

LESLÉA NEWMAN (U.S.A., B. ?)

THE FENCE
(that night)

(for Matthew Shepard)

I held him all night long
He was heavy as a broken heart
Tears fell from his unblinking eyes
He was dead weight yet he kept breathing

He was heavy as a broken heart
His own heart wouldn't stop beating
He was dead weight yet he kept breathing
His face streaked with moonlight and blood

His own heart wouldn't stop beating
The cold wind wouldn't stop blowing
His face streaked with moonlight and blood
I tightened my grip and held on

The cold wind wouldn't stop blowing
We were out on the prairie alone
I tightened my grip and held on
I saw what was done to this child

We were out on the prairie alone
Their truck was the last thing he saw
I saw what was done to this child
I cradled him just like a mother

Their truck was the last thing he saw
Tears fell from his unblinking eyes
I cradled him just like a mother
I held him all night long

13 WAYS OF LOOKING AT 9/11

I.
First thought:
This is not good
for the Jews.
Second thought:
This is not good
for the lesbians.
Third thought:
this is not good
for me.

II.
Even now—especially now
the body has its demands:
The belly cries to be fed.
But food can't push past
the lump of tears
stuck in my throat
too terrified
to spill from my eyes

III.
The cats, usually so aloof
except at feeding time
stay close
unaware, yet knowing
something heavy
soft and purring
is needed on my lap

IV.
Born in Brooklyn
raised on Long Island,
I moved to the East Village
to make my fortune
then fled the city
twenty years ago.
Still, in my heart
I am a New Yorker
so people call,
wanting to connect
wanting it to be their tragedy, too.
"Did you lose anyone?"
they ask, almost hopeful.
I am almost sorry to disappoint them.

V.
The nation is on high alert.
I stock canned goods in the basement,
stash two hundred dollars
under my mattress
thinking, this and a token
will get me a ride on the subway.
Then I remember
where I live
there is no subway

VI.
The search dogs get depressed;
there are so few bodies to be found.
One team stages a mock recovery
to boost their dogs' morale.
A burly firefighter
puts down his gear,
lies down in the rubble
and like a dog, plays dead.
Soon the search dogs start to bark
and wag their tails
and lick his face.
Soon the firefighter rises from the ashes
and slowly walks away

VII.
Bags and bags of body parts:
finger, ankle, elbow.
I remember lying in bed with you
looking at our feet sticking up
from under the blankets,
yours so brown and slender,
a perfect size six with ballerina arches;
mine so pale and squat and flat.
We joked about knowing each other in a crowd
solely by our feet.
Now I try to wrap my mind
around the unimaginable:
a knock at the door,
a strange man
brings me your right foot
and I am grateful even for that.

VIII.
It doesn't take long
for the newspapers
to quote letters
blaming Israel and the Jews.
It doesn't take long
for the newspapers
to quote Jerry Falwell
blaming the feminists and the gays.
It doesn't take long
for me to stop reading
the newspapers.

IX.
In my little town
at my little grocery store
a cashier refuses to check out
a woman he calls a "turban head,"
a woman I call a cancer survivor.
X.
It is the longest we have gone
in thirteen years
without making love.
Finally I let you touch me
though I feel like glass
because those who died
will never enjoy
this gift again.
How dare I waste it?

XI.
A blank notebook page
an empty computer screen,
What is the point of writing anything?
Then an unbidden email from a fan:
"Thank you for bringing so much
beauty into my heart and the world."
Tears tumble from my eyes.

XII.
I dream a child stands
on the twin towers
of her sturdy legs.
before she disappears
and I am running
across the Brooklyn Bridge,
naked and burning,
my skin falling away
like the Vietnamese girl
in that famous photo.
Everyone I ask for help
asks me, "Are you an Arab
or a Jew?" I tell them,
"I am a human being"
and everyone who hears my answer
vanishes like smoke

XIII.
On Rosh Hashannah
There is a discussion group at the synagogue.
Our leader says when she first heard,
she was so angry she wanted to kill
somebody—anybody—and everybody
she spoke with felt the same way.
"Is there anyone here
who isn't furious?" she asks.
I look around the circle,
then slowly raise my hand
like a white flag of surrender.

SESTINA FOR BUDDY

Oh for the days when AIDS
was a candy cube I ate to lose weight
my only goal in life to be skinny
as Buddy is right now, all eyes
and bones in his hollow face
still lovely in the early morning.

Buddy sleeps all morning
now. Even the hospital aides
pause to stare at his chiseled face.
I sit at his bedside and wait
for him to open his left eye,
the right one lost forever in a fold of skin

swollen and purple like the skin
of a grape. In fact, this very morning
boasts three new lesions I
kiss one by one by one. I'm not afraid of AIDS
only of this never-ending wait
which is sure to end too soon. Will I be able to face

Buddy's death when it comes? His face
is a battleground: mottled skin,
sunken cheeks from lack of weight.
Will this morning be the morning
Buddy loses and AIDS
wins? It's a question I

don't want answered so I focus my eyes
once again on his dear old face,
so familiar yet so strange since AIDS
has rearranged everything under the skin.
Who can bear this sight first thing in the morning?

I swallow hard and wait
for my courage not to fail me, wait
for Buddy to open his one good eye,
wait for the waiting to be over and the mourning
to begin. I memorize his face:
the unbearable translucence of his skin
wracked by this monster we call AIDS.

If I could aid him in ending this wait
to leave his skin behind and fly, I
would face him toward the light and let him go this morning

JEFFREY OAKS (U.S.A., B. 1964)

Little What

In the darkness. What a sonnet. When muscle
grunts, gives, accepts, resists, sucks its breath,
even aches. But is not broken. What is going up.
Not a wrong way. What is going in. What is darkness
but unseen. Where are those nerves? There. What
a sonnet. Like a bed with a penis. Growing harder.
Like a hallway after grief. A curse and a whisper,
an awe, out of which the wolf arose. On your lap.
Nails clicking, down the finally dark purple
each man sits on quietly, secretly. A hyacinth. That
strange boy dead, transformed into petals. My
God. What a sonnet, what a little song of nails.
Slap it. Wolf it down. Slip it in, sing on. The mouth
shivers and opens to be a moan, that moon.

Mistakes with Strangers

I pulled down a man's pants in public once.
I had said *I love you* earlier and I had meant it.
Don't ask me why. Two men later I was him,
betrayed. I pulled off the next man's wings
in return and I found out he went on to own
and run a large company that manufactured
a kind of shoe that was so beautiful you had to buy it
but so heavy it was impossible to lift. Some people died.
Help me, Rhonda, Jesus is not coming for me.
I stopped returning his calls. His wounds
made a boring centerpiece for conversation.
He kept asking me to stick my finger in them
all the time. The next man stuck me
with a three-hundred-dollar sexline phone bill
and vanished. I liked his thick body that was like
an ice cream cone I could not lick away.
Later, I was told he was a professional
ice cream cone, whatever flavor you wanted,
at the corner of 6th and Wood downtown.
So I paid. One man I stuck with a three
year depression—well, he said— that required
a therapist, two women chiropractors, three new jobs,
and four other lovers before it lifted. Later,
he thanked me for being so cool. One man
I left handcuffed to a bed, since he was always nicer
unsatisfied. Once I tried an orgy but found myself
thinking in the middle of it all, this: *we're a pack*
of lions clawing, eating, roaring over the body
of a crippled zebra, which is also us. Then I fell in love
with the least pushy of the bunch and acted as if
he alone meant anything. We fell off the bed
to be alone. I saw him again only twice more,
since it required an eight-hour drive and I was poor. After
the second time, he decided he had to write a poem
right then and I put my clothes back on and sat
on his screened-in porch. Crickets, katydids, big
furry brown moths came to cling on the screens.
I examined their armored, hairy undersides with
cocktail toothpicks while his typewriter clattered.
What was the meaning of such machinery?
Cats howled and screamed. The poem went on for hours,
it seemed, and turned out only to be a letter
to his mother, who he said was crazy. I apologized
and took the next bus home. The next week
I was paying for a therapist, looking for
a personal trainer I wouldn't fall in love with.
That was a mistake too, since it meant I had only
myself to impress and that trick never works.
Once I slept with a man right after his wife died.
He said it was her last wish. Once a man promised
to make me a star. Once a man drove his brand new car
directly toward a tree to see if I'd flinch or scream,
which is how he recognized care. I said

I'd welcome death and groped his crotch. He
turned away. I had late night dates with another man
who turned out to look so much like my father
when he was twenty five— in a photo I never saw—
thank God—until years later. I'd meet him
in his shower at precisely ten o'clock.
For a while I pretended to be the plumber
who needed to check out his pipes. After
that wore off, we'd usually end up sitting together
on the shower floor while hot water rained down. We'd
sit there and admire our feet getting cleaner
and cleaner near the drain. Usually he'd be drunk
before I even got there, and want to talk about
his first lover's suicide. When I wouldn't agree
to tie him up and then punch him until he fell asleep,
well, that was that. He yelled faggot at me
from a car once when I was walking on the street.
Once I slept with a man who was kind but
not attractive at all, just to see if I could make
what I thought was the right choice. Forget
running with scissors or dropping pennies off
the Empire State Building or swimming right after lunch.
There was only had to have, have, had, had it with.
One man I nearly killed myself over I ended up
laughing about. Another I laughed at then now I miss
like the best goddamned dog I ever knew, who
I could tell anything to, who listened even though
he could never help me which did help in the end.
I was ordering drinks on a plane to Europe
when he got put down. Sometimes I still
feel his big warm weight beside me in the night
and turn toward it before I think, oh, right.

DWIGHT OKITA (U.S.A., B. 1958)

Where the Boys Were

1. The Nightmare
It was the year Madonna
came into public view
and left her belly button print in cement
in front of Grauman's Chinese Theatre.

But it's the nightmare
I keep remembering
of boys falling from trees,
from the sky.
Boys landing in construction sites,
quarries, on top of buses, at intersections
where the lights go green all at once.

Turn your head to cough
and 5,000 boys fall from the sky.
It's frightening. Light candles
in Central Park to their shadows
falling all night. Push them back
into heaven with our little flames.

2. The Media
I met a man named Bruce
at an AIDS conference
who was getting better. TV cameras
closed in on him, lenses sparkling
with good news, they held him up
to the nation as a symbol of hope.
He's dead now.

And I read about Jim—
a man from Texas who has AIDS.
When he was little, his concept of heaven
was a canasta game with lots of coffee and cigarettes.
But recently in the shower,
he found a maroon splotch on his arm.
Maroon, like a color they leave somewhere.

And now heaven seems closer somehow.
He can almost hear the shuffling of cards
from somewhere high up and far away.

3. A Man Chooses His Funeral Urn
Sometimes a man sits down on stone steps
beside the pink and brown jar
which will contain him. It could be
a teapot but there's no spout. He's dying.
He sits down in the middle of the stone steps
as if in the middle of his life.

Lifts the lid,
the pretty, bubblegum-pink ceramic urn
with brown Japanese strokes
swirled in. He lifts the lid
and looks deep into it:
So this is where I'm headed.
So this will be my new home.

He's tired, he wants
to rest his thinning legs.
Wants to hold
that pink and brown teapot
gently in his hands, as it will one day
hold him. Whisper something
sweet and funny into the empty space
so that he will not be alone
when he gets there.
A nickname. *Baby Doll.*

4. Voice
When they look at my life
like a charcoal sketch
ripped from a pad, tell them
I wasn't done.
That there was color to be added—
oranges, pinks, greys.
That all the lines would eventually lead
toward the horizon, some vanishing
point past the paper's edge.

Tell them how finally
there was nothing left of me:
I ran out of dance steps on a crowded floor,
the parquet wood cracked
beneath my feet.
How I threw my name into the air
and it came down faded ticker tape,
unreadable.

I suppose I'll come hurtling down
from heaven, handsome again. Let me fall
where no one will find me
so you can go on with your life—
a wedge of honeydew melon rocking on a plate.
Pretend it's a bad dream.
Wake up from it.
Wake up from it as I could not.

Some Tattoos

Last night, John and I
went to sleep talking about
the tattoos we'd leave
on each other. Anchors, eagles—no,
not the ordinary things.
For him, I wanted an airplane
gliding across his left thigh.
For me, he saw a parachutist
coming down across the sky of my chest.
And we called each other
merciless in our planning.
And we could be spoons in bed,
sky to sky— the parachutist
and the plane he left.
In the morning, it made no difference.
We woke late, tattooless,
more naked than ever.

                        *

He had the sun tattooed
on his chest, I had the moon
and when we made love face to face,
we called it an eclipse.
The blue shadows we cast
on the bed below us, the sunglasses
we wore to look at each other.
And when you put your weight
on me, when the room went dark
and vast—it was hard
not to hear the planets whirring,
the stars coming on, hard to imagine
a time before Sun and Moon, this
eclipse.

                        *

When we leave the bar
they stamp our hands with
a rubber stamp and for a moment
we are passports—why shouldn't
our bodies say so? But even
when they stamp a navy blue eagle
on your wrist as if to say
the door is open, fly right in—
you can never come back.
Better to drown the eagle
in warm soap and water, better
to forget the places you have been
that mark you, that change you,
that leave you standing at
a bathroom sink at 4 a.m.
rubbing pictures from your hands.

STEPH PIKE (U.K., B. 1967)

Civil Partnerships and All That Jazz

we're getting civvied up
we're de-mob happy
the war is through
we're rushing out
to say, "I do, I do!"
we're very nearly
just like you
we're in the suburbs
with our 4x4s and 2.2
kids. we go on family trips
to International Ladies Day
hey, times have changed
we've won the right
to become racist thugs in blue
to butch it up in prisons
swing our keys
clank our chains
join the army
we're in the main-
stream now
we're getting carried away
we're celebrating this freedom we've found
with our beautiful, shiny, pink pound
we're pushing out the boat
we're afloat at last
are we fuck. we're all at sea
because this isn't a war that we won
we just crossed over to the enemy

Age 7

it was the year of that dress;
a lemon-meringue mess
of yellow nylon
and white lace trim

in that dress
she was not the girl
who bent a paper-clip
and felt the whip of your hand
on her face

in that dress
she was not the girl
who threw her first punch
and heard the satisfying crunch
of her sister's nose

in that dress
she was not the girl
you chased with a belt
and who, for the first time,
smelt her own fear

in that dress
she was not the girl
who disappointed your days
with her strange
and awkward ways

in that dress
she was all things nice
sugar and spice
her mother's pride
the apple of her daddy's eye

in that dress
she was straight-jacket calm
good as gold
with folded arms and knees closed
who tried and tried to please;

she was your bees knees

that was the year;
a little girl
in a bile-yellow dress
waiting to explode

JULIANA HU PEGUES (U.S.A., B. 1969)

Conception
For Sông Mikiko Haley Phi-Hu

conception, *noun.*
1. a general notion or thought
2. an idea of something formed by combining all its characteristics; a construct
3. fertilization, especially in pregnancy
conception, not to be confused with inception
even though you were there,
   in my mind,
   always.

to construct a child
to fertilize a dream
to compose a lyric, note by triumphant note

to conceive, *verb.*

to conceive meaning to begat
as in my daughter was conceived
by a Chinese woman with long legs
and a big nose
who came from a woman
fond of comfortable shoes
and deep discounts
who came from a woman
carrying her children across
two borders and a civil war
who came from a woman,
   came from a woman,
   came from a woman.

to conceive as in sperm
greeting egg like an arrow,
a missive, a salmon—sweet sliver
of silver climbing water,
sockeye coho king,
arriving to shallow pool
and gravel bed.
all upstream to the end,
   life meets death,
   meets life again.

to conceive meaning to voice
an alternate universe as in
turkey basters and sperm bankers
double dads and trannie aunties
birth mothers and other mothers
family style conceived as
capacious as our appeals

for life
and love

to conceive meaning to hold an opinion,
as in i can't conceive of a world
where a mama who must bear
the weight of a drunk driver's
tires atop baby girl,
running out into that street
only to get hit by a
            three-year
            prison sentence.

can't conceive of a world
where a mama must bear
the weight of a teenage son
beneath 8 leaden bullets
only to be told the
gravity of this force
is not extreme
when Youa Vang and
Raquel Nelson live
with an impossible
excess—dying children
            they carry
            always.*

this started as a love poem for my daughter
wanted to write a love poem for you daughter

but
the
world
is
a
heavy
place
i may be the poet
but you conceive the best ideas

live art as crayons on the wall

eat a balanced meal of avocado and veggie booty

our jokes a cat with a keyboard
and the Chinese word for fart
            fong pi, fong pi, fong pi

you, child, pull miracles out of your ass

you conjure joy against no hope

you magick my smile at the end of gray days

this started as a love poem for my daughter
and ends not with a promise but a wish:

may your small arms and legs
propel you fearlessly into
            your glorious and
            uncertain future.

After an impaired hit-and-run driver killed her son on a road in Atlanta in 2010, Raquel Nelson was convicted of vehicular manslaughter by an all-white jury (Nelson is Black) on the grounds that Nelson and her children were not in a crosswalk. Youa Vang is the mother of Fong Lee, a Hmong youth who was killed by a Minneapolis police officer in 2006 amidst questionable circumstances.

Miss Miscegenation

Me and my genes are all tangled up
and confused/rolled up slap happy
and amused/at the status
of things.

How it's gonna be for folks
like me/in a check-the-box
draw-the-lines and sit yourself
smack dab in it (don't talk to
your neighbor but be with it)
type of a world.

As a swirl girl I don't get it
but I do.
Miscegenation blues.

Kinda like the sky with a triple scoop
cone on a hot autumn day when my banana
nut melts with that double fudge cocoa
brownie/hitting that *ooh la la*
French vanilla on the way down and
mixes with mathematical superstition
in a cosmic artistic rendition whirling
dripping and dipping into that delicate
curve between my thumb and forefinger
before you deliciously lick it up
with a satisfied smirk.

GERRY POTTER (U.K., B. 1962)

The Soldiering of Soldiering On

*There are always turning points. Life moments that rock you out of your sensibility and
routine. Unfair on the surface and not necessarily about middle age. Respect to those
moments and their teachings, both horrific and joyous.*

This is not positivia.
I'm well aware a child somewhere
Is watching her mother die of AIDS,
That a trickle-down joy has made a smile.

A beach fire.
A scald.
A street party.

This is not a white-wash
Where we cleanse our chakras clarity blue.
It's simply the soldiering of soldiering on.
Because you have to,
Simply have to.

Unless you don't want to.
Can't.
That's a different story
And I understand it.

The wandering of wondering things,
The pond-life of pondering,
Because history isn't made up of ding-dong-dings.
That never happened.

This is water on a morning face,
Ting-a-ling-a-ling.
The mourning of a wintered state,
The demolition of fate,
Re-imagining of great.
It's a world, things happen.
It's the soldering of soldiering on.

This
Next breath I take,
Key I press,
Thought I hate,
Love,
Want,
It's filling time.
Stuff.
Nonsense.
It's the pressure of pressing on,
Because someone loves you.

Or will.
Or might.
Or can't.
Won't, even.
Not allowed.
Remember those amazing parties
Where laughter rediscovered humanity?

Because someone, somewhere, is making soup,
Brilliant soup.
Or crayoning a butterfly.
The lovely colours of crayons.

This is not positivia.
I'm well aware some people can't afford crayons
And we're training teenagers to shoot teenagers.
Simply the soldiering of soldiering on,
Because there's tea to drink
And monsters to manifest.
Toast.
Rages.
A stumble that makes you smile.
Those amazing parties.
There's a rhyme to hide in the miming of language.

Soup!
For God's sake man, there's soup,
Brilliant soup,
And we all know how that can taste.

It's ache.
It's kiss.
The murmuring of *Wuthering Heights*.
The jangle-woven danger of secrets.
The smell of a puppy.
Your first E.
That child's mother has died of AIDS.
Ting-a-ling-a-ling.
Snow.

Cake

Some men have no intention to stop.

How did The Man get so greedy?
Did he see the world like a great big cake
Baked just for him and the people he owns?
Crumbs!
Did he think all that cream could cleanse his soul?
A pussy milk, soured thick and curdling,
Bubbling intensely like the festering larder of a cannibalistic
B-movie monster.
A monster made from dead men, sultanas and bit part actors,
Baked to disorder and imperfection
By a misguided mad professor.
A misguided mad professor
Determined to imitate the greatness and perfection of God.

Did he think he could hide that sweet sticky stink
With a pomander,
Hysterically squealed from a make-over show?
A pomander reimagined from leftover Christmas cake, Armageddon and crackers.
You know the make-over show I mean,
The one with the two camp pretenders trilling overdose
And oblivion in television Scots.
How did The Man decide on this?
Och-Aye the noo!

When did he think it was a good idea to see people
Who might be great artists or builders
Grovel for cake or beg for what's left
Of the very last bits of the rotting cow?
When did he think this was a good thing to teach his children?
When did The Man decide other men
Could not be great artists or builders?

Is there a time somewhere I don't know
Where The Man stood alone
Atop his ivory tower and declared to the world
That his voice
Would be the only voice obeyed?
In that same time-space I don't know,
Did all the other men agree?
Was The Man's name God
Or Tony
Or Rupert
Or Margaret
Or Adolph,
Chuck or Rod,
Or a name made unpronounceable
By the very evil of its nature?
A name with more letters than there are scars in the sky,
Filth in the sea.

A name that created wanting in our hearts.
A name that carved hollow into empty.
There are names so old they can no longer be spoken,
Ask the lipless and invisible.
Oh dear!
When did The Man kneel
To the prissy blonde homicide of cash?
Why did he kiss it full on the mouth and call it "Sugar?"
Why did he get so greedy wanting more cake
And decorate it the way he did?
Why did The Man rape and murder or murder and rape
[take your pick]
Those children in the concentration camp
And why did other men cheer
And why does it still go on?

How much cake can any man want?

"Someone left the cake out in the rain
I don't think that I can take it
'Cos it took so long to bake it."

Crumbs!

Copse And Robbers

For the first time in my gay life I have started to enjoy the fruits of sober daytime cruising. Manchester's alive with secrets. Part of this adventure featured in BBC2's Britain in a Day.

Flowers hang their heads
Like Edwardian servant girls
To a brash beating sun.
Mystery's rotting in the orchard.
Breathing the sweet decay of apples
Is history.

Through the trees light splatters.
Ocean flecks
Dancing liquid green.
This is the pornography of dreaming,
The secrets of awake.
Hidden in the bushes,
The freedom of guilt
And the rape of religion.

For the faithless trapped by faith
This is Eden.

Heavy with machismo
The trogs affect men,
Lumbering leather and chains,
Look like Gestapo
Not like they fell from trees.
Middle-Eartha Kitts
Disguising effeminacy and grunting.

And by the apples, condoms.
Like a joke for Adam.

A sudden shift and storm,
Branches shake like *Night of the Demon*
"It's in the trees!"
And a queen with all her fairy
Screams
"I've just had three cocks
But I prefer the weather."
I recognise a witch
A sister,
We howl inside the wind.
Nature's bitches,
We are her wit.

IAN IQBAL RASHID (U.K., B. 1964)

Middle-Aged Love

5

Suddenly this offering
like a scarlet autumn heat,
or somehow understanding a foreign phrase,
the revisit of a happy daydream to ease
a dark, addled night.
A jewel swaddled in sawdust,
muscles long thought wasted
now plump and round with aspiration.

The two syllables of your name
butter my parched lips,
vowel, consonants, another vowel,
ready to be sung
to be rhymed with everything.

Another Country

All this new love of my parents' countries. We
have bought the videotapes together, bought the
magazines and books, all the advertisements,
 clothes and each others' responses. We watch the
slides of your visit. Your handsome face is tanned
surrounded by mango trees, planted above the
poverty. The moist beauty—which you think of
blowing up and then framing, building into your
walls—majesty imposed upon majesty.

Now I watch you watch Sergeant Merrick watch
poor Hari Kumar. And follow as the white man's
desire is twisted, manipulated into a brutal beating.
You are affected by the actor's brown sweating
body, supple under punishment. What moves you?
The pain within the geometry of the body bent?
The dignity willed in the motions of refusal?
A private fantasy promised, exploding within every
bead of sweat? Or is it the knowledge of later?
How my body will become supple for you,
will curve and bow to your wishes as yours can never
quite bend to mine? What moves you then?

My beauty is branded into the colour of my skin,
my strands of hair thick as snakes, damp with
the lushness of all the tropics. My humble penis
cheated by the imperial wealth of yours: Hari's
corporal punishment, mine corporeal... Yet this is
 also part of my desire. Even now, stroking myself
against your absence, I close my eyes and think of
England.

JOSEPH ROSS (U.S.A., B. 1958)

The Silence of Lawrence King 1993-2008, a requiem in two voices

To be a 15 year-old boy is tough.

Man, don't talk to him, he acts like a little girl.

To be a 15 year-old boy
and gay is tough.

He ain't nothing but a faggoty little girl.

To be a 15 year-old boy
and gay and in love with another boy
in your junior high school is tough.

Man, that queer don't know what's going on.

To be a 15 year-old boy
and gay and in love with another boy
in your junior high,
with Valentine's Day approaching is tough.

You got a sweetheart little gay boy?

To be a 15 year-old boy
and gay and in love with another boy
in your junior high,
with Valentine's Day approaching
and ask that boy to be your Valentine is tough.

What did you say, faggot?

To be a 15 year-old boy
who is gay, and in love with another boy
in your junior high,
with Valentine's Day approaching
and ask that boy to be your Valentine,
and then to come to school the next day
is to be dead.

Yeah, you can't say shit now, can you?

Stonewall Riots, New York, 1969

The lights rose
to police badge brightness,

exposing those who only wanted
to be seen at their own pace.

But this time, breathless
and nameless, they fought back.

Dancing hands balled into fists,
feather boas balled into fists,

men and women became
men and women,

each one carrying a paschal
memory of life in a tomb,

no longer willing
to settle for darkness,

their own,
or anyone else's.

MAUREEN SEATON (U.S.A., B. 1947)

The White Balloon

"To love something you know will die is holy."
          --Kaddish, AIDS Memorial, New York, 1987

The air is gravid with life,
the cloudless sky swells
with souls, ascending.

I'm in charge of one young soul
tied to my wrist
with a string that won't break.

St. Veronica's, the end of June:
You weep beside me, hold
a candle steadily near the flame.

Earlier we were two ladies
shopping on Broadway. I recall
your wire of a body,

the delicate arc of ribs
and small breasts above—this
as you quick-changed

in search of something radical,
feminine. Your terror of pink
amused me. You said:

Don't tell anyone
of this sudden reversal. I said:
I will, but I'll change your name.

Linda, it's the letting go
that terrifies, the night air
alive with rising ghosts,

the cries of strong men
grieving in each other's arms,
the ease with which we love.

When I was Straight

When I was straight I dreamed of nipples,
my dreams were crowded with cleavage and yin,
I read a book that said if you are fickle

about sex, note your obsession in dreams
then do the opposite in real life. This
made sense, my boyfriend said, although it seemed

oddly like a game of Exquisite Corpse
to me. We'd make love, I'd dream of figs,
that drizzled pink, and sometimes I'd lapse

into madrigals (meaning: of the womb), big
leap from the straightforward sessions in bed
of linearity and menthol. Legs

would cross and uncross in my dreams, heads
fall back with me at the throat. I adored
the winged clavicle, that link between breast-

bone and scapula. Straight as gin, I poured
myself into pretense and fellatio,
you could count on me for bold orgasms, for

trapeze art and graceful aerobics, oh
there is no lover like a panicked lover.
Once I dreamed of abandoning the Old

Boyfriend Theory of Headache and Blunder-
buss. Believe me, I said, this will hurt him
more than me, but the dream laughed! Torture

me, I thought, now that even my id
has turned against me, there is something fragile
here to lose, exquisite truth, and I did.

Sex Talks with Girls

When sleeping in the same bed with another girl, old or young, avoid 'snuggling up' close together...and, after going to bed, if you are sleeping alone or with others, just bear in mind that beds are sleeping places. When you go to bed, go to sleep just as quickly as you can.

—Irving D. Steinhardt, *Ten Sex Talks to Girls* (1914)

1

Girls may appear innocent, even girls
whose breasts develop early and who
calmly wait for their body to grow hair
down there and under here, places no girl
should ever look. Turn your thoughts to creweled
coverlets. Cook a moist turkey, tat
a pillowcase. There is no better way
through puberty than the fine art of Home
Economics. Cupcakes are a great dis-
traction from awkward sexual urges.

2

Remember that God made Adam, and Eve
fell for a viper while our first man
stood by munching a Macintosh. Pity
boys—they aren't equipped to compete with snakes.
For instance, where would we be if Snow White
had settled for wildlife? Fairy tales are great
guides for living. Like *The Lives of the Saints.*
Saints had their hands cut off rather than sin.
Don't waste your time on girls. It's like kissing
a mirror or rubbing against a stuffed cat.

3

It is never okay to hug a girl
who looks like James Dean. If you're unable
to stop yourself, invoke the name of your
patron saint, and think about martyrs. If
it's Joan, ask her to guide you through the fire
of your formative years. She herself died
too young to think about sex in her man-
ly clothes with her sword and her armor suit.
But remember: They burned her alive for her-
esy. (Even now, you've got to wonder.)

4

To summarize: Sleep quickly and alone.
Stay away from snakes, Joan of Arc, James Dean
flicks, and women's sports. Cook furiously
to appease hormones. Do not trust flowers.
Consider the seaside a possible
temptation. When developing a crush,
check for a real penis and stop yourself
if you don't see a white horse. Everything
should be Disney or saintly. Under no
circumstances should there be chemistry.

Sally Field

If I could be any actor it would be Sally Field. If I could sleep with any actor
it would be Queen Latifah. Field reminds me a little of me if I weren't

so phobic about flying. Latifah, you might say, has become a famous femme
in recent years—if you judge by the makeup and the glossy

magazine spreads. Still, the way she rapped in the old days…and that *Set It Off*
scene. The thing I like about Field is her seamless approach to her

life and work. Plus she's a mom and she says censorable things. I like that she
loved two men in *Norma Rae.* I've had trouble myself loving just one

person over the years. I could easily have three lovers at a time like a Mormon
or a beach cat. Latifah reminds me of the night one of my lovers

dressed up as a femme fatale and sang me a torch song. Not all butches can
do that. Some look like drag queens when they put on femme clothes.

Even in a construction hat and steel-toed boots I femme myself out. That's where
Sally Field and I have something else significant in common.

Cowboy boots just make us look cuter.

GLENN SHELDON (U.S.A., B. 1957)

First June in Our New House

wondrous face in moonlight

your arms windmill with delight

stare at stars to frighten their flicker

bird bath breaks by thirst of a possum

something answers you throaty

quiet symphony of yellow lights

uncertain to brush our chorus off

they mellow flights so we sleep there

luminous clock without arms

lets lie in our grass you say

but lightning bugs swell around our faces

you make frog sounds and

we creep into the mud room at midnight

on our shoulders

or bring them inside where cats will neuter

in brief human glow

AIDS Arrives at its First Sweet Door

Inside, beneath the downy quilt
the sailor holds a picture book.
Panama, where he was stationed.

This page of the Canal, this
specific angle makes its locks and
dams look like the scars of his wrists.

Alone, he chokes on a pill.
He panics, leaps up and crashes
into the wall. Coughing,
the pill comes up like a cloud.

"Goodnight," he growls to himself.
Now on his feet, he feels
for his body, presses down
on the flesh over here and behind there,
hoping to find something.

Placing his thumb firmly upon
the pulse of his ankle, he hears
his name being spelled out
by someone else's voice.

The goodnight sky swells
into a thunderstorm.
Watching out his window,
a lightning bold splices
his favorite cedar tree in half.

The red-tailed darts once
embedded in its summer bark are
randomly sprinkled all
over his muddy front yard.

He goes outside. The goodnight sailor
begins to cart the tree limbs
away. At the curb, he starts
to feel it: a bit of God still inside
the worn, almost pulsing, wood.

Anniversary Poem: May 3, 2001*
                for RA

I hear impulse: to speak your name,
to create circles in the sand, surround

your body with the syllables of you.

The floors of this empty house drink
dusty neglects: why sweep up sleeplessness?
Why polish the almost empty mirrors?

Now it is May, and I can open the naked
windows. Let the breeze be my maid! There has been
too much world behind the windows.

Soon you will be home; it will be Thursday
returned to Little Bee and me, your own bed.
Soon we will touch.

I will roast a pork loin; I will cancel my own trip.
I will pick you up at the airport; we can fill the day
with clever shadows, not destinations.

* written for my life partner of 28 years, the late Rane Arroyo, in anticipation of our 19th anniversary

When Someone Cold Comes Home . . .

. . . a school of lovers swim home with him.

This morning I woke, wet and
green in the bed: not plural *beds* for
it is always my one bed; merman are
attracted to me for I am captain
of the promiscuous heart that beats within.

One lover, smelling of brandy and aglow
with algae, froze overnight in the Arctic;
he had a hard-on straight as a compass
needle but pointed into a fifth direction.

Last night he came home cold and
I did not want him here; the police just rolled
their eyes at my story and I dared not blink
for something told me that blinkers look like liars.

I swore to them: I slept on the floor, alone, but woke
this morning more satisfied than having a school
of lovers; my hands had hurried home
to become the warmest of strangers.

Still that damned song floated up
through my dreams: *Pack up that heart
of mine and throw away the key.*

Now standing here in just a towel, fresh
from a much-needed shower, I know that
I, too, am an old suitcase of sea.

NATHAN SIEGEL (U.S.A., B. 1967)

Repugnant Translations

The Good News Bible for Children
contains the translation: "No man is
to have sexual relations
with another man; God hates that."
The Holy Bible Contemporary
English Version Children's
Illustrated Edition contains
the translation: "It is disgusting
for a man to have sex
with another man," and:
"It's disgusting for men
 to have sex with one another,
and those who do
will be put to death,
just as they
deserve."

Are these the verses
a child
finds
in the sacrosanct "Good Book"
today ?

How do
you feel
about
this
teaching ?
this
reading ?

Whose words
are these ?

I question
the pairing
of God
with hates.
In the Bible and out of it.

i oppose war

silence equals death
i oppose censorship
silence equals death
i oppose religious interference
silence equals death
i oppose racism, sexism, ageism, homophobia
silence equals death
i celebrate sex body life your voice my voice

DOROTHEA SMARTT (U.K., B. 1963)

gambian sting

A Gambian sting left her in Kwinella.
No money, no passport, nothing.
These brothers know what to say, run it like
a pre-recorded tape: play-pause-rewind.

No money, no passport, nothing.
These guys had promised overstanding,
said, "Yes, Rasta sistah!" smiling at her
dreads. Said, "Yes, you are home, in Africa."

These 'brothers' know what to say, run it like
a life line between me and the longing
they read in my eyes, the restless ghosts
of unspeakable times jostling for redemption.

A Gambian sting. Left her in Kwinella
at the base of a silk cotton tree.
Tears washing the red ochre, dusting her feet,
spirits thronging to give salvation to the restless.
A Gambian sting left her in Kwinella.
No money, no passport, nothing!
These brothers know what to say, run it like
a pre-recorded tape: Play. Pause. Rewind
the lash, the sting marking us both.

Eclipse Over Barbados

Look up man! Wha wrong wid d'moon?
D'sky clear-clear, an' a t'ousand stars flickering,
begging me look up. Dey are endless!
But wha'happen to de moon? Man she slipping 'way!
Cast over by sumtin', blot out, the dark rejoicing!
Disappearing, she staring eye interrupted! –
Is dis m'las chance to run 'way?
Get on d'ship?
Not get on d'ship?
How I is to read dese signs and portends?
How I is to know? She slipping 'way
but look, she peeping out de nex side,
coming back to me, whole I hope.
Maybe she got secrets fuh tell me
when I cast m'full eye pun she.
Moon? Wha' could mek y'pass yuh dark side pun we so?
The waiting ship?

Dey gon put me in the deep-down hole again.
An' all I could do is let dese quiet tears
fall and shake m'soul-case heavy.
Mek me dig m'hans in dis earth to keep me here.
The others, here to stay,
look pun me like I doom, like I is a traitor to leave dem.

I leavin? Or somebody takin' me?
It's not fair! Dey doan like me, 'cause I leavin,
leavin d'pickney gang;
leavin de steaming pot of molasses
and de hard-wuk cane, and de licks;
leavin de sun brooding down on muh back
searing de sores an' de scars from d'whip.
I leavin dem to boil in de rum factory,
to mash and tun, to be mash and tun.

I leavin
an' de dark moon telling me t' g'long
an' see what pun de other side.
Mebbe d'ship gon tek me back
Mebbe d'ship gon tek me back!

An' Mummy will be dere, pounding cassava,
an' Daddie will sing out a call to prayer jus' fuh me,
jus fuh me one.
Maybe.
Maybe.
An' dis disappearing moon? Dancing slow widda shadow,
whu she got t'tell me?
De full-shine o'she marking my face
with signs. There an' then,
there an' then, she made me her own.

An' I know
how much she want me back,
and I goin' on dis nex ship
and maybe,
maybe, jus' maybe,
it gon take me home.

PAMELA SNEED (U.S.A., B. ?)

Beloved

I want to tell you this before the book closes
last line written
my mother is not the same person
I knew as a child.
She is not the woman driving fingernails into my skin,
not the woman beating and denying me mercilessly—
She is not the woman who appeared to me at 6 years old
as my father's 2nd wife,
not the woman so frightened and afraid
of a new situation
and her husband's black daughter from another marriage.
She is almost no longer the person refusing
to buy me clothes, dolls, schoolbooks
and things that I needed,
not the woman responding with malice to my every
and seldom request.
She is not the woman in a picture
whose face was chiseled into hard mean stone,
nor the person to whom anger flashed
in her eyes perpetually—
No, over years and time my mother has softened some
and at 68 she has grown beautiful,
childlike, vulnerable
exploring, curious,
is a child herself for the first time.

She has taken to reading mystery novels
and talks of world history using new and impressive vocabulary.
She buys expensive dresses, and invests in her appearance.
She watches Oprah Winfrey on television
and went to see the movie adaptation of Toni Morrison's novel "Beloved,"
She also tells me her opinion and speaks of global issues—
She half listens when I talk now,
kissing hello,
she is able to kiss back,
though she is still not whole.
I know somewhere in the back of her mind
she still hears me screaming,
"You've treated the cats better," and asking,
"Why have you never said I'm beautiful?"
though her first instinct is denial,
I know she hears my voice in her
and she can't respond
except this birthday, my mother sends me a card
after 30 years I've waited
I receive it unexpectedly
when I've already sworn she's forgotten
and this card for some reason feels special,

not Hallmark,
but is one of those new fangled African American ones
with a picture of a pretty Black girl on it's front
it reads:
Daughter,
you are beauty, light& inspiration—
and on the inside it says,

"I am blessed to have you as a daughter and friend"
And somehow I feel that the sentiment expressed is not mistaken,
my mother has chosen
whether it's burrowed deep in her subconscious or not,
now is the time, she has purposefully picked to tell me,
I am loved.

Turtle Eggs

I'm laying on a beach in Mexico, just staring at the horizon
when this White gung ho surfer dude comes up to me and says,
  "Blissed out, huh?"
"Yes," I say, to which he responds by sitting down,
telling me how he's traveled the world, but he says, "It's my first time to Mexico,"
and it would be even better, he adds, "if they had some environmentalists."
"What?" I ask, but believing he's found a fellow confidante he continues,
"The other day I went surfing on this practically deserted beach
and I met two Mexican boys who tried to impress me
by showing me some rare turtle eggs.
They also told me turtle eggs are delicacies to eat,
I got mad and told those boys, if they continued eating the eggs,
turtles are going to become extinct."
It's obvious that the gung ho surfer man is proud of his statements
and assumes I share his perspective.
Instead, I say "Mexico is poor and the people's priorities are shelter and eating,
and until the quality of life for poor people is improved,
they won't look after and care for the environment."
Startled as if by a wave of politics,
surfer dude rapidly removes himself,
which brings back another point in my own Brooklyn neighborhood
whereas on a Sunday morning I'm awakened at 9 am to sounds of an electric saw
and my neighbor's two agitated rottweilers who are barking from yards over
into my bedroom window.
After working all night and feeling jolted out of a bartending stupor
I rise, open the window wider and yell
"Shut those fucking dogs up, and turn the goddamn saw off,
It's 9 am Sunday morning and people are trying to sleep!"
My neighbor barely responds and continues to saw,
which brings me back to another point, which I hate to say,
hate when it's said about Asians, Blacks, Irish, Puerto Ricans and Jews,
but it's true, WHITES REALLY RUIN NEIGHBORHOODS.

Five years ago, when I moved in, my neighborhood was eclectically mixed
with Blacks, Latinos, White working class, and it was quiet.
No, we all didn't get along, but it was quiet.
Then three years ago we were discovered as Manhattan's cheaper alternative
and suddenly there are Whites everywhere
buying and renovating half million-dollar homes, a block away from the projects—
Whites who've replaced indigenous, Latino cuchifrito shops and cafe con leche
with strict cappuccino.
Whites with dogs of every shape and size without leashes
allowed to run free,
not understanding everyone in the free fucking world doesn't love
or enjoy Puffy Wuffy.

There was a time in recent past where I lived and left my house in relative ease,
but now since the neighborhood changed
I'm accosted at the front door by two leashless, glaring rottweilers
and an owner who's half a block away. When I complain
he explains to me like one of those new-age permissive parents
how his obnoxious, tantrum-riddled rottweilers are just babies.

Not only is my street littered and peppered with dog shit,
property values are up!
So that once moderately priced apartments are twice the price
and artists are moving to Queens.

The Whites have also brought with them these strange little shops and
restaurants where you can't get a meal or sandwich for under ten dollars, so that a meal
around the block,
offering a minute green salad, can cost upwards of 20 dollars
and there is still strangely nothing to eat.
They're also into beautifying and improving the environment.
Suddenly there are private gardens cropping up everywhere,
construction at every hour, morning, day, noon and night
and every once abandoned, dilapidated building is now a billion, trillion dollar site
with ultra thin looking Vanna White showroom models. And agencies
like Verizon, Con Edison and cable who were once scarce
are eager to please, and on once quiet, relatively clear streets
there's traffic, tourists arriving by busloads
carrying maps
eating at outdoor cafes
staring as I pass by in casual Sunday sweats.

My new neighbors, like parents, are also angry, righteous and entitled
forming block parties, coop boards,
and offering millennial visions to determine the future of our neighborhood.
One of my friends who is White and lives next door is out one day
picking up the trash, trying to beautify the neighborhood.
He looks at me strolling by and says "Why don't Blacks do more?"
"Why don't they care about the neighborhood?"
I try to respond as if for the entire race, not withstanding my experience
is as far from project Blacks as it is from
that of the Whites populating our neighborhood.
Impatiently I explain, as I did to the gung ho surfer,
"Because we don't own half million dollar homes, and landlords exploit us,
until our everyday concerns for survival are met,
we can't care about the neighborhood."
My neighbor looks at me unconvinced, half perplexed,
as if we were discussing something as removed, distant and ridiculous
as turtle eggs
found by children on a Mexican beach.

For David Kato

To my students who say they don't read
follow news
know no details of what's occurred over the past two weeks in Tunisia, Egypt
never heard of David Kato, a gay human rights activist murdered in his home in Uganda
after a newspaper outed him and other gay activists
In a fit of fear care rage I say there's a government, system,
a whole world banking
that banks you'll be asleep
at the mall shopping catching a sale trying on jeans
texting lovers friends
meanwhile 24 public schools in New York are being closed those affected are predominately poor Black,
Latino, working class
still they're giving you credit cards, loans, mortgages and banking you can't won't read fine print
follow nothing except a twitter stream
that all this multi tasking has all but destroyed your attention span
you can't last five minutes before needing another hit of something mindless
I saw someone texting updating FB continuously the other night through a play/presentation of Tennessee
Williams, an American Master
Yes, there's a government, a world, corporations working overtime
so we can all feel connected, but banks on us being separate
not caring about your neighbor because we're all too busy
and isolation takes hold
Like Reconstruction after slavery
school lunch programs
affirmative action after civil rights
In South Africa they are trying to build anew after apartheid
where for Blacks laws were separate and unequal
separate experiences for Whites, Blacks, Indians, Coloreds
and then I think about here how everyone has a separate experience
one class from another
Blacks, Latinos, and those who are poor experience separate education,
separate knowledge
Last year, I taught poetry in a residency with a choreographer at Paul Robeson High school
one of those schools now designated to close in the deep pocket of Caribbean/Black Brooklyn
I remember how those kids expressed even then feeling less valuable, worthless with their school/ culture
on the chopping block
minutes after the school board announced Paul Robeson would close
they said it had been purchased by IBM
so all of the years of pretending the closure was up for debate was just theater
it was planned all along
the entrance will be citywide and competitive
so the whole culture of Crown Heights has been wiped out
so how am I supposed to sit here and do what history does
separate the narrative of Crown Heights Brooklyn from apartheid South Africa
How do I not see here a Bantu education
forcing children out of their native languages forcing them to speak Afrikaans
how do I not keep seeing the first casualty of the Soweto Uprising murdered by police a dead 13 yr old
Hector Pieterson draped over the arms of his friend
his sister wailing beside them
How do I erase that Black woman who told me how the massive township Soweto was built, forcing Blacks
to live separate

"There was only one road to get in or out so the psychology was that wherever you went
the government/police could find you"
like some massive video game brought to life
a real reality show

So how do I separate the narrative of Crown Heights Brooklyn
form the streets of Egypt today where people are fighting
for basic rights, opportunity
freedom from dictatorship
How do I say of all these groups Americans may be most disadvantaged
because we don't have a clue
as to what we're fighting.

RICHARD TAYSON (U.S.A., B. 1962)

Tracks

After we'd made love all
night, and morning like a gauze
wrapped down over us,
you slipped your arm beneath
my head, and I thought
of the needle you used to
jab into your skin. Four or five
times a day, seven, maybe eight
months of your life, in your room
or on a roof somewhere,
or in a shady spot
(park, bathroom, alley)
you'd crouch down and watch
the needle's eye enter
the used vein. The pure
heat raced in you,
spread out like a parachute of fire
over you, arresting
your breath, at first, then
helping you breathe, beating
a rhythm consuming
as sex. That is how

we found each other, standing
back to back on a glass surface,
drawing each other in,

holding
nothing and everything with one
motion of our arms
in the crowded bar, in the haze
of the alcohol glow, each of us
wanting to be held, given
shape, identity, anonymous
perspective. This is the beginning

of all stories recorded in history,
the need to lose the body,
the story
within the fabrication,
the lie ("I'll love your forever,
what do you think these six months have meant?")
inside the box, the body
falling asleep

beside you. Diastolic pressure,
systolic pressure, breath
taking you beyond the border
of the real:
your father
chasing you into the forest,
green the shadows of faces around you,
leaves large as adult hands
beating you, inner arms, upper
thighs. Then the pushing,
the pressing down of your face
into the square of wet earth
you've been gliding over
(high where the light should be)
and those two hands
(is this the true story?)
that made you, hands
that shaped you from the clay
and raised you up to stand
beside your mother's burning stove:
("be still goddamnit
can't do anything right
man you're an ugly kid can't do
anything right can you")

your mother in the other room with her paintings
your mother crushing her eyes in a vise

which is where the story becomes perverted
which is where the story becomes about _____.

Her painting of the sea is what converts
as you cook hatred in a spoon,
black as your father's heart (my love),
four or five times a day, seven
or eight months of your life, staring
at the needle's mouth
and wanting
to suck it like a mother's breast
or any man's dick
who will give you money, carry you
across the self to another whole

Self, pressing
the plunger
down
slowly, letting
someone else do it for you some days
 (O miracle God above, O heaven on earth above)
each cell filling up with the pure,
each cell breaking open
until you slept

as you now sleep, your arm
crooked beneath my head, vulnerable
at the inner elbow, point
of multiple entry, cave
into cave (Lead us not into temptation
where every eye doth dwell), every
delicate thing, this world
exposed, pin-
prick, track
marks, crumbs
through the forest I keep following you back to.

I DO

I bought the rings at R.J. White Jewelers
from the old man with cataracts
who handed me the black velvet tray,
like a silver tureen reflecting black
orchids at the reception after
we'd kissed. I took
the tray and as I started to shake,

he told me to try one on for size,
then turned his back and blew
dust and dried rose petals
from the mantle. "Been in business
forty years," he said, rubbing
his finger over a smudged
mirror. So I chose the one
with tiny grooves etched
along the edge, I put it on
my ring finger, left hand—what
was I doing, this was not something
I could have planned for
or foretold, once done
it could never be cancelled.
"That's nice," he said, and told me
how he'd opened the shop in 1963,
same location, two hundred thirty dollars
to spare and a love of metals
that alchemized to liquid gold
under fire. "Back then
there weren't too many boys like you
buying rings, no sir. This was
before Stonewall, of course."
It had been years since I was called
a boy, and I thought how I was seven
the day in 1969 those men
in skirts and high heels stood up,
three blocks away, for the lives
of people like me who would one day
walk into a shop and buy a ring
for another man's finger. "You sure
this will fit him," I asked, looking
down at that perfect gold
circle, like a halo that would taste
of fire if I put it on my tongue
and swallowed. He patted my hand,
the way a grandmother would
and said, "If it doesn't, bring him in
and I'll serve the champagne I keep
chilled in back for special occasions."
R. J. winked then, and a white
of names carved in the countertop:
Michael loves Robert,
Bill +Guillermo forever.

I started to get sentimental,
so I took the F train home and found
him on the couch in his underwear,
I held him for a long time, kissed
his lips and the room crowded close
around us, everyone we loved
took a seat, relatives alive
and dead, friends alive
and dead, everyone who had been
imprisoned for kissing in public,
the ones who were tortured
and had their tongues cut out,
the ones kept in boxes
the size of the body, the ones
tied to a fence and beaten
in the name of God. In front
of them all, I held the hand
of the man I loved
and said I wanted him in my life
for as long as I have my life.
His eyes welled up, and I tasted
salt in the corners of my mouth,
then I tasted his salt inside
my mouth as we
married each other
in front of the Van Wyck Expressway
at 6:15 on June 8th, a Tuesday
which will never repeat itself.

Sylvie's House

The first time my lover took me to his mother's house,
she made Guyanese pepper pot
and showed me her altar
of Hindu gods, in the center of which
stood a statue of Jesus, palms open,
facing you.

Rohan baked Christmas cake,
and after we said a prayer
for people without
houses or warm coats, kids
whose parents left them
at birth or stuffed them
into garbage bags
and put them
in a dumpster
somewhere in one of our
famous, rich cities—we had
a champagne toast.

She's seen the photographs:
her son in Jim's blue kayak
paddling down the Colorado river;
me in front of the Canadian ski lodge,
tanned and just down from the mountain;
Rohan in his pressed suit on our first date;
the two of us kissing
in front of Karahi restaurant;
Rohan, his son and I laughing
in front of last year's Christmas tree.

Over kir she says
she wants me to meet her cousin.
When I ask how she'll introduce me,
she says, "As my son's friend, of course."

SHERI-D WILSON - THE MAMA OF DADA (CANADA, B. ?)

Circus Beserkus

I've got the big top red and white blues
striped banana and bubble toe shoes
in a wacko world we got nothin' to lose.
So let's go Circus Berserk-us! Circus Berserk-us!
Let's buzz our kazoobie kazoos
out of our rhapsodic wazoos, in high C.

Yes, I'll be your red nose clown, that's me
and you're my blue heart clown, to the n'th degree
as we splash around sweet Paris
cause it's spring—it's rainy and we're zany.
And we're heading north to Circus Berserk-us!
Circus Berserk-us!

You say:
If people from Vancouver are Vancouverites
then people from Paris are Parasites.
We howl—

You and I, we're trippy-acolytes, sans a towel,
we're castanet bons vivants
imbibing at bohemian bars,
we're whores on all fours
turning our tarot up to riant stars.
Heading north to Circus Berserk-us!
Circus Berserk-us! Gypsy Circus
all the way from Transylvania,
soma, soma, soma—Roma! Roma!

I've got the big top red and white blues
we lost our damn umbrella,
so we're getting matching downpour tattoos.
Me and you, drenched metaphysical friends
going so deep underground,
I think I feel the bends. We reek
like Nosferatu sewer-rats, entrenched
in the Metro's lair; almost there, almost there
faces running—harum-scarum
bonjour retro-Baudelaire.

♪ Do do dodododo do do do do—do do dodododo do do do do ♪

We arrive at Cirque Romanes—
Circus Berserk-us! Circus Berserk-us! Before us
caravan wheels circle like ouroboros tambourines,
lace curtains mask wagon windows,
chimera to smithereens,   ghosting
baby jumpers, feet still attached,
clothes-peg-to-clothes-peg, eyes mismatched
—dissolves and gone—
is the black haired woman
who opens the caravan door with her back
in pants and skirt and sweater and shirt
with steaming saucepan in her hand
baby squawking for goat milk from deep inside the caravan
"Bonjour Madame, bonjour"
she disappears,   gone
sleek as a pickpocket tweak.

♪ Do do dodododo do do do do—do do dodododo do do do do ♪

Bam!
Bow-tied dwarf appears. Tells us to stay
comps us. Turns our night into flame breathing
dragonesque orgasma-centiceuphoritanian-belladalodius-hocuspocus-
entredumojoplazmatoryjism-schismism.
Bravo!
He disappears in a puff,
"Merci," we say.

On with the show! On with the show!
Old woman sings long-in-coming sorrow song
which lengthens in macabre light, boulevard of broken dreams,
disappears into the vanished night.

Roll on! Roll on!
Banished are the shiny black shoes of the gypsy king
dancing slick-haired Christ, arms outstretched, dancing on and off
the cross like a drunken skeleton, soles off the moon
—gone—
is the apologetic buffoon, with exploding flowers
—gone—
are the ingénue eyes, that seduce us and death above the center ring
captivating; flying man, eyes tightly on desire, mind securely on God
extends his hand to catch the babe-in-arms, the beatitude bod
blue dolphin tattoo on his shoulder
her blue is more blue, bluer, than his blue, she jumps
he extends his fingers to seize her. Death-defying act
death-defying, no net, no, not an act, no net

timelessness   hangs   on the   air
—in a circus of suspension—
check my watch, it's gone
time escapes, eclectic marquee

as she; free-flies in ageless awe
her diamond bra flirts with sapphire
in a wink; her nubile breasts blink, blink, blink
and all the beauty of this world moves in rhythm
with this flying gypsy girl, without net, eyes of eve
—gone—
is the lanky contortionist as she bends her legs
backwards over bodice, Goddess tongue to toe
—gone—
is the mental note of the tiny holes
growing in the soles of her slippers
we see her make, before she molds, unfolds herself
into another inconceivable shape,
crystal ball saw humanly impossible
woebegone, gone, gone
like the white cat who bends metal with her mind, gone.
And the gypsy king dances toward the firing squad
spotlight travels across his yellow teeth like cigarette stained minor keys
plink plink plink,   extinct,   he has vanished,   gone
stubbed out.

Left with old man in old hat,
band drenched with sweaty brow
violin bow singing devil's sonata
the cries of annihilation
through wailing strings   waterfall of tears
and the woe of struggling years,
"La neige, le vent, les étoiles, pour certains . . . ce n'est pas assez!"

Can you hear the ghosts of Gypsies singing?
They're drawing down the moon, mirror, moon.

Can you hear the ghosts of Gypsies singing?
Shrieking strings and deep-song calls.
As poetry dies, can you hear the cries?

Can you hear the ghosts of Gypsies singing?
Circus Berserk-us! Circus Berserk-us!

Gone.
Gone.
Gone.
Gone.
Gone.
Gone.
Gone.
Gone.
Gone.

Gone.
Gone.
Gone.

The remains of the great Romanes, phantom sparks explode
nomads fling themselves on the pyre, fire   skull and bones
Gypsies expelled, deported,
disappear without rights.

Timepieces return.

There is no more lore,
my dear blue heart clown,
no more lore forever more.
My dear blue heart clown,
no more.

STONEWALL – FIRST DIAGNOSIS OF AIDS

(1970-1981)

RACHEL AMEY (U.K., B. 1970)

Feminine Hygiene

We've sanitised the past
Knees together
Given ourselves a New Look
Way past '47
Drawing the lines
Up the backs of our legs
To oblivion
Not a communist
Amongst us
Unless we were posh
And therefore
Forgiven
Not a political thought
Since Pankhurst, apparently,
- and she a terrible mother, so they say-
Did you know suffragettes
Burnt
Down churches?
And all in the name of
Democracy
It often appears to be
Unclean
The means
By which we
Really set ourselves free

The hunger strike was female
- by the way-
I guess that we invented it
Because
Its origins
Are not
Well documented

(Besides, we've been doing it for years
Though the jailers have retired
The cat and mouse of dieting
Is all that is required)

But I digress
Constance Markiewicz–
First U.K.
Female M.P.
Couldn't take her place
Too dangerous you see
- no, really-
Uprising. Easter.
1916

She was still in jail
When they came
To call out her name
Now, commentators, teachers, are careful to repeat
Lady Nancy Astor
Was "the first female U.K. M.P. to take her seat"
It's not a lie
It's the truth disguised
Paint, appliqué, deoderise
We're busy pressing transfers
On rents in pristine sheets
Rinsing doubts with borax
Down spotless kitchen sinks

Be careful
When we choose
To discuss
Handbags and shoes
That we're not
Being sold
An old
Story and
Told
That it's new

Exchanging homemade crochet
Patterns
To make a new set of chains
Waiting for the pretty lady with the magic wand
To set us free again

Well, I bagsy be the thirteenth fairy,
And I'd like an invite—quick!
Or we're sleeping girls
We're sleeping

In whose interests are we keeping
A powder puff of history
In a neatly be-ribbonned box
Parading brave but suitable heroines
And scrubbing out the faces of those that are not
Oh come on!
I bet some of those witches
Were bitches
Misunderstood
Herbalist healers my arse
We reclaim nothing
Sisters, nothing
If we only sieve gold
From the past

Picture Perfect

(Section 28/Clause 2A stated that a local authority could not "PROMOTE IN ANY MAINTAINED SCHOOL OF THE ACCEPTABILITY OF HOMOSEXUALITY AS A PRETENDED FAMILY RELATIONSHIP." This was brought in by the conservatives in 1988 and repealed in Scotland in 2000).

Right children...today we're going to draw families and places where we live...
And...yes John?...yes dear...they'll go on the walls, of course...
So...there are your pens and there is your paper...
And Stuart? ...... as we're doing families—can you not draw yours?

Now Denise...I'm sure mummy's hair isn't green...
Well...it's probably not spiky like that...
And those are what, dear? Oh, all her tattoos...
I tell you what lovey...let's draw mummy... a great big hat.

Yes Stuart? Why can't you draw your family?
Well... Anna, say, has a mummy and daddy...who'll be married from beginning to end...
And that means her family is what we call real...
Whilst yours ...is only pretend....

Yes Shirley? Yes, you just live with your mum...
No that does not mean her mum is a queer and that is not a very nice thing to...
Shirley! I don't care what she's told you darling...
......We don't need to hear.

Stuart, you're drawing! Well...yes...the actual flat you live in is real...
And no...your brother ...isn't pretend...
What I'm trying to say here Stuart...is that it's O.K. to draw your daddy...
But can you just not draw his friend....

That's a very big house dear...
Are you sure you really live there?
All those children...no mummy and daddy?
Oh sweetie...of course...I forgot...you're in care.

Stuart! I thought I said....Oh he's your Uncle
Does he come round a lot?
No he's not your real Uncle is he? Oh till he marries your Aunt!
Well you could draw the wedding.?.............but you'd rather not...

Now you have three houses, don't you? And you live with your Nan...
And what about this one? Oh this one's for sale...
I'm sure your mummy lives somewhere very very nice...
.......Spell it how it sounds, dear...Cornton Vale...

Now what's this?...mummy, daddy, brother, sister...even a dog!
Anna...this is just what I've been looking for...
Tell you what, sweetheart...without making a fuss...
Do you think you could draw me some more?

Stuart stop! In fact everyone stop...
Yes, Shirley...that means us all
Cos although you've drawn some very lovely pictures...
Only Anna's here can go on the wall
Yes I'm sure that's very upsetting...

Yes Stuart…I guessed that's how you might feel…
But although your families are very…"interesting"…
They're not what the government calls "real."

Ah, ah, ah!! The pens and the paper are already out
And we've half an hour left to go…
So…we needn't tell anyone…but if we all copied Anna's…
We'll all have something to show…

Yes? Please? Right. Pay attention. Like this…
Brother, sister, dog, mum and dad…
And Stuart and Shirley…can I make this quite clear…
There is nobody else I would like you to add….
Yes Stuart? This is your one final question…
No. I suppose I can't argue with that…
It's not wrong to be different Stuart, no—and I'm going to let you be different, Stuart— just this once…
I'm going to let you—swap the dog…
…..for a cat.

[THE END]

We've fucked it up, the fucking

we've fucked it up, the fucking
made it something it never was

middle page spread and staples
more internet and porn

we've sold out to plastic couplings
and coupled with no choice

denied our adolescents
an informed heartfelt voice

we've fucked it up, the fucking
—or maybe it always was

we come from a past
of Droit de Seigneur
—that's the right to fuck the wedding night bride
of every man in your employ

and we all know the age old story
where the son of the house
has the parlour maid
as an introductory toy

and rape is now a war crime
it's an ancient strategic idea
to penetrate the enemy lines
and populate their minds with fear

and oh dear god don't tell me
yes, the church is still to blame
I'm sorry, if this is predictable
there are some things we still need to say

we've fucked it up, the fucking
and we pretend it never was

we hide the
contact
adult to child
that underpins
our world.

call it
an occasional
outrage, whilst it
permeates
this life in which
we're immersed

we've fucked it up, the fucking
made it something it never was

If abuse has become

such a

regular
headline

cliche

then we need to take a closer look
at the part all the rest of us play

we've fucked it up, the fucking
made it something it never was

we've fucked it up, the fucking
I fear we've fucked it up too much

and now I'm here
alone
with you
we're of a mind and an age
it's fine, it's the time we might touch...

but we've fucked it up, the fucking
we've shamed the name of lust

so
tonight
you and I
let's try
to find
the time
the mind
together
to

unfuck

Cos we've fucked it up, the fucking

And we need to unfuck it all back up

CHRIS AUGUST (U.S.A., B. 1976)

An exercise in empathy

Gentlemen—
If you have a wife or a girlfriend,
Talk about her a lot this week.
But when you do,
Call her Kevin.
As in:
Kevin and I went to PTA night on Tuesday,
I bought Kevin the hottest little lycra mini skirt,
I had amazing vaginal sex with Kevin last night.
Kevin.

To your coworkers, to strangers, to your mother
Call her Kevin.
Monday and Tuesday may find you catching yourself,
So used to speaking your love by name,
But now afraid of the looks your moustached mouth will garner
When it utters the word "Kevin."

Sure, your friends know you,
Will understand what you mean,
But how can they not laugh at happy hour
When they speak of their Jennifers and Jasmines
And you swig your beer and talk of Kevin.
Even if it is about how big Kevin's titties are,
How much Kevin's smile reminds you of your mother's,
How much Kevin's perfume reminds you of your childhood.
Your silence will be worth the anonymity;
You will not mention your girlfriend Kevin very much.

These two days are roughly equivalent to twenty years,
Fifteen if you are especially lucky or enlightened,
Twenty-five or more if you are not.

If by Wednesday you grow tired of Kevin,
Feel free to switch out the proper noun for "partner":
My partner and I are taking the kids to the aquarium,
I woke up wrapped in my partner's sweat more sacred than a shroud—
Be sure that all of your friends understand
That the woman who lives inside your breath,
The woman who owns every hair on the back of your neck
Is basically a business associate.

God willing, on Thursday you will grow tired of code speak and quietness
And become bold—
You'll paint "I Heart Kevin" on all of your wife beaters
So that by Friday, Kevin will be an effortless utterance,
Your lips' two favorite syllables.

You will not ignore the confused responses
And nasty looks on Saturday,
But you will understand how little they have to do with you.
If, before this week, you harbored any false notions
Of what is and is not a choice,
Reconsider them on Sunday,
It is, after all, the Lord's day.

You will not feel the same on your first Kevinless Monday,
It is hard to avert your eyes
Once you have stared your own privilege in the face.
But don't turn away;
Spread that privilege:
Smile at the girls holding hands on the sidewalk,
Invite your brother and his boyfriend to Thanksgiving dinner.

And when a law comes to vote,
Check yes
As easily as uttering a lover's name,
Let it read like a thank you note to society
Signed by Kevin and you.

Person first

I was trained in "person first" vocabulary.
It ensures that I constantly indicate to others
that I see their humanity before I see their flaws
no matter how untrue that actually is.

For instance, my autistic student
is really my student with autism,
and his wheelchair bound fifth period math teacher
ought to be his fifth period math teacher,
who is in a wheelchair.

One day I took my class to the post office
during a trip for our Community Based Instruction class.
Or, "to the office of services that are postal for our class
on instruction that is community based"
(if we were to extend the lingo to objects that are not animate).
The purpose of this trip was to teach
Danny, my student with a brain injury,
and Lisa, my student who has Asperger's,
to make appropriate conversation
with workers who are postal.
And they were getting it.
Brandy, a girl with orthopedic challenges,
found all of the accessible entrances.
My students on the autism spectrum
made eye contact while purchasing stamps.
Everything was going swimmingly.

And then a hot Asian midget walked through the door.
Let me clarify: *midget* as in his head just cleared the counter,
Asian as in distinctly brownish (despite my inability to discern nationalities
due to my sensibilities, which are white),
and *hot* as in I was panting. In front of my students. In a post office.
I couldn't even think of what to encourage the class to call him:
A hot midget who is Asian?
A person who is hot, height disinclined and of Eastern descent?
An individual whose comparatively low stature is eclipsed by his vaguely honey-turmeric complexion,
 yielding an inappropriate degree of attractiveness?
(probably not that one.)

My brain was so frantic to address the person in words
that I almost missed the amazing thing
that was happening to the person in real life.
That thing was nothing.

Lisa and her autism said hello,
never even thinking about where his eyes were.
Brandy and Danny stumbled over their own injuries
to open the door for him when he left.
Nobody called him anything.

As for me, the closest I came to seeing
his humanity first was calling him *hot*
before acknowledging the reality of his history or his body.
I am not like my students. There is not much of me
that sees the person first. And so my mind and my mouth
work overtime to make up the difference.

SAMIYA BASHIR (U.S.A., B. 1970)

Planck's Law

What else made sense but
the push to climb one another

hand over hand and grab at
whoever was near enough?

The season groaned on
into November; crows bled

branch to sky; stone upon
stone upon stone towered

toward a heaven that flushed
its three-day-old lie of bruise.

Snowflakes threatened war
the moon split town and

swore not to return for days.
Your flicker and turn a lighthouse

and a storm. At quarter to six
the sun went down forever, so

what else made sense but to
climb one another hand over

hand and cleave to whoever was
left and near enough and would?

At the Altar

Rubber gloves, cotton mitts,
sweat coats brow, sprinkles lips.
Reach up for the kiss.

Stole the pink plastic cup
from the clinic kiddie korner;
used the enema tube bought
at the 99-cent supermarket.

Sometimes it's best fresh,
sometimes frozen.

Younger brother has
much to give, needs
minimal notice.

Want to moan, raise hips
to meet hand, reach into
forest of hair, whisper.

Fight the urge to run back
into the wardrobe, cower
behind denims and silks.

Reach down for the kiss;
close lips around communion.
Wait for answered prayers.

DOMINIC BERRY (U.K., B. 1979)

Solid with Stardust

Mother and rising son
alone.
Thatched Britain burning.
It's a witch hunt.
Mum is single-minded. She will protect
with not even a broomstick to call her sword.
Me, I'm a baby goblin,
Warm-blooded reptile with a lion's tail.

Those who were friends would now watch us burn.
Watching, whispering,
"Dirty girl."
"Yeah," Mum smiles back
"Dirty."

I marvel Mum's strength. Solid with stardust.
Woman powered beyond comprehension.
Shows me life's sparks. Dark, mystic arts.
Lizards and butterflies ink dance her skin.
Flower fairies leap in bedraggled glamour.
Eyes speak of wardrobes that all lead to Narnia.
Sweet and sour truths brewed by midnight
candlelight, cauldron deep.

A witch's familiar,
this black cat's tight round Mum's ankles.
She's always been proud
when the good people have come down,
crucifixes in hand,
preparing our bonfire.

If she had died, then she would have been human

but I know she is supernatural.
Love will lead me,
spellbound.

Not My Father

Tomorrow, I'll go dancing
because I am not my father.

Buying books on How to Breathe
because I am not my father.

Buggered at Goodwick Youth Club
because I am not my father.

We're there, so fun at weekends,
because I am not my father.

Read Six Women Poets on a cliff edge at night
because I am not my father.

You'll have to come back in the morning
because I am not my father.
I'm sorry Mum
because I am not my father.

Sometimes I'm a bit Elaine Paige
because I am not my father.

A pin-stripe man with his briefcase leaves
because I am not my father.

Yes, I do like being violent
because I am not my father.

Never say I love you
because I am not my father.

I would take a bullet
because I am not my father.

Call me any name you like
because I am not my father.

Call it "the little death"
because I am not my father.

Tell me I won't leave you
because I am not my father.

Can't let this poem stop
because I am not my father.

Time Travellers

Time travel to our past,
Manchester, 2006.
I always wanted a man who could hold nails in his teeth
and you look dead sexy holding nails in your teeth.
You know how hammers work!
Understand screw drivers!
Your arms, strong enough to lift me when
I fall apart in Tesco's, sat crying in the biscuit aisle,
my chewed up nails spiking teeth.
You're a man who can hold nails in his teeth
but never tries to mend me.
I'll never make sense in the way a spirit level makes sense.
My wood and bubbles are all wrong.
Sometimes I'd love to twist how I stand,
pretend I'm right angles, proper straight
but you love me crooked, weird and bent.
I do not look great with nails in my teeth...
but I do look dead sexy in fishnets!

Time travel to our present,
streets emptied, 2011,
time travel here.
You. Me.
Outside.
Yelling.
Broken words, broken yelling,
stupid words, breaking, not while I'm yelling!
My sentences are punctured, commas puss, I've severed colons...
I am talking shit.
You look like the sky, open, still.
Why was I yelling?
You used to be from Tunbridge Wells
but now we've rewritten our pasts
so I've known you since forever.
You tell me Tunbridge Wells would love a good yell,
to connect so heavy it hurts
but it can't even touch without wincing,
Tunbridge Wells couldn't ever just let us be us
all queer and sexy and yelling!
Hey!
Guess what?
We've yelled so hard
we've erased Tunbridge Wells from time and space!

One last time.
Twenty-forty-something.
People say you look like Doctor Who so I know you can do this.
Tell me a queer might be Prime Minister
or that gays can now be gays on daytime TV.
Tell me that Tunbridge Wells can exist
if it wears a fez
and that supermarkets now have to have
designated areas for panic attacks,
little rooms where they play B-52s,
give you stuff to make out of glitter, pritt stick and potatoes.
Tell me we're together, old,
our love keeps regenerating and I will still have
...hair.
Immortal hair!
Tell me you'll love me beyond end of days and
I love you.
I love you!
Let's make this Sci-fi epic love
where heroes will never die.

AHIMSA TIMOTEO BODHRAN (U.S.A., B. 1974)

Sage

In each place,
purple flowers, fuzzed tongue,
fragrance felt, rubbed, lifted to fingers,
nose, nostrils, inhaled in, no other
smell left possible. An overwhelming
of senses. Wood chip, dirt, stump
to sit on, clearing in the round,
each four, water on rock,
sizzle. Steam. Some of thin leaf, others
round, pointed, a different way to collect
water (counter-counter-clock-wise), bring
it to root, hopefully still
in soil. Dried for home
cleansing, each foot lifted,
then down the back, before
entering, a gradient of genders, each
place a space for us, left on altar
for after bad visit, magick, time
for battle/war, our aim a good one, no
bowl or rug, basket, for the wall, used daily,
before entering, leaving,
the breaking of ties, new love,
house
warming with sweat, peek of night sky,
stars, or day sun, warming rocks
fire, and the flap
closes again; we are here within
this womb. Each time we leave,
we are born again, medicine
deep within us, prayers,
songs, in memory, Mother on our
feet and faces. No Christian
saviour greets us at the door.

Our Ancestors are the ground
beneath us.

Towers

i.
A week after I am blamed
for the disappearance of buildings,
you tell me you are leaving
my skyline.
                    I wait six
months. You do not
reappear.

ii.
One block away, twelve hours to confirm
you're alive.

iii.
Columns of light,
dust makes us see.

iv.
You left me because I was Arab.
I can say this now.

My words pass over
your grave.

v.
Día los Muertos
has come early this year.

vi.
A week after I am blamed
for the disappearance of buildings,
you tell me that you are leaving
my skyline.
                    I wait six
months. You do not
reappear.

when i learned praying to be straight was not useful

the first time i brought a man to sweat, taught him to offer tobacco, i came full circle. it is here i first lit fire. and almost a decade later i return, with man. a year later i returned, after the prayers had betrayed me, after i had betrayed myself. and i tried not to judge the man i brought with me. perhaps we always judge those learning what we are ourselves. perhaps that is what we offer the fire: to burn and renew, Ancestors working through it for us in the flames. a year prior, here, praying to be straight, praying to be anything other than what i was: a lover of man. here i returned, unalone, with family. i had not expected to be the one teaching, guiding hand, voice, guiding body over rock and stump, through kitchen, over stream by log, snow flower, to a place where water falls, tumbling over rock and cliff, into the first round, out the second, sometimes all four, him still learning new lungs, through the heat and dark, new breath.

something healed in me there. who knew in the loving of another man, gentle, from a distance, i'd partake of new waters, smell pine anew, count lichens of trees, rejoice in swarmings of ladybugs on an evening shirt. who knew i'd offer words to someone who didn't know them, but heard them resonate in, quill, quiver, from before birth. who knew i'd be teacher, and in the teaching, taught: a new drum singing in my chest, rhythm playing through our bodies, all the notes.

JERICHO BROWN (U.S.A., B. 1976)

Romans 12:1

I will begin with the body:
In the year of our Lord,
Porous and wet, love-wracked
And willing, in my 23rd year,
A certain obsession overtook
My body, or I should say,
I let a man touch me until I bled,
Until my blood met his hunger
And so was changed, was given
A new name
As is the practice among my people
Who are several and whole, holy
And acceptable. On the whole
Hurt by me, they will not call me
Brother. Hear me coming,
And they cross their legs. As men
Are wont to hate women,
As women are taught to hate
Themselves, they hate a woman
They smell in me, every muscle
Of her body clenched
In fits beneath men
Heavy as heaven itself—my body,
Dear dying sacrifice, desirous
As I will be, black as I am.

The Ten Commandments

But I could be covetous. I could be a thief.
I could want and work for. I could wire and
Deceive. I thought to fool the moon into
A doubt. I did some doubting. Lord,
Forgive me. In New Orleans that winter,
I waited for a woman to find me shirtless
On her back porch. Why? She meant it
Rhetorically and hit me with open hands.
How many times can a woman say why
With her hands in the moonlight? I counted
Ten like light breaking hard on my head,
Ten rhetorical whys and half a moon. Half
Nude, I let her light into me. I could be last
On a list of lovers Joe Adams would see,
And first to find his wife slapping the spit
Out of me. I could be sick and sullen. I could
Sulk and sigh. I could be a novel character
By E. Lynn Harris, but even he'd allow me
Some dignity. He loved black people too
Much to write about a wife whipping her rival
On a night people in Louisiana call cold.
He'd have Joe Adams run out back and pull
Her off of me. He wouldn't think I deserved it.

Another Elegy

This is what our dying looks like.
You believe in the sun. I believe
I can't love you. Always be closing,
Said our favorite professor before
He let the gun go off in his mouth.
I turned 29 the way any man turns
In his sleep, unaware of the earth
Moving beneath him, its plates in
Their places, a dated disagreement.
Let's fight it out, baby. You have
Only so long left—a man turning
In his sleep—so I take a picture.
I won't look at it, of course. It's
His bad side, his Mr. Hyde, the hole
In a husband's head, the O
Of his wife's mouth. Every night,
I take a pill. Miss one, and I'm gone.
Miss two, and we're through. Hotels
Bore me, unless I get a mountain view,
A room in which my cell won't work,
And there's nothing to do but see
The sun go down into the ground
That cradles us as any coffin can.

Tin Man

In my chest	a slit of air.	Don't say love.
Drop a penny.	I can't feel a thing.	Remember
Cities shine gray.	Never believe	the color green.
No green is god.	I've watched color die.	I've killed it.
And every tree must fall,	slicing the air.	In my chest
A missing beat.	Skip it—	Hush, love.
Man made me.	Add a little oil,	drop one penny,
Pull the lever:	I chop.	Men made me
So I stop.	I am tired	of your woods,
Your whole world	unpaved, green.	Cities shine
The color gray.	Don't you want	something heartless?
Can I get you	an axe handle	for destruction?
Tired of your body?	Use mine.	Manhandle,
Beat time—	I won't feel	one damn thing.

J.T. BULLOCK (U.S.A., B. 1980)

Reclining Nude

She is 71
tilted back at 30 degrees
strung across a hospital bed like a puppet
a gastric tube connected to the stomach
gives her food she's forgotten how to eat
oxygen flows through her nostrils
cause her lungs
do not know when to breath
a foley catheter collects urine in a bag
that is glowing like a warm glass of beer

And in the background
on her television screen
the country music station
plays something to the refrain of
"Will you miss me when I'm gone..."
but she hasn't left
can't leave
must be
turned on the hour
because pressure against her bones
has been known to cause skin breakdown

So I do my best to take a minute
press two fingers across her wrist
watching the second hand of the clock
counting the beats
while her tiny earthquake palms shake
from Parkinson's, Alzheimer's, End Stage Dementia
acronyms I had to translate

And those who can't bring themselves
to wear this white uniform
might ask how I've found the means
but I'm avoiding the question

Because today I wore blue
plastic hospital gowns
a surgeon's mask and latex gloves
as a shield against the bacteria
resistant to antibiotics
swimming in her blood and sputum
for the simple reason
that she needs a bath
after leaking from the only opening not hooked to a machine

This is the first time I've seen a woman
full frontal
but not in all of her glory
there are still electrodes that need to be removed
IV lines positioned
stockings and boots taken off that keep her joints
from becoming rigid

And I know what you are probably thinking
cause I've said the same myself
so many times
it might as well become a living will
"Lord, if I ever get that way
take me from the bonds of this unbearable pain
to the eternal rest. But if God doesn't hear my prayer
I'm begging someone
Sign those papers
pull the plug
release me from the bonds
of this life no longer worth living…."
and we'd all like to think it's that simple

But you see
I've read her chart
the only visible means of support
she has is in the form of medicare
no relatives or dependents
some might call her a burden of the state
but I call her a human being
a masterpiece
the reclining nude
basking in an eerie glow
of this institution

And as I rub a washcloth
across the small of her back
I hear a mumble erupt from the unresponsive abyss
lips
form syllables
from a tongue and gums that no longer hold teeth
but she speaks all the same

And I could easily ignore her
go about my tasks
change the linens
take out the laundry
but something told me instead to ask
"I'm sorry, miss…"
"What time is it?" she says
"It's 9:30. AM."

And I smiled
because it was the most beautiful thing
I'd ever seen

Granted

You won
and I guess that's what
you always wanted
to hold the reigns
of a pulse run riot
beating fists
against the twisting of limbs
until someone cried uncle

But if you
care to keep record
remember
that I never did

Because losing your breath
is not the same as submission
it requires some sort of
informed consent
a signature
placed across the tight rope line
leaving nothing but leverage
in the hands of once tied
taught
tangled up

Surrender is granted
only when permission
has been implicitly given
and those words
were never birthed
so unless you
are hearing the ghost
of what we both wanted to say
but somehow
failed to mention
there's no reason to think
that I ever gave in

Because I have given up
enough times
to know the difference
quit everything I started
for the sake of believing
that walking away
is as easy
as kissing a stranger on the cheek

I've held steadfast to the notion
that all things in this life
are temporary
especially people
but I must give you credit
for helping me realize
how unfair it is
to speak poetry to an audience
that lacks the ability
to leave

Holding hostages
has never been a pastime
I've fancied
it is everyone's unalienable right
to be alone

But for those
who can't seem to bear the thought
I say this

Unless you were born a twin
you did not exit the womb
holding anyone's hand
and I can guarantee
you will not leave this earth
in the arms of another
so at any given moment
you are the only one
you've got

And I have danced to this mantra
from time-out chairs
in dark hallways
to after school detentions
through seven months
locked behind the steel bars of Bessemer-Cuttoff County
to the realization
that nothing would ever change
if I stayed where I was

So I leave every chance
that I get

Because walking away
is as easy as a one-night-stand
and Lord knows
I've had enough skeletons
and rendezvous
to fill a Smithsonian

So I guess I should be used to this

Which is why I left your apartment
for the cold November rain
declined the umbrella you offered
as a courtesy
so I wouldn't have an excuse to come back

But there was so much that could have kept me
from the subway train to 110th St
like coffee at your breakfast table
watching raindrops glide off the window sill
while Coltrane plays something in the background
that makes you feel the earth move

Instead I'll give this victory to you
if it was all you were after
I wish you would have told me
I would have given up
long ago.

Among pigeons
For Jason Ricci

Jason, you maniac
how the hell did you get in there
in that skin, I mean
inked up like a testament
telling the gospel according to whomever
proving that everything has its truth
as long as you listen
beyond the syllables
and the breaths

And I have heard you blow
a hurly burly churning corn cobs
into gasoline
boxcar engines running on hobo refrain
a lonesome kind of
nobody knows my troubles
and secrets are for the keeping

So speak in code, Jason
tell the allegory of how you fell asleep
by lobster traps in Portland, Maine
woke up with whiskers
on a catfish farm near Memphis
hitched a ride to Beale St.
bought a harmonica in some shitty tourist shop
that sold shot glasses
and magnets
with everyone's name but your own

You are a ghost
there's no way to hide it

Selling your soul where two highways meet
has already been done
this is the new South
rules have changed
so find the space between Kimbrough
and Burnside
be the only white guy
in a juke joint that has since
burned to the ground
wear the ashes like war paint
trace Amen
cross your forehead
let it slip that you're queer
as a peacock among pigeons
and make shadow puppets
across the backdrop of dimly lit dives
as fingers glide effortlessly.

REGIE CABICO (U.S.A., B. 1970)

In the Porno of My Life

you'd be the never
before seen bonus feature

& if masturbation made one blind,
I'd keep jacking off to you

so I could surrender
all my senses of the world
to your descriptions.

*

Your poetry is so lonely, Orpheus wants you to be his lyricist.

*

I feel affecktion not affucktion for you not that I don't
want to fuck you I want to feck you which is as close

to fucking as I can get or say. Fucking is easy as sucking
a 24 hour slurpee I'd rather curl with you as you speak

to me of strippers & wedding bands & we'd channel
our inner Clive Owen & bitch slap each other till the moon

smirks fecklessly & we're lying like empty salt & pepper
shakers, till the loneliness is seasoned in feck-able affection.

In Ireland, feck means fuck, so I'm a frustrated leprechaun,
without a pot to piss or a rainbow to fuck. The Scots refer

to feck as worthless & irresponsible & yes, I have fucked
up so much that I have reached the feckful pinnacle of my life.

I've fucked like a bronze Chevrolet rolling over muscle
& towels from Montreal to Seattle & given more head

than a soccer player scoring points in the net. I have sucked
Victory & swallowed so much Rejection, I left Simon

Cowell's nipples hard & Paula Abdul screaming, Next!
I have fucked all the male Mexican Folklorico dancers

in North America till I was a broken Filipino piñata,
I have sucked so much cock, my mouth is perpetually

the Year of the Cock with General Tsao's roosters
ruffling and crowing their way to the sunrise & I have

taken cock like a Chinese lion climbing every orifice
of my body straight up to heaven. I have fucked so deeply

my penis invented new prepositional phrases & I have
fucked so profoundly my dick reincarnated into Buddha

pulsating over a pair of lotus petals & I have done it
hard on leather hammocks so those screaming pretty

boys were pebbles in my slingshot. I was David
fucking Goliath till I was empty as sin, a glass of tonic

& gin at a piano bar fucking up all the vocal parts
in a Les Miserables medley & I have fucked too much

that all I can do is fuck things up & my fucking you
would be this feckless act where I am afraid that I'd

fuck you up so badly you'd just lay by my side
like a finished Starbucks cup staring at a lamp from Ikea.

                    *

If only I can fall into you like chalk, I'd wear your halo
& know what it feels when an Aztec's heart is ripped
out & on those tequila nights when you text me, *mis u*

because you're stumbling in the Tenderloin
like a colonized junkie looking for flesh,
I'm in Petworth, Georgia Avenue punch drunk

like a lost tacqueria truck texting you back,
wish we were drnking 2gther & when you text me
back, *wish we were in Spain*

or the Moon, I want to tell you fiercely that the world
is sturdy & that poetry can hold us up.

REGIE WANTED TO PLAY SHAKESPEARE'S PUCK
BUT THE CHECK NEVER ARRIVED & HE WOULD
TOTALLY BLOW MEL GIBSON TO SAVE THE WORLD
BUT THE PLANET SPINS & THE GLOBE GOES ROUND
& HANS CHRISTIAN ANDERSON IS LOOKING HOT
ON A CNN THURSDAY NIGHT & EVERY TIME REGIE
TAKES HIS CONTACT LENSES OUT HE SINGS THE
SECOND VERSE OF "WHAT I DID FOR LOVE" FROM
CHORUS LINE

Spread Your Wings
haiku skin

PrepareYe

ABC after school generation

Atari 2600   Ferris Bueller   the Great Work begins

Carry the crystal

That is your life with the ease of a goblet

To the lips of a sinner

If it slips pick up the pieces

Swahili   Yoruba   Hausa

Titanic tinny tinkle tunes

Flamingo roars

Infinity caught in the claps of baboons

12 Scottish pigs on stilts want me to teach them slam poetry

Google it yourself, I pontificate

I kissed a frog & the frog turned into Purple Rain Prince

I liked you better as a frog,
I deflected

Prince sang,

nothing
compares
2
U

& crawled away wearing a diaper of doves

Green memory is not A Money Memory

But A Memory with my time with the little Leprechaun

Who played the harmonica on the Marcy Avenue Platform

…setting up a wine house wine house wine house
setting up a wine house wine house
Wine louse now…

There is a syllable-less sea
Seething thru my
silent centless wallet

Hear the tofu get seared   showered with sugar   camouflaged in basil

Pad prik dreams   Try my prik   Prik great

Anderson & Gloria Vanderbilt barge in my apartment

I am war torn / have been raped by

Tony The Tiger   Count Chocula & Johnny Depp in Pee Wee's Playhouse

Don't take the milk from the fridge   I say over & over

*

Barbra Streisand does her 17th Final concert with Michael Meyers

The proceeds of Some Enchanted Evening go to me

*

Anderson sees me as a Pandora's Box of Ponderosas

We fit like green & red jello

Hope is the best lubricant for a thick hurricane

END: gold coins thrown in air

100s of wind-up clapping monkeys

JAMES CAROLINE (U.S.A., B. ?)

Kok*
for Sun-Kyung Cho, sister of Cho Seung-Hui

My brother was born from a teakettle
pink water afterbirth
stained with the raw
newness of him
callow becoming sapless
spilled from the safe brine of our mother.
He began to dry.
Cried tears that limped
and protested their leaping.
He was a baby once
circle mouth warping
with heat from his cheeks.
His face a blank mask facing our coos.
His voice air pockets in glaciers.
He fell often,
had training wheels longer than most.
I think I remember that.

He was sick sometimes
ate his belly sore on good days.
He loved summer
would come home sun licked
stand in the kitchen for a snack
he could leave with.
He liked honeydew, sweet and walled.
Sometimes his
cheeks streaked yellow from smearing
dandelion heads over a warm face.
He spoke so little
his slick skin growing and growing
silent
except for the weight
of his shoes
on the stairs
and always that door shutting.
He smelled like wind.

All families have some wicked
some fingerprint screaming on a mirror
long sleeves covering bruises.
The uncle who
beat the nagging mouth
of his wife.
The brother arrested
for selling heroin.
The sister's failed suicide attempt.

The grandfather who loved children,
clutched at them secretly
while they dreamt him
into a good man.
When you put
your own monsters in the ground
their teeth will dull
your judgment topple.
The retelling will be fit for brunch
for sermons.
Such good boys.

We forgive the dead enough
to lie for them.
Please.
There is so little left of my brother
that is safe to remember.
He is smoke,
God-mouth bulge at the hip
of a teenager's jeans
cradled bullet.
He is a bloodless
forever snapping moment.
I want him
to not be
unspeakable.

How he hacked at
and smeared your flowers over the classrooms
sprayed their colors over notebook pages.
How he saw nothing of himself in their screams
in the boiling run
the dotting of red in the back
of a girl tipping out the window
to escape him.
How he opened your children
covered rooms with them
but then bullet-to-skulled himself
off to hell
like a good boy.

* Kok- In the Korean funeral tradition is wailing as a means of expressing the sorrow and sadness of the
mourners after losing a close relative. It also involves the outpouring of guilt by the mourners who think
that it was their lack of pious actions which caused his or her ultimate demise. It is also believed that it can
prevent the spirit of the deceased from returning and doing any harm to the family.

Lil Girl Blue
for Janis Joplin

i am writing this in red
too bawdy for babies' eyes
trying to put blood back
into the chapel of your heart
follow you full tilt, Mama.
cock lovin /cunt lickin, baby girl
you busted into Port Arthur cars
to drive deep into Cajun country
leaving Texas as soon as you slid out
from the folds of your mother's delivery.

so you drove.
black pavement under sequined canopy of night
yellow lines of caution made meaningless by drink
singin Odetta for your friends
when the radio was busted.
crossed black snakes laying in the road
tongued grime from windshields
until your mouth stretched
to suck off the same blues
you were hunting the same blues
been at your heel since home
where they called you cheap   pig   freak.

puberty gouged grace from you
put more holes in your body
than men knew what to do with.
you bought junk to stuff into crevices lovers feared
        trimmed horse's mane
but it grew back
helped soften the recoil of cannon shot
you belted in songs carved with a lover's tooth.
from whiskey leaking scars
you squeezed the blood we crave.
your sweet piss tracked through the kitchen
by the boot of some young, hung fool.
gypsy skinned, doe-hearted, Mama
purple velvet cupping a tit tattooed with valentine
looking for love with violet eye.
runnin—little girl blue be
fuckin that horse for the ride
until long roads made cheap thrills expensive.
so it was loose
coverin bruise and
i know that song, Mama
i know sounds that can spilt skin
lovers that freak on the floorboards
cause the carpets been worn thin
how they loved the wound of your mouth.

you knew they wanted you
exhausted, anguished,
lavishingly decorated in the remains of love
held to the stage by the hands of an orgy
erupting to stop time

from the anatomic findings and pertinent
history I ascribe death to:
ACUTE HEROIN-MORPHINE INTOXICATION
DUE TO: INJECTION OF OVERDOSE
jackin off the mic
to make men pre-cum in tight jeans too soon,
make girls think twice too soon
or just goin down, Janis Lyn
wantsa ball but the chain pulls tight
makes you scream through tears
could harmonize with yourself
singing 2 notes at once
baby, your pitch
was perfect

THE UNEMBALMED BODY IS THAT OF A CAUCASIAN FEMALE,
APPEARING THE STATED AGE OF 27.

A TATTOO OF A BRACELET IS
PRESENT AROUND THE LEFT WRIST.

at home they were still trying to break your feathers
calling your parents and laughing when news came
that your larcenous reign had ended

THERE IS A SMALL HEART TATTOOED OVER, AND MEDIAL TO, THE LEFT
BREAST. NUMEROUS NEEDLE MARKS ARE PRESENT IN THE ARMS
BILATERALLY.

in song you complained
they're always gonna hurt you and they're always gonna let you down
birthed demons that were exhausted from calling you to heel
urged us to cradle our own.
sent desire bawling back to Texas
meek, unashamed
knocking on doors at dawn
hoping for a place to crash until it blew over
—that need.
singin that cruel bastard through the dark of holding on too tight
and trying to run free.
love took you to town
left you stranded in bars
clawing at the microphone for support
collapsing backstage trying to hold onto anything you had left   some scorched air,
     applause,
     and a nip left in the bottle clutched to your chest.

NO EVIDENCE OF MAJOR TRAUMA OR OF VIOLENCE IS PRESENT.

CHING-IN CHEN (U.S.A., B. 1978)

Mutant: a zuihitsu

Look at myself—small bean. Sprouting song, pigtail, smile. *She poured her child into such and such a container until*

who are you? Archiving spine when
did I begin to feel a container
a certain tension

Of lady-ness. A woman not refined, polite, and well-spoken,

a slut, says my mother. Though she did not say. Not her city of Grammar, not her country of Syntax. But the nation of Longing—norming ourselves to the proper binary.

In a poetry craft seminar, Amaranth Borsuk. An Oulipo strategy of definitional literature, each word replaced with a definition. So this is the first mutation.

Is my mother a woman of high social position or economic class. Any woman (sometimes used in combination), (used in direct address; often offensive in singular). Wife.

Together in solidarity, descended from a now-dead patriarch, this is the "what in the house" we build. *Are you a boy?*

In the house, to live or stay in a specified place while performing official duties, carrying on studies or research, awaiting a divorce, etc. *to be in control of her own body* I met a woman who reminded me of myself. She told me she was a "strategic lesbian."

Meaning, her body render the enemy incapable of making war, as by the destruction of materials, factories, etc: a strategic bombing mission. Meaning, essential to the conduct of a war. Meaning copper, meaning lesbian.

Let me explain my Chinese family, she said, as if I didn't woman loving another woman.

As if the house
makes me mutant
to love my own woman
to grow my selves, to tend to my gender(s). There are six I learned in Intro to Women's Studies, to my mother's dismay. *Shall we begin with the correct pronouns?* it became obvious
Her father's face is revenge,

What held her In the slang dictionary, a total jerk, a social outcast (Also, a term of address), such as: Stop being such a mutant. If she wants to be a strategic lesbian, why can't I/she
becomes her weapon.

And when I looked her up in my dictionary: "Researching the last sentence suggesting the making of a mutant, it can be a sweet dream and nightmare to become one." Make an example—a sport—out of that one *was the eventual conclusion, the place where she, future tense, would stop.*

And then

Queer Poetry: a zuihitsu

1. You asked me to write about queer as genre, poetry as genre—and all I can think of in terms of intersections is failure and scatter. What Kind; sort; style, asks the Oxford English Dictionary. I am obsessed with the zuihitsu poetic form, a hybrid Japanese form which utilizes subjective lists, journal entries, juxtaposition, fragmentation, etcetera, to create a sense of randomness which is not really random. Because it is messy, chaotic, contradictory, it is a form I frequently return to, especially when I do not always know what and how to say. It is a form which maps and contains my fear.

2. "My poetry is often guided by an impulse to fail. When this is the case, writing is an attempt to salvage something from the mess." –Douglas Kearney

3. I moved to Milwaukee from California and met five queer Asian people (not me, though I have been referred to myself multiple times—is this a mistake? Are others mistaking me for me? Do I look like myself?) This is totally subjective—I moved to Milwaukee for poetry, not for queerness. Yet the search becomes what I frustrate, what pushes me to lineate, what creates the next line, what is filled up here.

4. What are the essential qualities that make up this loneliness?

5. Queer sorts:

One moved with me from California for school.

One I met in a cafe with leafy greens overhead. We met there because he drank tea, not coffee (my uncle—a handyman—in another life dreamt of opening a teashop). I think he had been persuaded to meet with me as a recruitment/retainment strategy. One of us had been tricked to be there? My mother was visiting, and we talked about whether he would be comfortable if she came along. She said, you go ahead, I don't want to make him uncomfortable. It was a matter-of-fact conversation, and I cannot remember another one about this topic with my mother.

One told me the only queer (gay? lesbian?) Asians she knew in the city were her two siblings.

One told me he was glad to be moving away because he felt unsafe.

One spent a night with me in a red bar, coastal people, fast talkers both. When I met her, not wanting to assume, I asked—do you identify as Asian? Are you ____?

None of them are like me, exactly, yet I want.

6. In another blog entry, writing from the past, Bhanu Kapil: "I become so familiar with this scene that at one point, I lie down on the ground instead. I exchange my body with the body of another girl. I wait for something to happen, and it does."

7. When I left California, an old friend from my MFA program told me that she had seen my doppelganger in the MFA program. By the time she had gone up to her to say something, my twin had replied: I know, I know, I look like Ching-In.

I have never met anyone who looked like me. Or is this a lie?

8. Last week, at Las Dos Brujas Writing Workshop with Kimiko Hahn, poet who originated writing zuihitsu (as poetry? As essay? neither? all of the above?) in English. On Wednesday night, in the middle of the week, her reading was sparsely attended. I cried; it felt like a reflection on me. We are not interchangeable bodies, yet my body feels related to hers, familial. If she disappears (ridiculous!), will I not be seen (a fear), not be related to (a fear), not be recognized (a fear), not be made sense of (a fear).

9. In this extreme city, my bodies become multiple. How do you like to be addressed? Them, I reply, and they nod. At Kochanski's Concertina Beer Hall, where I have just performed with my band, the owner/bartender mistook me for a Sir and apologized. That's okay, I reply, I identify as multiply-gendered. A trans-man at the next table is indignant on my behalf and asks me how I feel. How I feel? These words all originate from my bodies.

10. "Because to fail to define your world, your nation, means disappearing from it. Latinos, they're banning your books in Arizona, and no one is saying anything about it. They're failing your children in cities across the nation. Your elders are dying off, and are being forgotten. They want you gone, forgotten. They don't want to hear your voice, because your voice complicates the story. Who's they? You tell me. A complicated story is a true story."—Rich Villar

11. I buy Kimiko's reading copy of *Toxic Flora* after her books sell out. She looks through the book for errant writing. I tell her I don't mind, but she says if she has made notes, she needs them. She writes me a note, but I lend my book out to another writer and do not see until after she has exited the premises: "Good to see you so often and now here."

12. "*From* indicates a particular time or place as a starting point; *from* refers to a specific location as the first of two limits; *from* imagines a cause, an agent, an instrument, a source, or an origin; *from* marks separation, removal, or exclusion; *from* differentiates borders.

    "Where are you *from*?"—Craig Santos Perez

13. Is the answer not a poem?

The True Tale of Xiaomei

This woman with my face   is not mine.
I do not love her   and she does not love me.

Her face would open
          as the ting announced my arrival.

She would sit me down
behind that plank doubling as counter,
          the Sharpie my weapon to nail her tongue onto placard.

I look her in the fierce eye and say,
          No, that's wrong.
          You are not saying it right.

She would halt her recitation,
press her thin peach lips,
          like she was glad I was worth something.

Other twilights, I said nothing,
          daring her to hang her failures in the window.

At school the next day, the girls would gather 'round and I would unfold
The Great Outlandish True Tale of my pathetic mother,
          married off at age three,
          to an evil rich man as second wife/concubine.
          How she squeezed sorrow out of her pounding chest.
          How he beat her for that first daughter (me!).
          How she squirreled away like the workday ant, coin after morsel.
          How one day the bus driver saw my fresh face and her haggard one,
                    two sides of the mirror of time   open onto his pale life.
          He fell in love with such courage.

          We a lovely family bought passage on the steerage section of the airplane,
          here to start a romantic,
          rose-tinted life,
          that classic immigrant story that breaks their little Pilgrim hearts
          and who could say otherwise—

                    my mirror of a face ensconced behind
                         a battling cash register waiting
                              for the munchies of college students
                                   or financial district secretaries
                                        on lunch break.

This face,
I the only authority:
translator,
writer,
communicant,
sage,
storyteller,
shit-talker.

How would you,
o foreigner,
know the difference?

How do you not know I am not secretly in love with this face,
which I have never hated,
as you first imagined.
This secret society,
            an imperceptible nod we pass,
                    a shit-talking language in which we say nasty things about all the foreigners we hate.

Even now, she is carving up her deep memories for me,
            I am scooping out her innards,
                    that long imprint of my family before her,
                            hand snaking up what she has stitched shut at the ass.

At the station, the old grandmother,
            mumbling poetic phrases in Mandarin,
a wrinkled-faced woman who could have been my grandmother
presumed I was part of her family.
Filial obligation
would move me to point her

                                        in the northern direction towards our tribes.

And that bleak day,
I wanted to talk loudly in another tongue,
shaming her for not knowing my other language,
for marking me with my difference,
a gift from my mother.

But I stuffed myself back into my skin.

She could have missed this smallest turn,

                        sweet opening,
                                but her finger crept up,
                                        touched that nerve,
                                                and spilled.

Until I picked her up with my split tongue,
            we bartered for those multiple years of bloodshed,
                empires,
                        emperors,
                            mandates,
                                for our shared failings as daughters,

                                perhaps not businesswomen who could lift up an
                        oppressed family with one finger,
                                        we stood parked

in front of that multi-hued subway map
at the mouth of the entranceway,
that immigrant port city of all the world.

Never having a lover with my own family face,
I headed home to empty bed.
I cried for all the erasures within myself,
for the sand I had thrown on my mother's memory,
for my hard back.

To love your own violent histories,
the remembered soup of your failings,
and to forgive those who have failed before you,
generation upon generation,
of the most mad,
the most terrible,
the deadliest secrets crossing the ocean.
We do not bury our dead, but hack them into shanks we lay on our backs,
bearing them forever into each new world.

I mention this because   this woman with my face is meeting her end.
I am still the translator,   her fate within the shallow breaths of my hands.
Her eyes ask me to tell her the honest brutality, the fate which only I can deliver.

Again and again,   I am her murderer.

I have been training all my life to place each word in front plainly:
Not to say without saying,
as is the tradition of my family,
or my tribe,
or my country,
or my people.

To love this only woman with my face.

ELIZABETH J. COLEN (U.S.A., B. 1976)

JANUARY WINDOW

I had a dream I was lost in your hair. The rain had started, so everything shined. I had started out near your ear, just my mouth on you there, just my tongue creeping up the outside of it, just a little. I know it tickles, so I was hesitant, respectful. You seemed to like it then. You moved against me in that way you know I like. Then I got distracted and found my way into the mess of you. I started at the ear, but I have no idea how I got to where I was, lost. When you're on someone's scalp or the roads of tendrils coming from it, it's so easy to lose your bearings. I know you think, just follow one strand from start to finish, follow it all the way out or all the way to the start of things. But it's not that easy when a girl is lying down. I found myself so close to the way you wash yourself. Your skin was red, raw from rubbing. You clean so well, you shampoo like you're angry. I saw it once, while standing in the shower next to you. You faced the faucet, face in the stream of water, your back to me. I watched the curve of the water from the showerhead fall onto the curve of you, down your back and then I lost it. You're legs are beautiful, but I hardly ever get to them when I look at you. Your fingers were in your hair, like they are now looking for me. When we got into bed, clean and leaving small circles of wet on the sheets, I mentioned the anger I had seen and we never took a shower together again. Sometimes I sit on your couch and think about you in there, what your hands are doing, how strands come away on your fingers.

ERIN BROCKOVICH

You keep the valentine up on the fridge: cardinals beak to beak and a red heart behind them. Be mine. I say I met you on the treadmill at the Y, dual runners facing the window, turning up the speed to impress, getting shocked repeatedly. The old, old equipment. And how hot our hands were, tuning our hearts into the machines, beat after beat until they added up to something. The burn zone. But none of that is true. Personal ads for anonymous sex sometimes breed love. But it was your mountain bike I got, light rust and its various speeds. The sex that day was elsewhere and mediocre, in a dirty apartment I left itching and still hungry. You and I laughed a lot. You held on to the bike for a time and I looked at your hands. We talked about movies and TV. Arrested Development and CSI, but mostly about Julia Roberts and how maybe she and her brother Eric were really the same person because we'd never seen them on film together. "Maybe he doesn't exist." "Maybe she doesn't." Erin Brockovich was not the answer to anything. There is a space between us that day that one could park two bicycles in. I'm not even close enough to grab your arm when you say something witty. My hand touches air and returns to my side. "We should ride together sometime," I say. But you've just given me your only bike.

JONA COLSON (U.S.A., B. 1979)

[from the wrist and reaches]

It is hard to remember him,
but I can see my father in his quiet August:

A young man, handsome and blue-eyed,
his smile not yet crooked and small.

I see him in the garden picking tomatoes
from their strangled green vines—

the time of year that opens from the wrist and reaches—

he smells of summer and dirt. Hot and alive,
a wire in my throat.

My Father's Dream

My father wanted me to
wrestle alligators in
central Florida
and eat fresh rattlesnake
meat down in San Antonio.

But I slept through
my father's dream
and woke up holding
a bundle of yellow tulips
that looked like the

early afternoon sun
of New York City.

TANYA DAVIS (CANADA, B. 1978)

Lost and Found

(Lost)

I found God!
And then I stumbled, I fumbled and I fuckn dropped him
OMIGOD!

And then I had to stop and look and so I took a moment's pause.

And then you wanna know what happened?
Well, then I smelled flowers where once I had not.

They were...strangely familiar
resembling dreams of childlike wonder
childhood fever
childishness keeps me believing in either and other
and so contradiction is really no bother

Both short and tall flowers
both long and squat stems
told me of both life and death
and so, for a moment, I forgot to care where it was that God went

But then something shifted.
Or the wind changed and I changed with it
and I worried that a life without him in it
would mean more questions and less givens
less answers more chances for shivering
'cause I'd be less shielded
therefore delivering me from evil
would be less easy
therefore more difficulty
alongside increasing
deep and meaningful joy

I lost God and found elusive holy spirit to explore.

(found)

lost: god
found: people
lost: jesus
found: reason

lost: answers
found: questions
lost: flock
found: others questioning

lost: tradition
found: tradition in its wake
lost: institution
found: freedom in its place

lost: repent
found: rejoice
lost: blind obedience
found: voice

lost: confession
found: share
lost: convention
found out I don't care

lost: guilt
found: responsibility
lost: little stale wafer
found: vibrant community

lost: him
found: them
lost: trinity
found: holy, nonetheless

lost: heaven and hell
found: earth
lost: big boss looking down
found: her

lost: a congregation
found: lapsed Catholics
lost: isolation
found myself surrounded

lost: certainty
found: freefall
lost a robot
found an animal

lost: judgment
found: critique
lost: assumption
found: belief

lost: church
found: stars and space
lost: religion
found: faith

Broken Poet

Remember, I was a broken poet
holding on to the drama of life in the doldrums
you were a strong lover
in both heart and muscle
you could have been my mother
for all those tears you caught

Remember, I was a fucked up writer
more depressed than inspired
you were sick and tired
of all that I cried
and our lion fire
must have surely suffered from the rain

Remember, I was a young one searching
you had a young one, still nursing
and I was lurching back and forth across the country
I was going more often than I was coming
and I knew nothing of love
            and I didn't help you pay for much

Remember, then?

To every woman I ever disappointed
I'm sorry for the way that I ran
how many tears I shed
how often I shed them

In an early narrow life, I filled books with pain and strife
while my lovers, loyal by my side
did serve the time it took for change
or no change

            and I'm sorry
            that I love you all for that

JULIE ENSZER (U.S.A., B. 1970)

IN MY FANTASY SINGLE LIFE

I am hooning[1] around
with lots and lots of women
because for some unknown,
yet incredible, reason,
I am able to stay awake past 10:30 p.m.,
and I am not spending that time
watching TV and figuring out the conclusions
to all my favorite shows,
which I have missed in my real married life
when I fall asleep before 10:30 p.m.,
oh no, I am hanging out at bars and clubs
and other hip places where hot lesbians
are gathered, and I am flirting
and I am dancing and I am seducing
hot women and eating their pussies
in bathrooms or my car or my hip
fantasy single life city condo

and I like it and I want it
to continue (who wouldn't?)
until one night this really fine woman
is fucking me really good and really hard
and just as I am about to come, she says
I love you (who says that in someone
else's fantasy?) and I have to stop and say
No, you don't love me
this is sex, not love and
I say it firmly and I mean it
because all of a sudden

I remember this is my fantasy single life—
where I have wild sex without love—
but I live in reality somewhere and there,
in that reality, there I remember: I know love.

---

1   Australian for behaving recklessly

HANDMADE LOVE

In kindergarten, I carried a schoolbag
my mother made from fabric with fairy tale scenes.

For three years, it was my most prized possession.
When I was scared, I would look at the bag and recite

fairy tales to myself. Goldilocks, Little Red Riding Hood,
the Golden Swan. These girls faced fear and survived.

In my carefully buttoned bag, I carried books, rocks, pencils,
and other childhood treasures. At seven, teased by children

for my handmade bag and matching dress, I demanded
store bought clothes, a back pack. Now my briefcase

is leather and bulging with files, but I yearn for my childhood bag
still in my closet. Sometimes when I am alone

I pull it out and carry it around the house filled with special objects:
papers, pens, stones, and books, items not so different

from when I was a child. I value handmade things.
I believe that there are two kinds of love in this world:

inherited and handmade. Yes, we inherit love
but my people, my people make love by hand.

FOR JUDITH REMEMBERING GRACE PALEY AND JANE COOPER

You are sad about losing two
one generation ahead of you;
I read your grief on email
but don't feel it with you.
Yes, I'm sad—both poets I love—
but also relieved. This is death
in its natural order, as it should be:
women my grandmother's age die,
and women like me scramble
to buy black stockings for funerals,
because we don't keep mourning
in supply. For me, it wasn't
always like this, which I can't tell you—
it would be like last night at dinner
when I was short with a friend.
She was outraged about people
protesting dead soldiers' funerals
How can people protest a funeral?,
she asked, as if this was new,
and even though she's on my side
I was harsh, *Americans are dying
in Iraq because we embrace the gays*,
which is true at least for the protesters,
but my words were caustic,
they startled her. I didn't care;
the sudden attention
because of the soldiers,
my friend's newfound outrage,
where was the anger
when my friends died?
James, bloated even in the casket,
skin stretched over hardened flesh.
I remember his mother's shock—
two weeks earlier, she learned
her son had AIDS, was gay.
At the funeral home—the only one
in the city that would embalm "the AIDS"—
we learn of James' brother
two years earlier, also dead, AIDS, gay.
Before his final coma, James
was still working, everyday in our office;
planning a benefit, attending meetings,
but wasting, wasting away
so with him we all ate like crazy.
I gained ten pounds and
at his funeral, walking behind suited,
white-gloved pall-bearers,
the black stockings I'd already worn
to three funerals that month
chafed my left inner thigh.

BRITTANY K. FONTE (U.S.A., B. 1977)

How to Woo a Closeted Gay Republican—Circa 1980's

Let's say you see a woman across a room, a woman whose "Save the Rich" button you miss on her designer red lapel, and whose Volvo key is hidden in her purse, or vulva, tight as tax day.

Let's say she is so beautiful you look past the Jim Bakker book open in front of her, past the beef on her lunch plate, miss that she's passed the firemen on the street collecting change in their charity boots.

Let's say, just for a moment, you actually want to date a woman who looks up to Newt because you've never heard her speak, and her make-up is flawless, and her flaws are hidden like Joan Collins'.

If you talk to her, see her WWJD bracelet, clear as day, and hear her say, in opposition to this, that she doesn't feel as if Robin Hood is a heroic Disney character, particularly, and that she appreciates, much more, the men of yore who raped Pocahontas and stole her land, and, STILL, you feel you can change her, you might try the following:

1) Ask her out for a milkshake. At Carl's Jr. Milkshake dates are reminiscent of the 1950's and the Woolworth's counter where Webster was never allowed to sit. Milkshake dates don't necessitate preemptive talks of IUDs, DUIs or rhythm methods, retracting welfare, creating warfare, or feeding someone else's children with Sally Struthers. Milk is white, wholesome, hearty—as long as it comes from cows, and not human breasts (in public).

2) Ask her over for a television date; watch "Growing Pains," and eat In-N-Out Burgers. She might, at first, poo-poo the popular sitcom as racy, what with a mother who works outside of the home and reports real news and a father who stays home to head shrink the needy-and-sometimes-without-insurance, but she'll think differently when you note Cameron's Born Again status, or read John 3:16 on the cola cups.

3) Before you even try to kiss her, however, or turn from ABC to the 1,2,3's of the lambada, bridge the physical gap of the leather sofa: you sitting on Santa Claus' North pole of gift giving and she on the South pole of recession and Reganomics. Try to tout the pros of Henry Kissinger, condemn your neighbor (who's Asian of some non-descript variation) of communism, finger your cross. Do not speak of "the gay plague"; do not suggest a dental dam. Perhaps Sandra Day O'Connor is a safe subject…. Or Oprah, if you truly live up North.

When you have her in your grasp, in your lap, lapping at your suggestion of a "kinder, gentler nation," when you've cried together over Christa McAuliffe and promised to make that pilgrimage to the Vietnam Veteran's memorial, despite the way she feels about homeless veterans, who do not work, do not work, do not work, when she's napalmed your heart with three open buttons on an alligator-imprinted shirt, and her cat's imprinted on your Donna Karan purse, when she's clutching at your severely-padded shoulders, just whisper:

Jimmy Carter for your Cartier, sister.

Because My Inbox is Filled with Messages: CougarTown, AARP, and Senior Singles.

Dear Little Girl swaddled in still-elastic muscles and a cherubic smile: I am older than your "vintage" jeans and wider than the hips they cover; I have genes I can no longer pass on to children. My eggs have run away to a retirement home: fried. They'd rather have sleep than lovers. They dream of flannel sheets and down comforters. They turn down sperm, dried; they learn nothing new. (Don't flirt; hide now!) I could have been your "Babysitter," your Elizabeth Shue. (Were you even born in 1980, ummmm, 7? Dude.)

Dear Pretty Girl with the side-long steps, yes, you, who does sets of 150 ab reps, drinks whiskey, and literally litters glances at my feet: When I use the word "hot," I'm referring to flashes; I'm being referred by a physician; I'm feasting on rosehips, and I'm reddening roots with Clairol. I'm looking for a sale on Depends. I still send handwritten letters, because emoticons can be read wrong. I warm myself in fuzzy slippers and swarm like bee to Botox. You see, I can't let you see the spot between my eyes. I….(sigh) It's 8:25. Past my bedtime.

Dear Smarty Pants in the smart pant suit taking graduate courses I could likely teach—I was around when they penned the Constitution—Your voice often voices sweet ministrations, sexual frustrations, or maybe that's my maternal, hopeful brain's citations: APA, MLA, LMFAO. I stand clear of mirrors and feel "sexiest" after two (or three) "Cheers!": white wine spritzers, skinny cocktails. No c----, uh, males. I miss "Dynasty," don't understand Wii, have never peed outside, aside from waiting in line for Bon Jovi tickets. Confession: I might have Rickets.

Dear Child-Not-Mine: Since when did my horoscope sign say "Cougar"? When did I flatter and purr? I don't lure nearly as well as worms; I confirm my stomach's still on stage with Spanx, demure. If we dated, I would have to shield your eyes from the white light of my cellulite thighs, then chastise you for lotioned elbows on latent dinner tables. If I segwey, now, it's only past my unshaven legs, my paint-chipping toenails. You are a round hole; I am a "Square Peg." (Do you remember that show?) And I cannot live on the "down low."

This is not to say I'm hopeless. Trust this:

I can write love letters in three different languages, read them in four; I give the best massages and kiss to the core.

I know how to adore a woman who deserves it; I've studied philosophy, art, music, and 19th Century British Lit.

I can bake a homemade cheesecake better than the one your mother makes: naked.

I can talk a two-year-old out of coloring on your Coach purse in Sharpie, bold.

I can walk through fire, glass, clean up vomit and still make dinner, while vacuuming, squatting, and working on the muscles in MY ass—wearing Jimmy Choo's.

I knew where the G Spot was before Map Quest, before Rand McNally, before cell phone GPS, and baby, I knew how to woo before you were born.

I can buy you Starbucks, cash, and, should you spill on your Egyptian cotton couture blouse, instead of driving back to your house, know I carry a Tide-to-Go Pen in my Michael Kors.

I am MORE than you can handle.

KAREN GARRABRANT (U.S.A., B. 1970)

Admissions to My Ghost

Confession 1:

Sometimes I drive past your old house
on my way home
slow down
talk to you
and share news.

I try to sketch in the summer backyard
parties
we were supposed to have
instead of the coffin compartments the rooms
became.

Confession 2:

I am grateful
because of you I now *KNOW*
there is an after-this.

A bird at midnight
on the patio
after poetry
sang my faith.

Confession 3:

There are still pieces
I haven't been able to write
the one about that day...the one
about how your mother also passed
or the one about how
my friend Sonia
held me together
with silence.

Confession 4:

You will always be
in my phone.

I call you, hear the ring
and hang up.

Confession 5:

I have held some of your opinions
long enough, had to let them go
or graft them to my own.

I told on you, let some of your favorites
know you loved their words, could have loved
them.

Confession 6:

I miss you, cry sometimes
even though I know you're
everywhere now.

Confession 7:

I knew you weren't finished
maybe we all have to make peace
with this hardest of possibilities:
the death of artists
is a death to art.

West Louisiana into East Texas

A yawn of border town bridge
spits you out in front of golden
and diamond light chandeliers
sparkling
grazing the earth.

You blink at the dazzling, glittering beauty
on the other side of the windshield
realizing
it's an evening gown of lights
fitted to frame
metal skeletons.

You inhale
and it's the perfume
of different kinds of cancers.

Petroleum, oil, chemical refineries
place themselves on the map as towns
reflecting names of odors and poison like

Sulphur, Louisiana, population 22,512.

This is the ass of nowhere on any night
truckers hustling, passing, rubber on asphalt, tar
for refill, for speed, for delivery with blood shot eyes
and nicotine veins.

You wonder about lungs and soft tissues under wiry muscles
and the wizened, underpaid factory jobs behind those lights
the wrinkled shadow faces of unseen men
in too-high baseball caps.

You only witness them
as the drivers sitting around the counter solo
at the Flying J.

The shimmer of lights gets caught in your eye to fool you
false Christmas
and party decorative
while cigarette stacks and pipe mouths exhale
and belch
toward a heaven obscured

up in smoke.

District of Columbia, My Polaroids

My city of firsts
spray paintings, highs, girlfriends, alcoholics, drownings
arrests, car boots, robberies, shooting witness, loves, crowd surfs
drunkenness, gay clubs, Traxx, DC Space, Old 9:30, cappuccino, spoken word show
rugby pitch, dirt in the teeth, protests, playing the police for bulls with dangled burning flags, marches,
 pride, castrating dildos with Lynnee Breedlove.
~

City of so much whiteness
you shaped me with so much metaphor
in the monumental monuments
Lincoln penny box
armored tit of Capitol
the Washington phallus
the closed fist of Supreme Court building
and the Jefferson diaphragm.
~

My city of bands and bars
swallowed into Madame's Organs
the grit of all of us
in our scruffy patches sewn with dental floss
we snagged the fabric of tourist scenery and dress blues
with spiked and dreaded hair.
We kicked up Mall dirt with Doc Martins
and made ribbons of instrumental noise; Fugazi, Dischord, Women of Destruction—WOD for short.
We screamed and shredded a power-lined sky
with no stars in sight
knocked four times to enter an after-hours attic
gulped swallowing licorice Jagermeister shots
deep inhaling pot from crumpled PBR cans.
~

My city of protests registered
Reagan-Bush tyranny youth, round one.
We wrapped Newt's house in a gigantic condom.
Marion Barry snorted coke off prostitute tit.
Bush stuck heroin needles
in the Middle East, seeking veins of oil, bleeding soldiers.
The world was apocalyptic ending already, like South East
like crack houses
visible from the Traxx club lines
gunfire air, the whole city shedding serpent skin
like Anacostia, almost the definition of anaconda
tightening in a two-class grip.
~

In my city
We were nobodies
hell-bent on nowhere, blowing smoke
eating a ten person table of food
at Kramerbooks & Afterwards
and forgetting to pay.
We tipped Black Cat bartenders
who held the claws of our nights
with Metrocards
and high fives.

BRENT GOODMAN (U.S.A., B. 1971)

Evaporation

My dropout brother swears a mouthful of freon
at the pressure gauge factory—his station
calibrated fittings for water mains, rescue
squads, crimson ladder trucks. Freon line
obstructed, he lifts the cool siphon to his mouth.
What were you thinking? Seventeen, saving
for his first kick-ass import MGB. Shift
supervisor scoffing, Skoal-yellow teeth:
Dumbass move, Goodman. He cuts a corner
and splices his blood in two. Grief begins with how,
not why. First week in oncology, Mark confides in mom:
Before I could do anything, it just evaporated
in my mouth. It was there, and then it was gone.
I wasn't there, sawdust concrete floor,
siphon rising to his lips. He came home
ghost-faced, went to bed. Dreamt he
swallowed sky until his blood turned
to wind. Shift supervisor retelling the story
at home over dinner, mouth spitting peas,
fork in his piggy fist. Mark cuts a corner
and swallows glass, his blood squeezed
thin as a microscope slide. *It was there, then*
it was gone. Grief begins with a story
I'm not sure how to tell. Eighteen years
after his funeral mom confides to us
a new religion that almost explains
everything. *Before I could do anything,*
it just evaporated in my mouth. That night
I came home ghost-faced, went to bed.
Dreamt us careening his convertible up Holy Hill,
switchback wooded moraines, top down
as it starts to drizzle. Dear dropout sick
of school, your blood swallows wind. Grief
begins with every story I try to tell. I wasn't there,
your hair thinning to nothing. My mouth burns cold.
Rain on the windshield disappearing fast as it falls.

Closet High School Girlfriend

Wintermint: the breeze in her mouth
opened a window I climbed through,
she going into journalism
or basketball, me small enough
to pick a lock or throw
a sparrow's whistle
into the nearby lilacs.
So she carried me around
like a lozenge, how a porch light
dulls through steamed glass,
her tongue the sky above
someone else's empty yard,
the whole world a breath in
or exhaled, rain moving
all the tiny things around.

BENJAMIN GROSSBERG (U.S.A., B. 1971)

A Middle Class Consideration of Lust

Olden days? I picture in cream and black
like a '20's movie, two men with round glasses
in summery bow-tied suits, sitting
across from each other in a train compartment
steaming through Great Plains states,
each with his nose in a small book:
Shelley, Byron, *Dr. Ansell's Headache Cures*—
who knows? Furtive, peering out like mice,
shielded by directions and dosages of quick
silver—eye contact happens: slicked hair
becomes tousled, and perhaps the scene
fades on one hand running around a shoulder,
flipping off the other man's jacket—
but real life doesn't fade: sure as sugar both
trousers come down.

It's different now, of course. At a gas station
in Memphis, my brother filled his van tank by hand
pump. His hippie hair and unwashed face, fumes,
the wet heat of the South, there must have been
romance somewhere. A man walked by him
from off the street, right by—within four feet
passed before him, close enough to smell
my brother's hair, oily enough to punch through
the petrol. At the perigee of the two bodies,
the soft word "blow job" filled the vacuum between
them. I have to admire the guy's courage,
but somehow the train seems nicer,
(would, even if it involved my brother—).

And then there are extremes: horrified first-
year college student, I read that the library
bathrooms would be shut down because of—
of—"glory holes"—
which, bored through the metal stall walls
by pure determination (I guess) served
for romantic access—like rodent-size gates
to heaven. The front-page story
included a picture beneath the caption—
"Alexander Bathrooms Closed"—of one such wall,
writing too grainy to read, holes clearly visible.
Someone must have kept it, taped it in a diary
to remember, blushing—coy and fond, and why
not? It really is just a question of degree;

my last encounter was no less
sleazy. Sure, we'd exchanged rings, but I
didn't want him anymore, couldn't
remember if I ever had; fully conscious of this,
I kissed the back of his neck and undid
his trousers with my right hand (fumbling my own
with the left). We were forty minutes
rhythmic as a washing machine, scant, oily,
and nearly without kisses. In the bathroom after,
he said, "I feel used."

I leaned down and kissed his face,
insides coiled like an over-wound watch,
not wanting to prolong contact.
I said, "I love you, sweetheart," barely

brushing his shoulder, "and I wish you wouldn't
feel that way." About an hour later he
kissed me goodbye, and we haven't spoken since.

BEETLE ORGY

Bloom up from the earth, blooming and curling
like ribbon, and at semi-regular intervals
sprouting leaves: almost the border art
of a Celtic manuscript, the vines up along the fence
of this old tennis court. Amid the wreck

of the net, the cracks of the surface, the rust
along the poles still standing, the vines
are a saving delicacy. Not jarring at all,
though incongruous—except as a reminder
that the school yard will gladly take this place

back in a few untended years, that between
the vines and grass, the tennis courts
will be ground into meal and digested.
I stop at one of the vine edgings caught
by even finer detail: the leaves themselves

are digested; they have been eaten to
irregular lace, and the perpetrators are still here—
five of them across one particular leaf, lined up
straight and even, like cars in a parking lot.
Beetles: their backs a lustrous green and copper,

taken from the kiln hot, thrown on a bed of saw dust
that burst into flame, then lidded over
so the vacuum could draw the metal oxides
to the surface. At first it looks like there are five,
but now I see that there are seven, no eight—

and that in three of the spaces, beetles
are doubled up, one mounting, back legs
twitching, as if running and getting nowhere;
and one mounted, also moving, slightly rocking
in back, close to the point of intersection—

or penetration—in any case, where the bodies
touch. And here I come to it—amid the advancing
vines and decrepit court: they're on other leaves, too,
all around—coupling in company, hundreds of them,
the rows melding to make a single metallic band.

Back in Houston, a friend had parties—
lawn bags in the living room numbered with tape
to store guest clothing; plastic drop cloths
spread out in the spare bedroom (cleared of furniture
for the occasion), a tray of lubricants, different

brands in tubes or bottles, labels black, red, and silver
—a high tea sensibility. The artifacts remained
uncollected in his apartment for days, even
weeks after, when I would drop by to find his talk
transformed, suddenly transcendental—

the communality, he told me, the freedom: not
just from the condom code (HIV negative I
was never invited) but freed of individuation—
nothing less than rapture, men more than brothers,
a generosity of giving and taking, to both give

and take greedily, that he had experienced
nowhere else. Could I understand that?
The room pulsing as if inhabited by
a single animal, caught up in a single sensibility.
Could I understand? I could read transformation

in his face, could see his eyes, feel him trying
to tell me something: to offer this reliable revelation—
what he always knew would come, but what always
in coming disarmed him. As he talked I looked around
the spare bedroom, attempting to see it

in terms other than lust—a couple of dozen men,
how they would have lined up, become a single
working unit on clear plastic, how their bodies
might have formed a neat chain. I looked around
and tried; couldn't I understand that?

So each beetle a tiny scarab, a dime-size jewel
that glints in the sun. I lean over and touch
their backs with the tip of my finger: running
up and down the bright, smooth surface
like piano keys, hard enough to feel resistance

but not to interject foreign music. Together they form
a band of light, a band of glaze, the gold leafing
that shadows the vines in Celtic manuscripts, a living art.
Maybe that's how it was at my friend's parties—
God leaning over the house on a casual tour

of the wreck of the world, noticing ornamentation
where it wasn't expected. Moved to add
His touch, He reaches a hand through the clouds, runs
His finger over the hard arch of their backs, covering
the length of each spine with the tip;

each man brightens at the touch, comes to know
something expected, unexpected, and tenuous—
and God, also, comes to some knowledge
as if for the first time, is distracted and pleased
by the collective brightness of human skin. . . .

Then I think of God fitting the roof back on
my friend's house, and exhaling, satisfied—
just like me as I walk away
from the tennis court, just like the men inside.

Out here the pull of bodies keeps
everything moving. Mass desires
mass, in even the tiniest quantities.
But what differentiates us, this
sentience, is that it isn't simply mass
that compels, but the idea of it:
the weighted notion, the notion
of waiting. A physics of our condition—
you might call it a strange force—
gives the dream of bodies more pull
than those orbiting close. It's as if,
human, your Earth suddenly tore
itself from the Sun, flung itself
chest first into the void, for the idea
of another: a sun whose conversions
were more compelling. You know
all gold's forged in a star's heart?
Well, it's as if your Earth lusted
for a sun that could generate better
luster. No matter the likelihood
of the planet spinning endlessly
forward—bowling ball (blue, marbled)
gliding on a never-ending lane toward
no pins. No matter that the star—
if it existed—might crisp it to coal.
The idea must be satisfied. But
I was going to talk frankly about
desire, wasn't I? Well, I desire
frankly: This dark is cold, and I
distinctly remember back there, still
pulsing, the place where I left my sun.

JACKIE HAGAN (U.K., B. 1981)

The Little that Tells a Story

Lopsided scars,
little staggering hatred,
curious oddball fears.
It's the dents that make you interesting.

Perfect silver sphere,
I prefer jumble sales,
The horsefly of the eccentric,
The smell of soil sewn in the scrap.

The broken bits fixed,
The broken bits broken,
The dark corners and under the table.

The loved so hard it hurts,
The loved too little,
The little that tells a story.

What We All Know

In here...
everything's broken: the activity cupboard's broken; the kettle's broken; this felt tip's fucked!
Just keep hitting your head against the wall; we know that works.

Come and have a nervous breakdown; it's something to do.
We wake up at 8, it's like an Enid Blyton boarding school
but the girls have all grown up.
Every day at 9 and 12 and 5 for meals we have food, that tastes like
food
and tomorrow for lunch it's
... food
and we smoke our fingers to the bone
and laughter breaks in
two.

Come on in—you might as well, it's like a holiday from life,
the view
from the dayroom:
men pacing and holding it in
until they don't,
crazy women in crazy women coats,
force-fed hope and tired of trying, we smoke.

Come on in, you're just in time—
Beryl's kicking off, screaming all that stuff we all already know
from the last time she kicked off,
with more arms, legs, tears, the nurse's face and blood and later
she'll come sedated into the dayroom,
tail-tucked and shamed that we all know
what we all know;
what we all know anyway.

Amy's stealing everything
with nothing to put it in
and Paddy remembers back
when he used to have opinions and a coat.

Come on in,
it's like an Enid Blyton boarding school
but instead of Matron
we've got Elaine the nurse who's overworked and going grey too early from empathy and no
time to care,
and Lucy, the young nurse, on who it's just dawning that this system,
it doesn't work.
But once a week we have ward rounds!
It's all straighteners and bobbles and Beth
think's she's got a chance to go home
and Erica's dying to see her kids
and we wait.

and wait.

and wait.

228

until the Lord Our Saviour!
(the psychiatrist)
is ready to look at us
in his peripheral vision
with his surprising lack
of interpersonal skills
(considering he's chosen to work with
people
and
psyches)

See,
some
psychiatrists need to learn one sentence:
when someone tells you something horrific that's happened to them
(which they will because you ask them *again and again*)
say this: *"I'm really sorry that happened to you."*

NATALIE E. ILLUM (U.S.A., B. 1977)

Quote me

When the reporter asked me about my sexuality

I told him the truth. "I fall
in love with people, not packaging.
Couldn't care less if it's a dick or a dildo
just give me a pulse I can measure

my laughter against." I want
my lover to show me where
my edges are.

And you can quote me on that.

But, he didn't. He forgot
my middle initial and turned
me into a lesbian activist. Which would
be fine, perfect, if I was one.

Yesterday, my coworkers from the Department
of Agriculture swallowed my favorite
LGBQT Alphabet Soup like it was

cod liver oil; spat out same-sex marriage rights
and complained about the growing lines
at the DC courthouses.

"We didn't know you were *that* kind
of poet," they said, "we thought
you had a boyfriend." It's unbelievable.
How I'm forced to listen to their psalms
and watch them trade church stories.
But I can't even write

a poem without a reprimand. I want
to tell them my bedroom is
classified information, that

my lover is my homeland
and it's a security
that can't be breached.

And you can quote me on that.

100 Reasons Why I Hate Facebook

#1-88: I found out you had a girlfriend even though your relationship status still says "single."

#89: The bitch tried to friend me.

#90: "Defriending" someone is the equivalent of a middle school temper-tantrum, so he and I remain "friends."

#91: "Poking" someone on Facebook is creepy.

#92: People have profile pictures of their dog or their child, and they update it daily.

#93: I still have access to the photos, him and his girlfriend, and I cannot help myself, which makes me hate Facebook even more.

#94: I cannot tell the difference between a group page and a fan page. My real friends explain this to me; I still don't get it. Facebook is lowering my IQ.

#95: I work at a computer for 9 hours a day. I go home and check Facebook statuses for another 2. I post answers to stupid quizzes. My inbox fills with other people's comments that I don't even know.

#96: I lied. It's more like 4 hours, which is why I never go out with my real friends UNLESS I get their event requests.

#97: People send event requests and reminders to ALL of their friends, even though I don't live in Chicago or Texas or Madrid. *Even I know* you can create a local list. Dear all 678 of my closest friends, create a fucking local list.

#98: Why don't I have more than 678 friends?

#99: My ex has 778. Please friend me.

#100 Facebook was created by socially inept Harvard geeks who couldn't connect with people. I am a poet—I used to do that all the time.

KAREN JAIME (U.S.A., B. 1975)

DOMINICANESS DEFINED

Am I any less Dominican
because I don't like
the taste of mangos?
The tart taste of guayaba fruit?
The lechosa with all of its seeds?
If fruits define me,
than I'm a nothing
for I'm not a big fan
of red American apples
or fuzzy peaches
that give me hives.

I'll tell you what I do like though
Un plato de arroz blanco
with thick ass *habichuelas rosa'*
cut up *guineo*
and some nice
carne guisaita on the side
with a tall glass of *refreco con hielo*.

All this
at 12 o'clock noon
with the hot Caribbean sun
beaming in
through the open *persianas*,
the cool air
wafting in
through the open doors
that we never close
except at night.

Family
gathered around a table
all talking sooo loud
it sounds like
you're in a wind tunnel.
The kind of loud you hear
as you walk by
on your way to *el colmado*
to get *un pedacito*
de dulce de leche
that's no longer
10 centavos
but that's damn good
as it melts in your mouth.

Loud
that makes people nervous
'cause it sounds like
we're arguing
when all we're doing
is enjoying the sounds
of our own voices—
loving each other
with raucous laughter
and slaps on the back
as we tell *cuentos*
until the meal is over,
the plates are carried out,
and *"El Show de las Doce"*
gives way
to *la novela de la una.*

After all this,
do you STILL think
I'm not Dominican
because I don't like
the taste of mangos?

Mangos have yet to define me
OR my Dominicaness...

I am as Dominican as:

- "Dios, Patria, Libertad"
- as the *plataneros* selling their *plátanos* every morning at 6AM
- as the Caribbean sun beaming down on *El Cibao, Santo Domingo* and my mother's hometown of *Barahona*
- as the sea water in *Boca Chica* with hot rocks that burn your feet on your way down to its clean shores
- as the cut-off Spanish that we're mocked for
- as the *merengue ripiao* that forces me to dance whenever it comes on
- as the people selling in the streets between the cars on *La Avenida Meya*
- as the faceless ceramic womyn that we have become known for

I am as Dominican as
el Malecon during *"El festival del Merengue."*

Neither mangos
nor you
will EVER define me.

Don't you get it?

I'M AS DOMINCAN AS

EL ALMUERZO

DEL MEDIO DIA!

I don't need no pride parades in June,
strutting seasonal feathers
for mass consumption...
I don't need no
rainbow beaded bracelets
worn under long sleeves at home...

I AM
NYC June in December

I AM
the West Village uptown

My sexuality is *not* dictated
by geography
or subway stops—
Hold hands on Christopher Street,
Let go on Newkirk.
Kiss me in Manhattan
and walk by me in Brooklyn.

If mom asks—
I was asking for directions
'cause West Indian mothers
ain't ready to talk about lesbians
when *looooong white* dresses
and good Haitian boys
are what they dream of...
and it's a long way
from 809 to 718
but your neighbor **didn't** *need* long distance
to call you the next morning
and ask you what you were doing
kissing a woman at 12:09 on New York Ave...
'Cause Haiti was in Brooklyn that night
and **I** forgot myself...

I *forgot* that it
wasn't June but August
and that this was Flatbush
NOT the West Vill.,
and that I was miles from home
But YOU *still* lived across the street.
I *forgot*
that the distance between us
was greater than
the hour and a half train ride.
It went *beyond* zip codes and area codes,
it went *beyond* our 6 year age difference,
it went *beyond* butch/femme...

See, I could **never** meet you ½ way
because you expected me
to wear those heels
I packed up for Goodwill
in order to make walking
down the streets with me
easier for you…

I am just **not** into
fashionable discomfort,
and I've grown tired
of walking miles
in someone else's shoes.
I can't step back
into your closet
full of loose threads
that like lips,
make *this* one secret
that's too hard to keep…

And I'm tired of secrets,
and stolen glances
on subway platforms,
and sneaking in and out
of your parents' home…
and shame.
I am tired of
not fitting into social boxes
too small,
to contain all of me.
I am <u>NOT</u> your seasonal love,
your once a week
"L-Word" fix

I am Dyke TV,
24/7
on public access
no matter what channel you turn to—
So if you ain't ready to watch
then
I
suggest
you

TURN

YOUR

TV

OFF!!

JOSEPH O. LEGASPI (U.S.A., B. 1971)

Imago

As soon as we became men
my brother and I wore skirts.
We pinched our skirt-fronts into tents
for our newly-circumcised penises, the incisions
prone to stick painfully to our clothing.

I was partial to my sister's plaid skirt,
a school uniform she outgrew; my brother favored
one belonging to my grandmother, flowers
showering down his ankles.
By this stage, the skin around the tips
of our penises was swollen the size
of dwarf tomatoes.

As a cure, my mother boiled
young offshoots of guava leaves.
Behind the streamline of hung fabric,
I sat on a stool and spread
before a tin washbasin. My mother bathed
my penis with the warm broth,
the water trickling into the basin like soft rain on our roof.
She cradled my organ, dried it with cotton,
wiping off the scabs melted by the warmth,
and she wrapped it in gauze, a cocoon
around my caterpillar sex.

I then thought of the others at the verge of their manhood:
my brother to replace me on this stool,
a neighborhood of eleven-, twelve-, and thirteen-year old
boys wearing the skirts of their sisters
and grandmothers, touched
by the hands of their mothers,
baptized by green waters,
and how by week's end
we will shed our billowy skirts,
like monarchs, and enter
the gardens of our lives.

V-Neck T-Shirt Sonnet

I love a white v-neck t-shirt
on you: two cotton strips racing
to a point they both arrived at: *there*
vigor barely contained, flaming hair,
collarless, fenced-in skin that shines.
Cool drop of hem, soft & lived-in,
so unlike my father, to bed you go,
flushed with fur in a rabbit's burrow
or nest for a flightless bird, brooding.
Let me be that endangered species,
huddled in the vessel of the inverted
triangle: gaped mouth of a great white
fish on the verge of striking, poised
to devour & feed on skin, on all.

[a subway ride]

His artfully unkempt strawberry blonde head sports outsized
headphones. Like a contemporary bust. Behold the innocence of the
freckles, ripe pout of cherry lips. As if the mere sight of the world
hurts him, he squints greenly and applies saline drops. You dream
him crying over you. For the duration of a subway ride you fall
blindly in love. Until he exits. Or you exit, returning home to the one
you truly love to ravish him.

LENELLE MOISE (U.S.A., B. 1980)

gift a sea

after i became
grandfather called me dry
nasty names
stood small in my kitchen
baking hisses at midnight
praying rocks
against the women
in my love

but before
when i was tiny thirsty
he bought me a vintage typewriter
heavy & teal it splashed under my palms
a thrifted gift a sea in my blood
the first tool
my damp fingers used
to cool & name myself.

& do you see how much i love you

if the baby don't exist yet
come through me
& i have not prepared
have not seen a physician
a nutritionist

an overpriced therapist applied
for medical insurance
applied myself & earned
good credit
a driver's license

a PhD
before i'm thirty
thirty-five
forty-one or good
or ready

if i have not paid
the back taxes paid back
those fucking student loans
stopped cursing
purchased a country

home
in a state where gays marry
near water
near good detectorless schools
with good gay teachers

who will get us lord
who will get us?
if i have not written my book
ten books
committed every inch of my trust to my lover

to a daily dose of yoga
to lifting up my spirits
to stomping out my anger
to american citizenship
if i have not renewed my passport

flown
over water-grave ancestors
to places
where no one but god
speaks my language places

where
i'm forced to get by
on good looks
expressive hands
& the kindness of strangers

if i have not fully converted
to buddhism or won a million
two million three million dollar lotto ticket
a genius grant or tenure
my lover's whole heart

if i have not lived to build
a few steps toward social justice
lived my own true free full life
nomadic & shameless
before another life depends

on me & physical stability
financial sanity
emotional hygiene
selfless love
unconditional protection

then i am so afraid
that when the baby don't exist
yet comes through me
i will cringe when she cries
snap or spit when she fails

challenges my patience
questions my authority
demands my attention
when i am trying to dream or do
when she's convinced my name is mommy

don't want to sound like
my poor mother lord
(and by poor i mean broke)
who shouted
when her unpaid bills met

my clumsy teacup bashing
shouted
"should have had an abortion"
so many echo times
claimed to "sacrificed too much"

for my burdensome existence
cursed "you're just like your father."
who was so close by
but absent
& maybe i was like him lord

& maybe i wasn't
my child will not have a father
my child will be the 8 pound result
of unconventional love
desire

tenacity only
& the money
i will raise
for the cause
there will be science:

a bright good-looking man picked out
of a sperm bank's book
of headshots & credentials
or scandalous stories:
an unsuspecting man picked up

at an activist conference
poetry bar
alvin ailey concert or
in provincetown where the men
know about these things

will my daughter be conceived
in a brave or stupid one night
stand in a three star hotel room
the way dykes dared it
in the seventies? or

will my itchy womb bloom after
a safer sweeter ceremony
in the dimmed romantic privacy
of my small city apartment
sade playing in the background

partner playing fertility doctor
warm turkey baster in one
determined hand
my trembling cheek in her other
once i asked my partner

if she thought she could
fiercely love
a baby
she had not pushed out herself
she said "you & me—

we don't
share blood
& do you see
how much
i love you?"

lord i am full of fear
& hope
& logistical frustration
everyday now i mutter earnest
premature prayers

pray my lover will stay
to hold me
& this idea to flesh i keep
imagining
a girl child

cherished long
before she meets
this bumpy
broken world & long
after

GABE MOSES (U.S.A., B. 1981)

How to Make Love to a Trans Person

Forget the images you've learned to attach
to words like cock and clit,
chest and breasts.
Break those words open
like a paramedic cracking ribs
to pump blood through a failing heart.
Push your hands inside.
Get them messy.
Scratch new definitions on the bones.

Get rid of the old words altogether.
Make up new words.
Call it a click or a ditto.
Call it the sound he makes
when you brush your hand against it through his jeans,
when you can hear his heart knocking on the back of his teeth
and every cell in his body is breathing.
Make the arch of her back a language.
Name the hollows of each of her vertebrae.
When they catch pools of sweat
like rainwater in a row of paper cups
align your teeth with this alphabet of her spine
so every word is weighted with the salt of her.

When you peel layers of clothing from his skin
do not act as though you are changing dressings on a trauma patient
even though it's highly likely that you are.
Do not ask if she's "had the surgery."
Do not tell him that the needlepoint bruises on his thighs look like they hurt.
If you are being offered a body
that has already been laid upon an altar of surgical steel,
a sacrifice to whatever gods govern bodies
that come with some assembly required
whatever you do,
do not say that the carefully sculpted landscape
bordered by rocky ridges of scar tissue
looks almost natural.

If she offers you breastbone
aching to carve soft fruit from its branches
though there may be more tissue in the lining of her bra
than the flesh that rises to meet it,
let her ripen in your hands.
Imagine if she'd lost those swells to cancer,
diabetes,
a car accident instead of an accident of genetics—
would you think of her as less a woman then?

Think of her as no less one now.

If he offers you a thumb-sized sprout of muscle
reaching toward you when you kiss him
like it wants to go deep enough inside you
to carve his name on the bottom of your heart,
hold it as if it can—
in your hand, in your mouth
inside the nest of your pelvic bones.
Though his skin may hardly do more than brush yours,
you will feel him deeper than you think.

Realize that bodies are only a fraction of who we are.
They're just oddly-shaped vessels for hearts
and honestly, they can barely contain us.
We strain at their seams with every breath we take.
We are all pulse and sweat,
tissue and nerve ending.
We are programmed to grope and fumble until we get it right.
Bodies have been learning each other forever.
It's what bodies do.
They are grab bags of parts
and half the fun is figuring out
all the different ways we can fit them together;
all the different uses for hipbones and hands,
tongues and teeth;
all the ways to car-crash our bodies beautiful.
But we could never forget how to use our hearts
even if we tried.
That's the important part.
Don't worry about the bodies.
They've got this.

JULIA NANCE (U.S.A., B. 1978)

Crazytown

You said: *How can you even like me?*
I Drive You Crazy.
We were having one of those beer-lit front porch reconnections
fueled by bittersweet make-ups and bickering
And Goddamnit... You DO drive me crazy,
You drive me to the best parts of Crazy
give me the grand tour, the clean sweep
You make me feel like the Queen
Hand me the keys to the city
throw a party in my honor
and everyone comes
because you're the fucking mayor of Crazy
You run the place
The festivities hit a frenzied peak
and you light the parade on fire
the children start balling
their mothers put dishpan hands over their little eyes
turn them away
just a typical Saturday night
here in Crazy
the locals cheer you on and wave
You spent years on committees,
practically wrote the charter
you flash a crooked smile at the littered bombardment
of Baggage strewn in everyone's yards
the dirty laundry in plain sight
There's a therapist's office every 2 blocks
people rattle bottles of anti-depressants like tamborines
they shout your name like a mantra
a victory cry
just when I've finally gotten used to the insanity
you knock me over the head with a left-field observation
something poignant and totally out there
Throw me in your trunk
and say the tour's over,
You do drive me crazy baby
You drive me to the best parts of crazy
but you know
I wouldn't have it any other way.

What would you do?

What would you do?
An off-key crescendo
from behind the driver's seat
As my girls sing
They feel this one particularly
From the group home to an NA meeting
You can hear it in their pleading voices
Loudest on
In and out of lock down
directed right at me when they scream
so for you this is just a good time
but for me this is what I call Life!
Life.
It's the only thing these girls got a lot of.

And what would you do?
When she cries
Deep shaking sobs
Pushing her knees into chest
Heaving ears red with effort
Put your arm around her?

It's not enough—
But full body contact
Not permissible
Possibly mistaken as sexual
By a 13-year-old
Who only knows the volatile touch
Of father brother uncle
All adults put into a box
Labeled and taped shut— "don't trust"
And I'm not allowed to give her a hug.

And what would you do?
When you saw new track marks
over track marks 2 years old
on age-17 arms
The slim crease
in her elbow
Scarred—
Scared
Leading down
to a homemade tattoo
"doesn't hurt when you're high"
she shrugs and
I'm not allowed to give her a hug.

And what would you do
When her caseworker calls
Tells her: her baby's daddy's in prison
A laundry list of reasons
She listens as her eyes fill
She can't write him,
tears spill
No more contact
And oh yeah, that ain't his real name
She bites her lip
until blood runs down her chin
Lock-up on a holiday weekend
Her face in the pillow
Sobbing "what about the birth certificate?"
Her baby's illegitimate
Now she doesn't even have his name and
I'm not allowed to give her a hug.

What would you do?
When she runs
Clued by a few days
of her closed face
And sullenness
Nothing to stay for
because it's not getting any better
after a full day in court
finds out there's no home to go home to
you have to watch her legs move
long and free
disappearing into woods
and on the other side
men who know what to do
with a 16-year-old from a group home
men who will take or rape or
maybe she'll come back
maybe she'll come back
bleeding, strung out,
pregnant, broken—
I'm not allowed to give her a hug.

These girls,
Our girls, flinch at words
Unpredictable reactions
Triggered by memories
I have no access to,
I am constantly on guard
To avoid lighting the fuse
That ignites the explosion of
Rage,
Pain,
Confusion—
And I'm not allowed to give her a hug.

LETTA NEELY (U.S.A., B 1971)

Forward Home

Imagine your body
as the universe in concentrate
think how we desecrate this place
we call home—divine spot,
we keep it too hot or too cold
most of the time
not knowing our temperature,
we venture into a rat race
becoming uniformed soldiers
fighting wars about which we are
uninformed
these formations we build are internal
are funeral pyres
we make our own death beds
and not recognizing phoenix
when we rise, we lean over and piss
on our ashes, crying
talking about next time will be better
bigger different when we're in the next time
right now.

Still we
forsake our loves, ourselves, become selfish, fold into
inferno after inferno seeking the finish line
when we haven't even begun to crawl home;
just stand burning or
stand stagnating sticking to stinking rotting flesh
waving it like a disparate banner

I have been here before and it's a lonely place
wearing skin that didn't fit/ elocuting voices
that were not mine/ diction a perfect fit
for someone else not me/ and you clapped, sometimes
and I smiled but I was not happy. I pushed me into the farthest crevices
Of my own unexplained unexplored territory
I went
In search of something sacred and ended up on a brick
Road when I'm from cracked sidewalks and dirt

I ended up here before at this crossroads where jesus and legba
salsa and do line dances, sip crown royal and throw back
tequila shots,
been at the precipice of this cauldron where witches
decide on brooms or bicycles or buses or hitchhiking
and I've sat so long and chosen nothing
except to snort a line of coke to prolong the waiting
make the anxiety of stepping into pain or
into power go away;
I know fear she runs like the Tigris,
Like the Euphrates, like the Mississippi
From my aorta to my great grandmother's
All the way back to my umbilical chord

I keep ending up here again.

And I died and was reborn. I die and am boring
My way into life again and again from the other sides
And I know Infinite Sustenance, she runs like
The Tigris. Like the Euphrates like the Mississippi
From my aorta to my great grandmother's
All the ways to my umbilical chord

Here is where life begins
Imagine your body as the universe in concentrate
Think how we decorate this place we call home—
Divine spot, we keep it holy, wholly freely able
To roam in our own skin, our own dreams,
Think how we magic the music in our
Muscles how we exorcise unwanted visitors
How we sit down to eat at our tables
How we see our skyline how we walk
Our shore how we believe in beauty
Which is before us, which is behind
Us which is below us, which is above
Us
Which is us. Which is us. Imagine
Us free and we are free
To be home
In ourselves

The Ghosts of Blowjobs Past

Suppose you're invited to a Christmas party
and when you arrive at the condo lobby
something feels familiar,
which is strange since it's not your kind
of building and you don't recall
ever coming there before.
Suppose on the flight up
it hits you that the building
sits on land that once occupied
one of your favourite nightclubs,
Luv-A-Fair or Love My Hair,
as you so affectionately called it,
and even though the elevator plays Christmas carols
your head starts to fill
with the thump-thump-thump
of the club along with visions
of your favourite bartenders,
the punk rock cocktail waitresses,
the woman with the long brown hair
who you swear wore the same black dress
as she danced on the speakers
for a decade's worth of Tuesdays,
all this and more comes back to you
as you exit the elevator
and just as you knock knock knock
on the door you're taken back to the moment
a beautiful stranger pushed you into the stalls
and gave you your first anonymous blowjob
and as the host opens the door
instead of saying hello you say
Someone gave me a blowjob here
twenty years ago
which makes him a little uncomfortable
and you a lot ashamed.
This isn't the first time
ghosts have haunted you
as most of Vancouver feels like a graveyard
of nightclubs past
and even by just walking around
you're bound to realize
just how many of your pivotal moments
have been cemented over
like Jimmy Hoffa.
Maybe it's just ego
not being able to let go
of the geography
or your need for connection,
a little bit of ownership
in a city you'll never own.

ALIX OLSON (U.S.A., B. 1975)

Box Spring in New Orleans

Poor Statue of Liberty

Stuck in all that water
Her head must have drooped in shame

When she heard her President proclaim that
"People in this part of the world are suffering"
and "this part of the world" used to be Her America.

Well, I remember
The bridge, the body, the barge, the body,
the boat, the body,
the breech, the body,
the school bus,
the scream, the stench,
the water, the window, the water, the waiting, the water
the crash, the crush, the coast, the crime

I remember the explosion.

The decapitated dog on the post
The dolphin in the pool
The crocodile, the cow, the bloat, the drown

Now, I remember
Seven days of wait on a roof
Seven days of rape on a roof
Seven days of pray on a roof
The helicopter
And how it never came

How they called it catastrophe, calamity, chaos.
But the police gun-pointing our bus seemed organized enough

I remember
The prisoners who were people
In wheelchairs in handcuffs
In the basement
And wondering how long
I remember the Convention Center
The Superdome
Pissing on the floor of our new home

I Remember
St. Thomas
The Desire
The Fisher
B.W. Cooper
The Lower Ninth Ward
Jefferson Parish
Sam Jackson

But mostly I remember
Balancing my baby
On a box spring
And sending her towards goodbye

I am now
Cold lunches
The National Guard
Charter schools
Subcontractors
Detention centers
Insurance adjustors
Blackwater
Formaldehyde
FEMA
Trailers in rows like tombstones
Toxic graveyards
Demolition
Bull dozers
Donald Trump
Decaying lots
Disintegration
Closed day cares and clinics
Commissions
E coli
Conflictions
Condominiums
Corporations
Well-connected elections
Voodoo tunes jazz gumbo blues
And I am wondering, Red Cross, where the money went
Because I am now
No playground
No recess
Black children
Criminal trespass
No gangs
No loiter

Because I am now
A ten year old daughter with a sign:
"Missing parents plus two brothers"
I am now searching through the rubble for my grandmother
I am now
"Teachers, this is just a reminder that today's PTSD workshop is in the library."

I am now
Your poems
Your pictures
Your politics
Your thesis
Your CNN segment
Your cause
Your conspiracy
Your songs
Your sympathy

But I am still

In Baton Rouge
Houston
Salt Lake City
Little Rock
In Denver
In Dallas
Holding a sign "In Desperate Need of Assistance"
I am still a refugee in my own damn country
And I am waiting for America
"To get my ass home."

Dear 16 Year Old Me

Dear 16 Year Old Me:
Men have begun to tell you to smile on the street so for the next ten years
You will pull it out completely automatic like a beaming pistol
Like a stun-gun grin. But one day you will realize that smile was never for them and like all of your fragile
things you will want it back. So when you pack it up,
Pack it in tissue paper.
Dear 16 Year Old Me:
You are all blue eyeliner and moral conviction you are a carpenter of things you are pounding them
together with Greenpeace stickers and Indigo Girls songs. But underneath, baby, you are blue blood Judy
Bloom heart break. You are sealing out the world before it can seep in, your sarcasm is a glue gun, your
stubborn is just in your wiring. You have a premonition that your taboo ethics might save you, you have a
strong suspicion there are girls out there just like you. Still there are so many stupid things you are pursuing
you will spend so many years undoing. Don't kiss that girl. She will play your heart like a Chinese jump
rope. That girl is black magic, she is full of tricks of tragic and there is nothing you can do to make her love
you.
Dear 16 Year Old Me:
I am standing in the bones of your ancient infrastructure,
These are the ribs where your fingers dig for fat, this is where a stone slices into your kneecap,
you never stop to inspect it,
Self-neglect is your best strategy and you intend to protect it.
This is the liver that faces the barrel of a bottle, this is the torn aorta you inherit from your father,
These are the lungs you hold hostage, these are the stitches from your last binge from when you drank so
much you could hardly stand, from when you drank so much you could no longer stand yourself.
And you have no idea how many promises will be harmed in the making of this life.
And no matter how much charm you harness you've got to know that this is true,
That the point is not to please them but to make room for all of you.
And loving yourself is not a condition of your existence but it sure as fuck will make every breath forward
easier. Because what happens is this: One day there' s a rapist, one day your dignity swims so far from shore
your shoulders slump like a widow and still you bounce back grinning cause you've been taught to bear it.
You've got a springboard of steel that will vault you towards tomorrow, spinning, doing somersaults and
tossing out victory signs.
I wish you could see the view from here. You are breathtaking. You are all bold voice and mistaken
intention, you are heart-wrenching, baby you are a goddamn dreamboat.
Don't you think I wish I could tell you to kick back and relax until you get your shit together,
To show you this coin from when you finally figure out what you are worth?
Don't you think I wish I could just hurl you where you need to go, or swoop down and knit you a nest of
newborn rules and neckties or disguise you as the future until your presence blends in?
Don't you think I wish I could tell you I am coming for you?
One day I will deposit you in the company of women with a love as ancient as constellations,
They will teach you to two-step with the world you thought you had to tackle,
They might unshackle your spirit
They might ask you just exactly what it is you plan to do with this one wild and precious life.
I wish I could pack parachutes in your pockets, guarantee a soft landing
Towards the ground
From where I'm standing
It's going to be spectacular.

SHAILJA PATEL (U.S.A., B. ?)

For The Verbal Masturbators

How big is your
voice? Bigger
than your dick?
Longer than the litany
of your self-importance?
If it smashes
into the woman in the fields
with the force of a fist so she
clenches her thighs, flinches
a hand over her pubis, if your voice
leaves blood in the crevice
under her tongue,
does that make it
bigger?

How wide is your big?
Wider than this room?
Does it open out your skin
to the passage of the planets?
Does it crawl, lurch, stumble
beyond the specificity
of your particularity,
the gendered animosity
of your physicality,
does its linguistic density
transcend the trite geography
of what's between your thighs?

If your wide maps
the exact elasticity
of the gap between

I feel   *I fear*   *I failed*

and

I Know.

I Am Right.

Not My Fault!
the nanometric calibration
of your self-protection,
does that make it
wider?

How fierce is your wide?
More fierce than your fear?
If your fear slams walls
around the mic but your fierce
lays type on the press at 3am,
by paraffin lamp, listens
for jackboots, alsatians,
if they came for *you*
in the knife
of the night
to silence your fierce,
would your walls
be
worth it?

How much is your fierce?
How much would you pay?
In shillings, dollars,
rupiahs, shekels, rand,
if you costed your words
and each
one
cost—
how much would you pay
for your fierce?

If a word cost your lover
would you pay?
Your job, your right to vote
would you pay?
A schoolplace for your child
a hospital bed for your AIDS-riddled
mother, the rationed insulin
you need to live, the visa
to flee the bombs
of those who have *never* paid
for one of their words—
would you buy your fierce?
How much?

How loved is your much?
Will it grow, be enough?
Do you delve its splendour
or rape it of content,
vomit it up half-digested
just so you know
that your much is loud
and your loud is big
at least as big as your dick,
and that preempts
the cold hard space
where you dare not face
the worth of your words or gauge
the love of your much.

How brave is your love?
Brave enough to walk
the perihelion?
To be the hands laying type
on the page
when the jackboots come,
to pay for the words, for every word
with the fear of your flesh,
with rain for your people,
if we stand in this room together,
in the wide of our much,
in the fierce of our brave,
my words cross yours,
need food
for the journey,
I have to ask:

how loved is your brave,
how much for your love,
how fierce is your much
and would you pay?
How wide is your fierce,
how big is your wide,
how voiced is your big,
how big
is your
voice?

OLUMIDE POPOOLA (U.K., B. 1975)

water running from my mouth

I

that call
before the tide
ripped and bowed
stripped
not
memories
clipped
not wings

walked
walked
on water

II

that call
mother said
it wouldn't be too long
she'd swallow, like she can
she'd tear away from seams
of un-proportion
but it doesn't work like that
in stale water
that too she knew
so they spat and burned
and cursed and fled
from the inside pockets of dis-hope
bursting into confused enigma
of re
ality
let's call it real estate

maybe on the moon
we flog again
maybe

II

that call
mid-air
which was thick like concrete
mother said
(actually she didn't speak just then
but in retrospect
we could interject
need
here.
need for words)
mid- way
necessity broke
the atmosphere hard
hitting all the usual
synapses
"cool down, cool, you person"

that call
was cleanse me not cleanse me now
because

I need to come and heal with you
I need to come and heal
with you

III

I never said
I couldn't swim
I just said
I'd drown easily

IV

tide wrapping
offering
entblöst sich
manchmal muss man einfach nachgeben
surrender they say
is the hardest form of acceptance
sie sagen
das es das Schwerste ist
am schwersten ist
sich hinzugeben
noch schwerer, wenn man nicht weiss
wenn man einfach nicht weiss
das andere Ende, so ungewiss
vielleicht gibt es keine Himmel
vielleicht gibt es aber auch kein auf Erden

surrender they say is
the hardest
form

they say

of acceptance

V

that call before the tide
clipped wings
ripped
apart
not memories
but
that thought
that it was easy

that call
before the tide
Said
go home
that call
said go
and don't know where you are

to speak against what your heart
cannot take
if only once
if
only once

VI

no need to drown

walk on water
walk
on
water

VII

Mama—
she led me
free
over
bricks and stones
tears and ravage
asking keys of ancient grounds
spillage made for expansion
Oshun was waving
off-shore

we boarded
delightful
this seems to be our resurrection
it is not that when you drown you have failed
it is your choice
it is not that when you have drowned
you failed

go home
go
even if you don't know where you are
go

VIII

to speak
against
what your heart cannot take
if only once
if only
once

IX

that call
before the tide
ripped and bowed
stripped
not
memories
clipped
not wings

walked
walked
on water

BARUCH PORRAS-HERNANDEZ (MEXICO, B. 1981)

The Pursuit of Taco-ness

Hello
my name is Baruch
I am a Mexican
and I like Taco Bell.
I know it's a shame to my culture
but it's sooooo gooood.
I love me some Taco Bell.
Yo quiero Taco Bell.

Every time I eat Taco Bell
I can hear my ancestors
screaming in the back of my head
"NOOOOOOOOO!!!
WHYYYYYYYYYYYY?!!!!"
From their tiny little graves
all the way back in Mexico,
but they say it in Spanish
so it sounds more like
"NOOOOOOOOO!!!
PORQUEEEE!!!!!?"
But then I remember
they spoke Aztec,
Or something like that,
so maybe I should stop eating Taco Bell
Cause man
it is making me hear things.

I hate it when white folks try to correct my Spanish
white old ladies spend a summer in Acapulco
suddenly they're Spanish professors

Gringa please!

World traveler white dudes
I know you smoked some good mota
on top of the Sun Pyramid in Teotihuacan,
but I don't care how Mexican you feel,
don't correct my Spanish.

But please keep visiting my country,
we really need the money.

Never tell a Mexican when or where
he can speak his language
I was in line at the bank the other day
with my brother.
We were talking about our crazy parents,
so we were speaking in Spanish
This white lady out of nowhere says

"Excuse me! Excuse me! You need to stop!
You're being rude, this is America, right?
We speak English here!"

The little Aztecs in the back of my head
started screaming
'SACRIFICE HER TO THE SUN GOD!!
SACRIFICE HER TO THE SUN GOD!!
IT NEEDS BLOOD
AND THIS BITCH IS ASKING FOR IT!!!"
I whispered to them
"Shhh! Guys I can't, look at her
she's not a virgin."
She screamed "What did you say!"
OH FUCK. I said that out loud
It made sense she was pissed,
They're not her ancestors,
she can't hear them
Besides, she looked more
like a Jack 'n the Box girl to me.
So before she could punch me I said
"Hey! How about some Taco Bell?"
It is amazing what a Crunch Wrap Supreme
can do to fix any situation.
Half an hour later
we're at the Taco Bell parking lot
eating Taco Bell.
She's happy, I'm happy
sour cream at the corners of our mouths
she says "You know,
eating Taco Bell,
that's not very Mexican of you,"

I say "Yeah, telling someone
what language they can and can't speak
In the land of the free,
that's not very American of you.
When I become a citizen, lady,
I'm going to think of you,
cause you've reminded me about
the kind of American I never want to be.
You better get used to hearing
people speak other languages
Cause we are not going away,
and there are a lot of us.

Enjoy your food,
bon appetit."

Puppy

Is a hate word for gay men in Iraq.
        Gay men walk around holding puppies in the Castro.

You can find the word carved into the foreheads
of murdered young gay men.
        In San Francisco, gay men hold their husbands' hands.

Iraqi gay men's bodies are stuffed into garbage bins
or left in neat rows along the streets for all to see.
        Gay men in San Francisco stand in neat rows
        outside the bars and shops wanting to be seen.

Hundreds of gay men have been killed in Iraq since 2004.
        18,605 men have died in San Francisco of Aids since 1980.

Militias and Iraqi Police kidnap men off the streets
break into their homes, torture them before killing them.
        Some gay men in San Francisco dress up like policemen
        some love to be tortured; safe words are important.

Some families punish their own kin in Iraq for being gay
        Some San Francisco gay men have little sex dungeons
        built into their homes, love being punished.

Some fathers kill their gay sons. Honor killing.
        Which one is called Dad? Which one is called Daddy?

A gay man in Iraq gets his anus sealed with industrial glue
        A young gay couple buys a butt plug

he is force fed laxatives by the fistfuls
        they shove fists up into each others anuses

until his digestive systems explodes
        this is done willingly, considered "sexually pleasurable"

they flee from Iraq into exile
        they consider moving to Oakland, the rent is cheaper there.

Posters encourage: dispose of the perverts
for the good of the community
        posters with a young boy no older than 18 for a local club

the posters note where they work,
        show the boy naked, bent over, his bottom in the air

posters note where they live
        looking over his shoulder with a leg raised up like a dog

basically, it has become normal in Iraq
to kill gay men
          there is a little star covering his anus

          his face looks innocent
          his eyes beg you for something

          this makes him look like a Puppy.

Unicorn on Fire

One night
I sat in my room wondering
whether or not I should kill myself
for being gay,
I didn't want to make it past 16.
Then my wall exploded!!!
And a red flaming unicorn
galloped into my room and said

SNAP THE FUCK OUT OF IT!
THERE'S NOTHING WRONG WITH YOU!!
I am a creature just like you!
Mysterious! Fabulous! Pure!
Except you get to walk around the land of the living!
So stop being a little bitch and LIVE YOUR LIFE!

Snap.

He disappeared.
My curtains and my room no longer on fire
I finished my homework
and went back to masturbating to images
of Tom Cruise from the movie *Legend.*

I was 14.

Rogue Love

Rogue has been one of the most popular and consistent members of the X-Men comic book since the 1980's. She was, at one point, one of the X-Men's deadliest foes, until she decided to join them and become a superhero. Her mutant power was uncontrollable; any skin to skin contact would absorb the powers and memories of anyone she touched, and it could also kill them.

Like you, I knew:
just one touch could kill.
Touch a man and you drain
the strength from his body,
memories from his brain,
breath from his lungs
still, you are beautiful.

Raised a villain,
outcast even among mutants
fueled by your anger with the world,
the X-tra gene in your DNA
that gave others the power
to read minds, control the weather,
transmute sound into
breathtaking sparks of light,
but cursed you,
unable to touch the ones you love.

Yeah, you could fly ...
but staring down at the earth
just made you feel more alone.
Being bullet proof just meant
suicide wasn't an option.
So you took off your gloves,
forged yourself into a hero,
swore to protect a world that
hated and feared you.

When you fell in love, you fell
in love with a thief,
to keep him from stealing your heart
you floated a quarter inch above his,
letting him feel the heat from your flesh
but not the goose bumps,
blowing streams of kisses
like little laser beams from your lips
to his chin, neck, chest—
your hair a mere tickle.

You only kissed him when it was the
end of the world.

You juggled tanks, destroyed giant robots,
pummeled hundreds of bad guys
and gave me the bravery
to walk through the halls of my school.
Closeted boys were cursed like you:

what just one touch
could unleash on us ...

but you made me want
to bare my chest to the wind
to let the lighting in.
Bring on the missiles!
The spears, magnetic bolts!
Bring on the bullying,
the death threats, even the fear
we both had
of ending up alone.

The last comic book I read as a kid
you were leading the X-Men
through their most dangerous adventure
with your thief at your side.
And now, as I, myself, fall in love,
I take off my own gloves,
plant my lips onto his and kiss him

like it's the end of the world.

AMIR RABIYAH (U.K., B. 1978)

FLESH OF MY FLESH

I am a little girl walking with
a giant of a man the giant grabs
my hand   squeezes four times
to communicate do-you-love-me?
& I squeeze back
yes-I-do

father twenty years later   you ghost
my daily rituals & howl my routine
you stop by unexpectedly   sit
at the kitchen table reading
the newspaper   drinking coffee
comfortable in your robe & slippers

you behave as though you have always lived here

I leave my own house   I walk around the lake
you goose bump my skin   father
you take my hand but I do not stop

you taught me about
the importance of appearances
so we say nothing

silence is our creation story
codes all we have known

I have become a son   you cannot pronounce

father the worst of the growing pains
come from being born   from absence
from taking my own rib   & putting
my own rib back   to breathe life
into my own lungs   to make myself

whole

to do this without you

so I sometimes tell myself lies:

> I don't miss a stranger
> I don't miss my blood

but you ghost giver of my flesh
always find a way to return
father sometimes when I walk
you grab my hand
& you squeeze four times
& despite it all   I always respond

always answer back
Yes-I-do

THE TIGHTEST LINES

every time I come through
the barbershop doors
I sweat   all eyes simultaneously
peer up from sculpted heads & scope
me out   access every inch of me
from my fitted hat to the sag

of my jeans
to the way

             I pause

before I stumble into the territories of masculinity
like a kid trying to walk in his father's shoes

in the shop brothers talk
politics & their mamas they boast about
cell   phones blowing up with
calls from last Saturday   sometimes

men are heavy   metal   teeth   clench
into steel traps
unhinge the mention I got laid
off   fingers   curl into fists

& a low groan spills out of grills
moans   She's gone

in another corner
several men sit on a leather sofa
they watch the television & cheer
& punch the air

a player scores a point
in a game i don't know the rules to

me   I learned to keep quiet
not a regular anywhere
you could say I keep searching
for the right place

ever since my last cut
ever since Ray disappeared

when Ray first leaned in
& threw his cape over me
& raised my chair
I learned what trouble smelled like

when he grabbed my shoulders
I confused his tendons for lightning bolts

when he placed his forefingers on my temples
& asked   *hey blood   what do you want?*
& I almost stammered you

But instead I said   one
& a half   all the way around
with sideburns long
everything defined & even

Ray turned the clippers on
began to work my scalp
my hair dropped into pieces
of intimate pileups

I pretended to be chill
but Ray's hands pressed hotter
than any blade I had ever known

He continued to guide
my chin to the left to the right
on occasion stopped
to see how things were coming along

You want me to use the razor?
he asked I nodded
he baptized his razor in alcohol & water
& tilted me back

keep still, don't move, good, that's right
the veins in my neck throbbed
as he began to cut the tightest lines

When he finished
he dusted me off
with a powdered brush streaked
a cotton ball soaked in stinging Bay Rum
lowered the chair   the chair sighed

goodbye

I left
I went back to my apartment
I tried to read a book
but my eyes began to burn

Ray beamed through
the window of my skin
made me pour onto the floor
& seep into weeping

My friends all thought I went
to the barbershop
to stay looking

fly

but really some days
I just needed
some days I just needed
a brother to touch me

JASON SCHNEIDERMAN (U.S.A., B.1976)

Moscow

For a while I was alone,
so I dated whoever's work I was reading,
but the relationships always ended badly.
I wasn't smart enough for Wayne,
I wasn't caustic enough for David.
Kevin & I were doing well,
but then I met his real boyfriend,
and it turns out I'm not his type.
Sometimes I broke it off.
Jean got to be too depressing.
Fyoder was a bad provider.
After Franz, I started dating myself,
and that was nice. Of course, then I met you
and I had to stop being the man in my life.
I miss me sometimes, but we'll always have Moscow.

Pornography II: The Capacity to Love

These naked girls really love animals
in ways that I just don't. My therapist
thinks it's because I never had pets
growing up. These naked girls must have
had pets, but not clothes. That's how
they grew with the capacity for animal love
in the buff. I only grew up with the capacity
for didacticism and fear, bitterness,
the ability to judge myself by what I can't do.

Like what that girl is doing with a donkey—
I couldn't do that. I'm not flexible enough
or dedicated enough. My therapist wants me
to work things out with my Dad, but really,
I think I need the unconditional love of a dog
or monkey. I think that's what would set me
on the right path. Did these girls have weird
displaced Oedipal complexes that they somehow
brought to their afterschool job at the stable?

I'm sorry, women have Elektra complexes.
I'm the one who couldn't get it Oedipal.
If I had managed an Oedipal complex,
I would get to be straight, but gay as I am,
I'm not gay enough to take a donkey-cock
like that. My therapist says I'm a narcissist,
and I guess it's true, because that girl's
fucking a donkey and all I can talk about
is myself.

THE BUFFY SESTINA
(first episode of the new season, before the opening credits)

Buffy is upstairs sharpening her large collection of stakes

when her mother comes upstairs and says, "Would it be bad,

just this once, not to go out staking vampires again tonight?"

After all—she had just defeated an apocalyptic force! Time

for a break? Buffy never has time for a break. Angel gone,

her stakes sharp, she kisses her mom and hops out the window

into the back yard. Buffy is familiar with this small window

at the beginning of every season (school year), when her stakes

are enough to fight her battles, and whatever the big coming

evil will be— it hasn't started to build yet. What big bad

will it be this season? She pulls her coat against the night

and there's Willow! Her best friend! She certainly has time

for Willow! They walk, explicate the summer, say, "Time

to go back to school." Suddenly, a vampire seizes this window

of relaxed defenses, and grabs off-guard Willow. Oh this night-

ly threat! Willow screams and resists. Buffy turns, her stake

at the ready. "Meet my friend, Mr. Pointy!" she says. Bad

blood-sucker, he lets Willow go. He wants to fight. He goes

at Buffy with everything, and Buffy (blue coat, boots) comes

back at him hard. The fight is oddly even. For a long time

(forty seconds, say), he gets in good blows. He hurts her bad,

she looks finished. She isn't getting back up again. A doe

leaps into the cemetery. All are distracted. Willow makes a stake

from a broken bench piece and the vampire tries to run into the night.

Xander arrives, blocking the exit with his own stake. This night

is going terribly now (for the vampire)! The vampire goes
around to a crypt and tries to run inside, but it takes time
to pry open the gates. Too much time; Xander almost stakes
the vamp, but he stops to quip, and the effort goes bad.
The vampire throws him hard into the boarded up window

of the crypt. Willow runs over, and pulls a board from the window
for a new stake. Buffy's back up. Oh, what a luxury this night
is! Forever to fight just one, lone vampire. Xander's bad-
image soundtracks the fight. Willow lunges and misses, coming
close, but too far left. Buffy kicks the vampire in face, stake
brandished. He goes down, and she's on top of him this time.

Buffy stakes the vampire. He's dust. Whew! Wait. Bad. Crypts
don't have windows. The night is heavy and dark. That took a long time!
What's coming begins to come. Let's un-board that window.

ADAM STONE (U.S.A., B. 1977)

Final Draft For The Moment

And why should romance lead anywhere?
Passion isn't a path through the woods.
Passion is the woods.
—Tom Robins
Half Asleep In Frog Pajamas

Wyatt has scratches on his corneas . from all the men who got lost in his eyes . died trying to claw their way out . the day we broke up . he told me there would always be a special place in his heart . just for me . I had been hoping for something a little more spacious . with a little less black

Elvis was my twenty-first birthday present to myself . boyfriend so out . he had a wind chill factor . an eighteen year old student of Baron Munchausen . majoring in revisionist history . a parasitic Pinocchio . every time I caught him in a lie . his dick looked bigger . he seduced me with broken home stories . his mother . the cancer that closed his father's throat . a wicked stepfather with a taste for Elvis's forbidden fruit

I was the fairy prince . with the glass wallet . that fit perfectly in his pocket . I spent two years . and forty-two lovers . expunging him from my credit report

Graham wouldn't touch me with the lights on

Ryan kissed me . like I was the exhaust pipe on an idling car

Matthew told me that I was the most beautiful . imaginary . friend that he had ever locked in his closet . I never felt so ugly

Precioso was the first lover who made me feel beautiful . he told me I weighed so heavily on his mind that he couldn't sleep nights . I started buying groceries in bulk . seasoned my steaks with weight gain . I would watch him . flipping through my old photo albums . caressing my twenty-four year old cheek . smirking at my seventeen year old sideburns . his love was better for my posture than milk . yet I saw every smile not flashed in my direction as an act of treason . counted seconds during handshakes and hugs . soon . our late night phone conversations grew so tense . fiber optics became brittle . cracked under the weight of our words

Wyatt developed a passion for pesticide ingestion . he skipped town to follow Phish

Elvis got lost . in the enchanted forest of the South Carolina Penitentiary System

I never heard from Graham again

Ryan carved cuneiform across his arteries . dabbed bleach behind one ear . ammonia behind the other . the darling of the Gay Goth Scene

Matthew . and his wife . lived blissfully ignorant ever after

Precioso . I'm sorry I used the cement in our relationship to build a bomb shelter strong enough to survive our past . instead of laying a foundation for our future . I'm not sure at which page in the photo album . I lost my ability to see the present for what it's worth

Hallelujah, It's Raining Men

The pity parade was canceled when it started raining men
Broken jaws and shoulders littered the main street

All these men broken before they fell
Now heaped into piles for the sanitation crew

Love is a felony that will never be expunged from your record
no matter how you plead
or whether or not you're acquitted

Your friends will tell you to roll with it
but your body has too many angles for that kind of motion

Have another drink
something so fruity it burns holes in your tiny umbrella
then call me   like you do
Tell me how much it hurts to be in love with someone who doesn't love you back

I am laughing
because it's better for my voice than screaming
and I'm afraid of all the tiny men swimming in my tear ducts

Crossing The Flock

When my aunt folds her arms across her chest
and announces *They're called Canada Geese*
not Canadian Geese
I begin to understand their urgent honking
the violent hiss at children offering bread
all this anger at being named for a nation that refuses to claim you
a nation you visit but is never home

In an article on one of my upcoming shows
my hometown newspaper referred to me as a Gay Poet
I assume because I occasionally sleep with men
though more often I sleep alone
but nobody refers to me as a Chaste Poet

I don't know why being labeled Gay
offends me any more than being labeled Poet
as I've been writing mostly prose for the last couple of years
maybe because I plan on reading poetry during my show
while I won't be fucking any men

I will spend my show hissing rants into a microphone
while across town
wings skim over water
and the geese are honking *Fuck Canada*

Whatever Lifts Your Luggage

for Larry Craig, Mark Foley, Ted Haggard, Glen Murphy Jr., Bob Allen, Roy Ashburn, Richard Curtis, David Dreier, Jeffrey Ray Nielsen, Jim West, Paul Crouch, Bruce Barclay, Phillip Hinkle, Ed Shrock, George Rekers, Eddie Long, Troy King, and all the hypocritical politicians and religious leaders who fought against gay rights before they were outed as homosexuals

The nun teaching sex education
rolls the condom the wrong way over the banana
in a room full of starved monkeys

The sheep in wolf's clothing tells you to master your own destiny

The chickens are giving lessons in proper lipstick application

Every frightened old faggot in a red white and blue balled suit
wants to cure your homosexuality with his star spangled asshole

The praying mantis preaches monogamy and non-violence

The suitcase wishes you'd never leave the house

The Republican drafting Anti-Gay Marriage Legislation
only sucks dick for research
It's not like he's getting enjoyment out of it

The sequins sing the praises of subtlety

Lions roam from college to college
educating students on the benefits of veganism

Plankton are trying to save the whales

Senators tapping their feet in airport bathrooms
are just practicing Morse Code

ANNA SWANSON (CANADA, B. 1974)

Shirt collar

You're standing by the mirror,
and I watch your fingers
slip cufflinks through buttonholes.
Your shoulders ease back,
as if the world finally had room for them,
as if your skin fit differently
under this shirt. Your small breasts
press out, unexpected
in these starched folds.

For you I would learn
the forgotten motions of my father's hands,
the foreign ritual of folding a tie
in on itself, anything
for an excuse to reach behind your neck,
slide my fingers up under your shirt collar,
that sharp cool crease.

When women were clouds

Back before control top pantyhose,
before the notion of too much woman—
when women were clouds,
we were consulted about everything.
We decided when the ships would sail and if
they would arrive. Men blamed their wet dreams
on the fog. Everyone sketched out secret plans
for a flying machine. It was a good time,
all in all, when women were clouds.
The rain never tasted better. We got more
airtime on the radio and there were many
and better words for women
who put out.

Loose woman

I figured it was like the difference between skinny-dipping and going swimming at the rec centre. Too many times I stood on a diving board in an old bathing suit that was never enough to cover all the right places, especially if you didn't shave, and I didn't. Always an aquafit class somewhere and a gym full of people behind a glass wall at the side of the pool. No one was looking at me but it felt like they were all watching because everyone there was always watching. And is it any wonder I never learned to dive as though my body were beautiful?

The first time I swam naked in daylight there were thirty of us. Imagine it. Enough naked women to sink a small dock. I swam out from the others and floated on my back. With the sun on my skin, I felt my muscles release, let my arms and legs loosen. Slowly I learned the lake would still hold me if I let go like this, my mouth barely above water and my breasts perfect islands beside a blooming continent of belly. I opened my thighs to the ripples that women's bodies were making somewhere, until my limbs made a star and I was looking up at the sky. The clouds moved so easily. Later someone said, *You looked beautiful out there.* And I believed her. That was the summer I learned to dive like I meant it: every arcing part of me.

ROD TAME (U.K., B. 1975)

Renaissance Man

In the beginning,
there was darkness.

In the Garden of England,
seeds of self-loathing,
sown by our Father,
fell on fertile soil.
Deep-rooted fear took hold.

Blessed Adam and Eve feasted,
gorged on lush fruit.
Cursed Adam and Steve starved,
denied earthly delights;
no serpent's temptation.
Sin-less desires smouldered
in a personal hell
of peaceful obedience.

Neon Northern lights
heralded a new dawn.
Venetian blinds pulled back,
revealed enlightened dance floors.
Statuesque David
moved among florescent frescos
with perfectly proportioned cherubim,
Mona Lisa smiling.
Venus rising
unafraid and unashamed
in a Queen's court of refracting colour.

Heart-reviving humanists
took to the stage,
faced the inquisitor's challenge,
"Dance or death?"
I danced.
Broke free from barbarian chains,
found a non-linear perspective,
and flourished in a heartland
of thirsty scholars.

Old World view shattered.
A thousand fragments of brilliance
reformed.
This man advanced.
Reborn.

Unreality

His hand on my knee.
Meals shared.
Sunday morning sex.
Under duvet,
watching Queer As Folk re-runs.
These images repeat,
flickering bliss.

But I am just a guest star
of semi-regular episodes.
Interchanged with
next weekend's storyline.

One man leading
to the next,
and the next,
and the next…

Must change the channel,
give up this unreality TV.
But I would rather
this quasi-domestic drama
than one-off spectacles
with could-be boyfriends.
Sometimes press the button,
dip into different shows
where a Hollywood ending
could actually happen.
But the protagonists
bore me with predictability.
His story hooks me
with a cliffhanger moment
where hope springs determined,
before normal subservience resumes.

Flick the switch
OFF.

Technicolor lies fade
to black-and-white truths.
Inglorious silence surrounds me.
But I won't be lonely
when he is back with me.
His hand on my knee.

Saint George is Cross

Three booze-crusaders,
Paddy, Andy and a boy called George
walk into a pub
and beat up a Welshman.

Looking for Blackpool lights
on a Spanish night,
they toast the flag above the bar:
A flag
red as a sunburned skinhead,
white as an untanned torso,
and blue as the language of Brits frying on a costa,
basted in the grease of an all-day breakfast
and wearing Union Jack shorts.

A symbol
of unfulfilled lives, football-padded out
with the glories of false idols,
overpaid martyrs in Burberry plaid,
whose fans overstay their welcome at away games.

Paddy performs his party piece
to impress the senoritas:
ten tequilas all in a row.

lick, swallow, suck,
lick, swallow, suck
lick, swallow, oh fuck

Stomach-lining is eroding,
its acid exploding forth
mixed with half-digested paella and chips.
Though, it is kind of a neat trick
how he catches it all in one pint pot,
a bull's-eye shot, not spilling a drop.

Andy rejects such high-brow seduction,
taking the lower tone.
He slurs, "Hey Chiquita! Cop a load of this!"
whips up his kilt
and releases his Loch Ness monster.

Fails to live up to the legend.
Our third patron has had such fun
drinking in the midday sun.
Mad Dog George and his flagon of ale
finish a bout, ding ding,
barman calls time out.

Georgy-boy shouts,
"Oi krauts, remember '66!"
Ironic, given his being born in '86
but he still gets a kick
from a victory long gone.

Tragic really, no boast more recent
and this behavior indecent
results in a high-spirited game of hide and seek
in a crowded street.

Our heroic lads lose.

Hell-raising their way into a cell,
they can but dwell
on how three saints are reduced to knaves.

SONYA RENEE TAYLOR (U.S.A., B. 1976)

Why We Hold Our Tongues

To say I had an abortion is to join a blood coven, be sister with the worst of our ilk. Sister with the one who strapped hers in seatbelts, sent car skipping like rock dropped in a lake. Sister with the hand that pressed five children to the liquid casket of a bath tub. This is to say I know how people will clutch their grace until I bring them an amulet of sorrow. How this hive expects all my cells turn regret; "If not a baby, at least give us the surrogacy of your shame." To say this word abortion is to say I am a shamed thing, a womb turned urn. It is to say I killed, died, am dead as I speak to you now. It is to say even my teeth wish to flee my mouth, the leper of my gums. I must be liar. Please be liar if I say I am not sad. To say I am not sad is to say I am monster. I am heartless as tile, as physician's claw; is to say I am receptacle. I am a food made rancid by its own hand. Can you smell my stink, the rotting of me? To say I called the clinic on a Tuesday night, made an appointment for Wednesday morning, is never to say I was 19. He was 19. Our teenage mothers began dissolving our futures in crack pipes when we were 5. Never, he washed the dishes of American Dreamers till his hands calloused; never my wince at their touch. Never that a Black girl's tuition for a better life is 14 hour work days, classes. Lest the glass slipper fairytale of a stripper's pole, an old man's semen snatch her. Never that I almost chose an old man's semen. To say, when the nurse handed me a photo, a marble of tissue growing, I only asked if I would feel better when it was done, is never to say: We would have just been another thing for you to hate. A nigger baby, food stamp, tick, fat lazy breeder, dead beat prison number, white trash trailer hitch, A RAPE, a black boy with a gun and no daddy, a bitter exhausted nail holding up our own crucifixion, a thing to pity, promote, donate to, a poverty gutter to gather your own raining self-esteem in. To say, I cried for my best friend as I took down my panties laid on the table, is to sever the stitch of shame, let the milk of this choosing spill from me until I am fresh vessel, is to unlatch my wrist bound in penance to the unhelpful, the watchers with only burrs to give. To say, the doctor's face was a blur of soft cotton, his voice a crisp steel speculum is to free the pigeon of truth from its cage so it might return dove. To say, in the recovery room I smelled twenty shades of crimson escape fleeing down all the women's thighs is to say, I am seer and historian, conqueror and scared teenage girl 13 credits shy of statistic. To say, I have never spent $350 dollars more wisely is to hang my two degrees in house whose shoulders refuse to slump, to stare down the brick or back hand of this world without reproach. In a land that has only desired to fuck or forget us. That would sooner see us orphan than owners of our own flesh, to say I did not chose to keep that which I know would have been beautiful and brutal is to say unashamedly, I absolutely did choose life, mine.

What Women Deserve

Culturally-diversified bi-racial girl,
with a small diamond nose-ring
and a pretty smile
poses beside the words: "Women deserve better."

And I almost let her non-threatening grin begin to
infiltrate my psyche
—till I read the unlikely small-print at the bottom of the ad. 'Sponsored by the US
Secretariate for Pro Life Activities
and the Knights of Columbus'
on a bus, in a city with a population of 563,000.

Four teenage mothers on the bus with me.
One Latino woman with three children under three,
and no signs of a daddy.
One sixteen year old black girl,
standing in twenty-two degree weather
with only a sweater,
and a book bag,
and a bassinet, with an infant that ain't even four weeks yet

Tell me that yes: Women do deserve better.

Women deserve better
than public transportation rhetoric
from the same people who won't give that teenage mother
a ride to the next transit.
Won't let you talk to their kids about safer sex,
and never had to listen as the door slams
behind the man
who adamantly says "that SHIT ain't his"
—leaving her to wonder how she'll raise this kid.

Women deserve better than the three hundred dollars
TANF and AFDC will provide that family of three.
Or the six dollar an hour job at KFC
with no benefits for her new baby—
or the college degree she'll never see,
because you can't have infants at the university.
Women deserve better
than lip-service paid for by politicians
who have no alternatives to abortion.
Though I'm sure right now
one of their seventeen year old daughters
is sitting in a clinic lobby, sobbing quietly
and anonymously,
praying parents don't find out—
Or is waiting for mom to pick her up because
research shows that out-of-wedlock childbirth
don't look good on political polls.
And Sarah ain't having that.

Women deserve better
than backward governmental policies
that don't want to pay for welfare for kids,
or healthcare for kids,
or childcare for kids.
Don't want to pay living wages to working mothers.
Don't want to make men who only want to be
last night's lovers
responsible for the semen they lay.
Just like [they] don't want to pay for shit,
but want to control the woman who's having it.

Acting outraged at abortion,
when I'm outraged that they want us to believe
that they believe
"Women deserve better."

The Vatican won't prosecute pedophile priests,
but I decide I'm not ready for motherhood
and it's condemnation for me.
These are the same people
who won't support national condom distribution
to prevent teenage pregnancy—
But women deserve better.

Women deserve better
than back-alley surgeries
that leave our wombs barren and empty.
Deserve better than organizations bearing the name
of land-stealing, racist, rapists
funding million dollar campaigns on subway trains
with no money to give these women—
While balding, middle-aged white men
tell us what to do with our bodies,
while they wage wars and kill other people's babies.

So maybe,
Women deserve better than propaganda and lies
to get into office.
Propaganda and lies
to get into panties,
to get out of court,
to get out of paying child-support.
Get the fuck out of our decisions
and give us back our VOICE.
Women do deserve better.
Women deserve choice.

GEOFF KAGAN TRENCHARD (U.S.A., B. 1978)

Another Matter Entirely

If you are talking with an unfamiliar group of men
and everyone is sharing anecdotes
it is better that you tell them
that you have beaten another man half to death
than that you have loved one.

The story of the fight should have details lush
as the under side of a tongue. They'll want to hear
the dull knock when his head bounced against the curb.
Did his face clench or just settle into your fist-like catcher's mitt?
Was there a wet rip of skin under your boots?
Could you feel the scrape of his teeth against your knuckles?

The story of loving a man is another matter entirely.

If for some reason you do end up talking about it, it
should always just be the fucking. The act should have
all the tender necessity of an ATM withdrawal. Just an off
getting of rocks. A kinked nut rubbed out. Do not talk
about the comfortable weight of his head in your lap.
The way his face held a goofy grin and then fell
to a calm slack. Do not claim to know anything
about the snug settle of hairy leg over hairy leg.
The soothe of being on the receiving end of razor burn.

Even if you tell a very good story of the fight
it will not become your defining characteristic
unless you tell it many times.

This is not true if you say you have loved a man.
You only need to tell that story once.

The Hottest Places

I don't believe in hell
but Junior High gym class
did a great job of making me fear it.

Chris and I were part of the huff
40's and blunts at lunchtime bunch.
He had a jaw like a Jack Daniel's bottle

and a stepfather's temper. I imagined
his lips tasted like the cigarettes
I longed for through nic fitted detention.

It was an awful act of will to avert my eyes
from the bit of his hip peaking out from his boxers
as we changed each day into our PE uniforms.

I was acutely aware of what would happen
if I wasn't careful about what I didn't do about it.
Even the implication of queerness

always drew blood.
The one out kid at my school was a redhead
Mexican named Gabriel who flamed like magnesium

and had a locker in the same bank as ours.
On the day Gabe caught me looking at Chris
rather than ratting me out he flashed me

a shrewd smile. Chris looked up

just in time to catch Gabe's grin.
Decided to defend my manhood

with a battle cry of *faggot*
as if to ward off this disease.
I don't believe in hell, but if I did

it would smell like my Junior High
locker room during a fist fight.
Nothing says violence more desperately

than a thick cloud of cheap deodorant
that still doesn't cover the musk
of unchecked testosterone.

From where I stood I could see the gleam
of joy flash in the eyes of the crowd
with each dull thud. I didn't hate myself enough

to join in as Chris pounded his image
of masculinity into Gabe's face.
But I didn't care enough about Gabe

to do anything to stop it.
Eventually our dung beetle of a coach waddled
out of his office to break up the fight.

Then we all ran laps that lead nowhere
as a fat man with a clipboard
told us that if we stopped we were bitching out.

Gabe got marked down for getting blood
on his PE uniform. Chris offered
to split a cigarette with me once we got

to the far side of the field.
I held each drag till I got lightheaded
even though they tasted like sulfur and brimstone.

PAULA VARJACK (U.K., B. 1978)

The affair behind London's back

When I left London
We said it wasn't a break up
But all that
Darling, you're the only one I ever have
Ever did, ever will
Already felt false

I saw London yesterday
It had been months
It felt like years
Our embrace was stiff
I miss you, when are you coming back
She whispered
Coming…back?
And as I wondered
My hands found familiarity in her curves
Roving but not really wanting

I saw London yesterday
She had that warm watery look
In those grey eyes
That I still loved
But maybe felt
Less engaged by
And her curves were too familiar
I miss you
She said again
I miss you too
I said too quickly
Placed a large wine glass in her hand
That she drank as quickly as I poured

I saw London yesterday
I took her out for a meal
Candlelit… romantic

But then
Berlin walked by our table
Brushed by me
"accidentally"
enshuldigung
she walked off
shoulders tanned and bare
she was glowing

was it from last night
more likely this morning.
meanwhile London was talking
about her failed attempts to give up smoking
Berlin came up behind me
indulgently exhaled tobacco and nicotine and…
her smoky breath danced along my neck
and I froze with how fiercely
I wanted her

I slept with London last night
And it was good
But not great
And I wouldn't say Berlin is a better lover
But she has this way of
Getting to me
When Berlin kisses me
She keeps one hand free
Finds my sex quickly
Eyes gleaming wickedly
Moves to another
Turns to me mouthing *Join me*

I tried to tell Berlin I had to leave
I told her this could only be temporary
There had been too many nights out
Ending at sunrise
Nervously I suggested
Maybe I should try to take it
Easy

Berlin lacht
Pleite, aber immer geil
London had been calling, texting, Skyping, Facebooking
I told Berlin
I'd be gone for a little while
Or rather I tried to tell her
But it had been too loud in that bar
She was ein bisschen betrunken at the open air
She was a little occupied with that couple at the after hour

I'm going I said
Stay she said
Pressed several pills into my hand
And definitely didn't notice when I left
I saw London yesterday
She was moody
We ended up having
Make up sex

But it was a struggle not to call out Berlin's name
London knows
Won't ask what I'm thinking
Feels me reconsidering
I saw London yesterday
And all I could think about
Was Berlin...

Clarification

The girl I briefly dated who said
It's just that I want to have kids
I mean I know I'm only like twenty but
I'm already thinking about them
And I am attracted to women
But what if we got serious
And we wanted to have kids and

I...am **not** that

The girls who throw themselves
At each other in the bar
So their boyfriends can watch
Or make out madly in the middle of the club
To drive all the men around them
Mad with lust

Noooooooooooooooooooooo
I . Am. Not. That.

But I am no less attracted to men
Because I've had relationships with women
And I am no less attracted to women
Because I love leggings and high heels
And I am just as likely
To arrive at your dinner party
With a girlfriend or a boyfriend

But my life is not
This rich pageant of threesomes
and free sex
although sometimes I wish
that rumour was true

I knocked down a walk-in closet
Full of dresses to come out
To my mother and my boyfriend
Before I was of a legal age
To vote, or drink

Back in the days
When I first hit the gay scene
I quickly worked out a few things
Like very few women wanted women
Who also dated men
It was already suspicious
If you were feminine
And I wanted in

So I ditched bisexual for lesbian
Shaved my head
Threw all my dresses in the closet
Carefully tucked behind them
Any passing interest in boys I came across

And I believe that sexual identity
Is not a decision
But it is worth mentioning
It exists on a continuum
So after close to ten years
Of being a card carrying member
Of the lesbian tribe
I…met…this…guy

And the thing about repression
Is if you dam the waters long enough
When they break
Get ready for floods
I remember so vividly
One summer morning
Walking down grey London streets

When it seemed as if every bus stop had
Some gorgeous tall
Broad shouldered guy
Baggy jeans low rise
Lazy arrogant swagger
Or some fantastically foxy curvy female
Legs elongated by sky scraper high heels
Hips swaying to a rhythm in my head

By the time I got to work I panicked
Because if this is what it was like
To be enticed by both genders
How was I ever gonna get any work done again
And if you think it must be great
To have both sexes at your disposal
That the opportunities for dates
Must be exponential
Let the record serve
When it comes to my scorecard
My track record consists mainly of
Going for guys that are taken
Or girls that are straight

And boys believe
The relationships I have with women
Are definitely serious
But gay girls take heed
Liking guys should not
make me a subject
of risk assessment

And if you're thinking
She must prefer sex with the same
Or opposite
Stop….
Let's just say
It's different

But if you're interested
Boy or girl
What I'm most interested in
Is if we can connect
Because I am more than ready
For that

Real

I used to love going to strip clubs. I used to spend the kind of money on strippers that would have sustained a cocaine addiction. I used to go to strip clubs a lot.

What did I get off on? Are you serious?!!

Everything! Beautiful women with perfect sinewy legs
Bodies in dimly lit spaces undulating to bass, trembling through thighs
with hip shaking beats.

But it was more than their bodies, what I got off on was eye contact.
I loved the eye contact, it made it more **real.**

The thing about table dances: A table dance is intimate, not as intimate as a lap dance but intimate enough. If you haven't ever had one, let me explain. You sit in a chair, legs spread as wide as you can, and then the stripper, she dances between your legs , bends *over, gets right up in your face, and* you can't touch, and the tension, well…that's part of the fun.

But what I got off on…was eye contact. I wanted to cement the fact that this was not just one of a million acts she was performing, no I wanted to make it clear that I wanted this, she was doing it for me…and twenty seconds later, I'd see a change in her eyes, a hint of a smile,
something in her understanding, that I was into her, only. Specifically…for the moment anyway.

It must have made it better than all the horrible men she had to dance for. She would understand I wanted her on a deeper level. It made the interaction more **real,** I thought.

There was one club I went to that was women-only on Tuesdays. I was such a regular that when I went on my birthday, several of the dancers were keen to get me on stage. One in particular was flirting with me intensely. She must be like that with everyone, I thought. I didn't take her seriously. I never expected to see her out of that club.

I'm not sure how long after that night it was. It might have been a year or maybe only several months, I was sat in a cafe in my neighborhood, ready to sink in to whatever tabloid newspaper had been left behind when a voice called out my name.

But the woman who had called it out wasn't someone I had ever met. I thought she must mean someone else, my name is common enough. But she called it out again and this time gave me a little wave. She crossed the cafe, sat across from me. I still had no idea who she was. I remember thinking I had never been so close to someone wearing so much make-up.

>   *live around here then?*

she said.

>   *yeah sorry I…where do we know each other from?*

She laughed. Told me a name, said it was her stage name, but she didn't mind me knowing her real name which she told me as well.

She told me I looked good, it was nice to run into me. She was happy to have my company, launching into her affairs with detail until something in her features finally clicked.

I hadn't recognized her, because she wasn't looking so great. Her foundation was caked, eyeliner winged at angles I couldn't work out. The grey hoodie and faded jeans hung off her emaciated frame, a far cry from the curves and glittery thong, and she was talking…a lot.

She was telling me about feeling lonely, not having many friends, getting bored with dancing but the money was good, and if she wanted the free time and the cash, she couldn't do anything else. And her love life wasn't so great, but now maybe running into me that could change. She winked.

She spoke of her son having trouble at school, and his father not being much help, and through all of this, I found it really hard to hold her eye contact. Because she was no longer someone I could project my fantasies onto, she had become far too **real.**

I avoided the cafe after that. Years later I went to a strip club with a girlfriend but it wasn't the same. I couldn't get off on it. I never went to one again.

BAKAR WILSON (U.S.A., B. 1977)

Fucking D.J.

So the night is summer warm.
We, a constant hot mess,
stumble to his TriBeCa flat.
Cars pass on Broadway.
We are at full mast.
He is a luxury that I do not always
get to know. We've been doing it for
a while. On our way here, he has already
blown me in a dark stairwell beneath
the street. Oh well, when you got to
you got to. He, of course, invites me
to the roof. I say "yes."
We go in and ride the elevator
past his sleeping fiancée.
The fiancée. She is a
woman who does not know
her man at all. She does
not know that he dreams of me
on a daily basis and is experiencing
me now in piping hot flesh.

As we ascend, the voices of my
friends begin in my head,
"He's engaged."
"What are you doing?"
"This is wrong."
My stock answer of course,
"Well, if it's not me, it's going to be someone else."
And then I'm absolved.
We reach the roof.
A warm garden of fauna and lust
and the view.
We kiss until our tongues fall down
each other's throats. He begins.
Two buttons and two zips.
Prophylactic.
He sits in my lap
And we gaze South
soaking in the Manhattan skyline.

S/M

Secular/Modernism
Scholastic/Manipulation
Sloppy/Meltdown
Satin/Malignancy
Savior/Misfit
Stale/Memento
Saintly/Masochistic
Supine/Mister
Sensual/Malediction
Salty/Marrow
Subtle/Minstrelsy
Sperm/Mess
Sassy/Monster
Shady/Marriage
Shaft/Magnet
Sadist/Memorabilia
Sweetly/Manhandled
Sex/Malfunction
Suddenly/Metaphysical
Shish-kebab/Meat

Spectrum: Black

Tar baby beauty flecks onyx and charcoal
wishes into a midnight sky, new moon
gives no light. Relish the darkness.
In this abyss of night, love flows and coddles.
One does not need to be afraid, finally negation
is something to be desired, something to cherish.
Ebony kings and queens come out to play,
go on cannonball runs, and write poems in
twilight zones. Give me this day's end. Let me
roll around with closed eyes and mouth open,
tasting the licorice of life, head lead heavy and
joyously lost. Be afraid of the dark no more.
Even in deep space, panthers roam around freely
anchored by their wrought iron wills.

Anti-War Haiku

1.
Forget the look of
the body as you know it.
War disfigures us.

2.
My sex is honest.
His is a thick mushroom cloud,
strokes nuclear heads.

3.
City streets fill with
the crunch of human traffic
ducking for cover.

4.
Go slow, the day is
war torn. Scraps float in the air,
softly suffocate.

5.
Survive. Survive it.
Gather yourself in the wake.
The body is not.

EMANUEL XAVIER (U.S.A., B. 1971)

AMERICANO

I look at myself in the mirror
trying to figure out what makes me an American
I see Ecuador and Puerto Rico

I see brujo spirits moving across the backs of Santeros
splattered with the red blood of sacrificed chickens
on their virgin white clothes and blue beads for Yemaya
practicing religions without a roof

I see my own blood
reddening the white sheets of a stranger
proud American blue jean labels on the side of the bed

I see Don Rosario in his guayabera
sitting outside the bodega
with his Puerto Rican flag
reading time in the eyes of alley cats

I see my mother trying to be more like Marilyn Monroe than Julia De Burgos
I see myself trying to be more like James Dean than Federico Garcia Lorca
I see Carlos Santana, Gloria Estefan,
Ricky Martin and Jennifer Lopez
More than just sporadic Latin explosions
More like fireworks on el Cuatro de Julio
as American as Bruce Springsteen, Janis Joplin,
Elvis Presley and Aretha Franklin

I see Taco Bells and chicken fajitas at McDonald's
I see purple, blue, green, yellow and orange
I see Chita Rivera on Broadway

I am as American as lemon meringue pie
as American as Wonder Woman's panties
as American as Madonna's bra
as American as the Quinteñeros, the Abduls, the Lees,
the Jacksons, the Kennedys
all immigrants to this soil since none sound American Indian to me
as American as television snow after the anthem is played
and I am not ashamed

Jose, can you see...
I pledge allegiance
to this country 'tis of me
land of dreams and opportunity
land of proud detergent names and commercialism
land of corporations

If I can win gold medals at the Olympics
sign my life away to die for the United States
No small-town hick is gonna tell me I ain't an American
because I can spic in two languages
coño carajo y fuck you

This is my country too
where those who do not believe in freedom and diversity
are the ones who need to get the hell out

THE DEATH OF ART

I am not a poet. I want to be rich and buy things for my family.
Besides, I am sort of popular and can honestly say I've had a great sex life.

I am not a poet. Georgia O' Keefe paintings do absolutely nothing for me. I do not feel oppressed or depressed and no longer have anything to say about the president.

I am not a poet. I do not like being called an "activist" because it takes away from those that are out on the streets protesting and fighting for our rights.

I am not a poet. I eat poultry and fish and suck way too much dick to be considered a vegetarian.

I am not a poet. I would most likely give my ass up in prison before trying to save it with poetry…and I'd like it! Heck, I'd probably be inspired.

I am not a poet. I may value peace but I will not simply use a pen to unleash my anger. I would fuck somebody up if I had to.

I am not a poet. I may have been abused and had a difficult life but I don't want pity. I believe laughter and love heals.

I am not a poet. I am not dying. I write a lot about AIDS and how it has affected my life but, despite the rumors, I am not positive. Believe it or not, weight loss amongst sexually active gay men could still be a choice.

I am not a poet. I do not get Kerouac or honestly care much for Bukowski.

I am not a poet. I don't spend my weekends reading and writing. I like to go out and party. I like to have a few cocktails but I do not have a drinking problem regardless of what borough, city or state I may wake up in.

I am not a poet. I don't need drugs to open up my imagination. I've been a dealer and had a really bad habit but that was long before I started writing.

I am not a poet. I can seriously only tolerate about half an hour of spoken word before I start tuning out and thinking about my grocery list or what my cats are up to.

I am not a poet. I only do poetry events if I know there will be cute guys there and I always carry business cards.

I am not a poet according to the scholars and academics and Harold Bloom. I only write to masturbate my mind. After all, fucking yourself is one of the great pleasures that solitude can afford you.

I am not a poet. I am only trying to get attention and convince myself that poetry can save lives when my words simply and proudly contribute to "the death of art."

LAUREN ZUNIGA (U.S.A., B. 1981)

CIRCLE DRIVE

My neighbor just came out to her husband. They have been married for 15 years and have three daughters. She has been in love with the same woman for five years but never once touched her skin. Never had the courage to explore the terrain of her sex. Terrified of what the neighbors would think.

Her neighbors are a rowdy house of queer women. They light bonfires and erect giant maypoles to celebrate the fertility of spring. They occasionally kiss each other. They sleep on the roof. They want a chicken coop but chickens are noisy and messy and illegal in the city. The neighbors might call the code enforcer.

The code enforcer lives across the street. He eats pastrami sandwiches every day and loves Bon Jovi. His wife is a dominatrix that he refers to as Mistress. She mows the lawn wearing black leather. Their boyfriend sleeps in the garage and works as a hair stylist. If he told his parents about the living arrangement he would be disowned.

His parents are retired and enjoy gardening and horseback riding. Recently, the mother has been wearing leopard print aprons and lace panties when she cooks. His father likes to have sex with her against the stove. She wants to scream until her grandmother's china shatters in the cabinet. She doesn't. She is terrified of what the neighbors will think.

BOSTON MARRIAGE

My mother says every straight girl has an Anne Heche Moment. Where they meet a woman so amazing they question everything about their sexuality. My mother's Anne Heche Moment was named Kate. We think this is how my sister really got her name. While pregnant, the doctors told her it was a boy. She cried so hard, she gave birth to a girl. There are no fathers in my family. Only men who marry mothers. Men who leave mothers. Sometimes I think if a man could hold me hard enough it would make my grandmother feel wanted. The first time I made love to a woman, we felt like two wooden matches with one eager head. An elegant factory mistake. When I told my mother I was engaged to a black man, she said It's just...so hard. Her throat pinched between finger and thumb of 1968: glass bottles thrown at her head. Students rioting in the street, shouting her name. I said, Mama, people don't act like that anymore. After the divorce, they told me the only way a woman in Oklahoma could lose custody of her kids was if she was a murderer or gay. The first time I fell in love with a woman I held her fist in my palm for hours. How strange that I could not make a baby with this swelling seed. My grandmother said they used to call lesbian couples Boston Marriages. When I held my love in the state capitol rotunda as they signed the Proclamation of Morality, declaring marriage between one man and one woman, I wish I had kissed her mouth so loud, it shattered the cacophony of hymns and protests but I stay silent. I stayed silent.

TALLY OF QUEERDOM {in no particular order}

4.
She lifts her suit trousers to reveal her rainbow socks.
Little sparkly letters spell out My Lucky Socks.
Quick sexy squint, sideways smirk. She is a bent light beam
in a grey cubicle farm. I will go home with her tonight.

11.
I am a whisky julep. Spread sweaty on the floor.
I've lost an earring. Sore hips. I am some shade of marmalade.
There is melted sunset all over the carpet. I have never spilled
in this shape before. She licks the inside of my ankle. Tells me
it tastes like peaches.

2.
The back porch is washed in the milk paint of moonlight.
The garden is showing off its unruly curves. Teasing me
with twelve shades of green and the sweet scent of curry.
I am alone with my body. More turned on than I can recall.
The highway behind the house shouts as loud as my veins.
I stroke the wisteria. Whisper, What have you done to me?

8.
We take turns giggling. Shifting from femme bones to
boy bones. Quiet maneuvering through the landscape
of energies. Identity is a swing. We are straddled like spider.

13.
She tells the catfish story to the redneck like she is sliding
a hook through his fat, watering mouth. Unlike his story
of the prize-winning Monster Blue, hers ends with a stringer
full of fish corpses, eaten alive by raccoons. I like her story.
Mostly I like how his face changed from salesman to friend
as soon as she dropped the trotline. Also, I like to imagine her
perched easy on red sandstone, speaking release to the shore.

7.
In the kitchen, she presses me against the counter and kisses
me madly. Her brother's wife saunters in to refresh her mint
julep and gasps. Fumbles awkward back to the living room.
Later, she confides, her husband has never kissed her so deeply.
She has never been caught in the act. We all have different ways
of fastening our sex shut. Slipping a nametag in our underwire.
Zipping up our strange beneath our pinstriped trousers.

12.
I am more terrified of monogamy/commitment/entrapment than
I am of lesbian/bisexual/wild woman/queer. Wedding rings look
like handcuffs. I do not want a circle drive or master bedroom.
I don't care what the neighbors think. I tackle her on the couch
just before the L-word snags my cheek. She knows how easy it is
for a poet to get all tangled in the reel. Instead, she says applesauce.
Asks me to be her jellyfish. I lick her accountant ears. Tell her they
taste like good sense.

1.

I am 13. On the bus headed to church camp. My first boyfriend
nervously asks me if I would ever kiss a girl. I explain my clumsy
theory of the spectrum for the first time. How we are shades
of masculine and feminine. How I kiss beings not genders or races
or wallets. Sixteen years later, he tells me the night before that bus
ride, he kissed his best friend, Greg. He never told anyone. He called
just to thank me for that.

AIDS DIAGNOSIS– BRANDON TEENA'S DEATH (1982–1993)

JO BEE (CANADA, B. 1992)

Disco

We're gonna dance disco
like the world isn't watching and laughing.
Innocent passers-by will not be prepared
for the magnitude of this.

Alone, I've got awkward alliteration, sorry similes,
and not nearly enough BRILLIANT in my life.
Together, we're like broken glass glued to a globe
and hung from the ceiling, dazzling other dancers.

There's more room in this kitchen
for an onion of complication,
like you.
Everyone will step out of their dark cupboards to see
the onion and the spice jar
dancing under rainbows from spinning window crystals—
I can see it now!

Don't be sad, my onion.
When you finally get to this kitchen,
things don't have to seem so serious.
Dinner will be beautiful!

And if those dreams are not the way you planned them,
we'll drown everything out singing so loud
the original artists will hear us,
wherever they are,
dead or alive.

And we're gonna play in a band—
No! We're gonna play in a
new-wave-
indie-pop-
hip-hopera-
wizard-rock
band—
and serenade the state
or the country
or the continent
or the whole gorram world
'cause no power in the verse could stop us.
Can't you see?
We're those girls laughing
in men's bathrooms,
blocking out footsteps
through the shower curtain
and hiding midnight music
in our chord hands,
'till our adventures add up
to OVER NINE THOUSAND,

and we won't stop
'till we've toured the world
enacting Shakespeare
on every bookstore floor—
'till we've spun tales
1,667 words at a time
and confessed to each other
how we're falling in love,
falling in love,
falling in love...

with Hermione Granger.

We'll stay up until we're high on life,
dizzy with the giggles,
and completely convinced we'll become famous
by filming our hallucinations
and turning them into reality TV shows.

Can't you see?
We're so frakking OTP
our friends write fanfiction about our love.
And yes, I may be a dolt with half a brain,
but I hear harmonies when you speak.
So I'm never gonna give you up...
never gonna let you down...
and we're gonna dance disco
like the world isn't watching and laughing.

Spiderman

I fell in like once.

I stole rhythms from under tables
and sent them to him as Morse code secrets
in the clicks of my shutter release button.
I nailed the metal backs of watches to my sneakers
and chased him for half a kilometer, flap-ball-changing
and screaming the Spiderman theme song at him
in the hopes that he would find it charming.

When he got home,
he put Spiderman Band-Aids over the wounds he'd acquired
running away from me,
sat down at his computer,
and proceeded to block me on MSN.
ALL of my Hotmail accounts.
Even the one I was sure he didn't know was me
because I'd told him I was 28, male, and from Australia,
and my screen name was
"PETER PARKER: I LUV U MARY JANE!!!"

Soooooooo
I realized we weren't going to end up side by side
in a Broadway production of
PATHETIC: The Love Story of a 13-Year-Old Boy and a 10-Year-Old Stalker Girl.
I would have settled for a community theatre production,
but when I emailed him for forgiveness
he made it clear that we would never again
share a pact of dependence on our hands;
we would never go big, so I had to go home,
and I did.

But it was okay, because I fell in infatuation once.

He captured my heart with the song under his breath,
and I captured his...boredom...with my...strangeness.
We ate lunch off paper plates and awkwardly conversed
about the height of vampires these days,
and I smiled at him hopefully
through the burning sunlight;
through the decaying walls;
through the distance that grew
like shadows at the end of the day as I walked away,
10, 20, 30 blocks, too giddy to stop.
I checked my wrist: 5 hours with him and I was 10 again.
I checked my wall: 5 months of stalking him online
and I thought I was fiiiiiine!
Until *you* told me I was "prohibitively creepy."

But it was okay, because I fell in love once...

I collected your smiles in old jam jars
to save for rainy days so I could dissect them
under daylight-bright-bulb bathroom lights for
SCIENCE.
I sang death metal from mountain tops,
trying to cause avalanches in the clouds to get your attention,
but when they finally came tumbling down
I couldn't find you.
My hands embarked on helicopter rescue missions in the dark,
and I tried to warm up your -70 degree breath with mine,
but all you could say was,
"You are my *Once upon a time.*"

I fell in love once...

And again.
I fell in love and there were spikes at the bottom.
Again.
I fell in love and it was a typo;
turns out I fell in ;pbr.
I fell in love, and when he asked me
to go halfsies on an ice-cream sundae,
I tried to keep my cool,
but when Mister OMGHAWTNESSLOL
invokes the whacky,
resistance
is
futile.

I fell in love, and I scraped my knees.
But it's okay, because now I have a box of Spiderman Band-Aids too,
and I swear on the giant, neon, East Van gang sign
that this time I didn't get them to impress you.

JAY BERNARD (U.K., B. 1988)

When the time is right
For Cece McDonald

When it's right, the white ball will be swallowed like a tooth.
She'll give you yellow beer and grin with indigo gums.
When it's right, no-one will have to tell you: You'll pick yourself up
and take the bus to the edge of the city and look at its other edge
iced with sixteenth century domes refrigerated in the twentieth.
No-one will have to tell you, you will take off your shoes,
empty your pockets on the pebbles, and when it's right, you'll slide

into the water and swim to the other side. No-one will know you are there.
Your breath will hold itself, you won't need breathing when swimming,
the current will keep you moving, its friction will keep you warm,
those buoys will call out to you in red and black ebonics, saying
twenty metres, forty metres, sixty metres, eighty—then

you can stand unshot, undetected, unseen on the other side, listen to
the rolling wheels of the normal cars and meet eyes with the normal kids
who look at you and up at their yellow balloons asking what's the difference.
Across, flat and southern, there is nothing to be seen, besides two figures
with their hands on their hips who watched you go. Their faces tilt
like broad leaves in torchlight. Go. Go. Come. If they don't see you
or hear you or detect the ripples of your body in the water,
if they don't catch you, if you get here, when the time is right.

leaf through , come in,
what page   , did you read,
hear or stop , or think
to ask what , what I might want.
heifer brown, back straight
"so sexy   , it looked so sexy,
when you   bent forwards"
well I'm glad, to bend for you
did you see , my perineum
how long   , do I have to ask
how often   should I turn away
or laugh   , I wrote dirty
rhymes and , photocopied chapters from
Kundera   , come now
give me it   , she did—
the sting   , I have wanted it,
I have spent, maybe, five, maybe ten
years   waiting to be prised
and then   , in Yogjakarta,
best bed   , mosquito whine
cracked   , chalk toilet,
there   ,
it isn't   what you think—
if this is new , its newness is
feeling full   , or going deaf
underwater , every sense
re-centered   , your gut is hollow,
it begins at , your lips
where you   kissed
why fear   , what you started?

is the sweat, any different
there   , can you quantify
the smell   , is it morning breath
or cashews   , doesn't it
ridge, isn't   , your palate ridged,
the legality , of this, I think
how close   , how near
to death   in Yemen...
            , they have
duped us , this
is so   , as it should be
like   , being read
which bit , of the book
are you   reading when
you   spread its legs
does it   face you or are
those   bent pages' cheeks ?
that's   inner wind
that's   the darkest exhalation
and you   , leaf through
no issue   well,
please put your hand there
keep ,   it there
please   , don't steady the stroke
or slow   , it doesn't hurt
that sting , I have wanted
it   , all my life.

FRANNY CHOI (U.S.A., B. 1989)

Ever After

I.

my mother once told me
american movies were too happy.
alien or cowboy enemies defeated,
he kisses her and they
fly off into the end credits
monogamous ever after.

we koreans
crave howling and tragedy
kneading our faces into gravel roads,
carrying with us
the holes and the sharp places
when finally we curl into the fire,
gently put life away.

II.

in the blue quiet of her mattress
she said i'm afraid
i'm going to hurt you.
who let her in
on the secret? for it's been
too much of a story
not to have a sad ending.

sixth morning after

hallelujah. the sheets
are stained with no.

so organs have exhaled their verdict
and here in the sliding weight of morning, it
starts to seep

away. now
the last threat of a family
darkens softly behind my hip bones.
now i begin the washing and the learning
to be new. now i try
not to wait for him
to come home.

MEG DAY (U.S.A., B. 1984)

On Nights When I Am Brandon Teena

I spend the smallest hours counting
the beats between the slamming
of the truck doors – the driver's side first,
    then the shot gun's –

    and the sharp squeal of the screen door
    as it's wrenched open & that first heavy boot –
    Nissen's, always Nissen's – strikes the threshold.
        Sometimes it's four

    more than feels likely; sometimes I get caught
    noticing the engine's still running, or that
    a car passes by despite the late hour & bad road,
                & the dream skips

    back to the augur iamb of slamming doors
    before any trigger finger slips inside
    a screen door handle on any farmhouse porch.
        Only rarely do I wake

    with the sharp stings of the coiled bedsprings still
    pressed into my back – but always with the sucked
    breath of filthy knuckles clenching bed skirt,
        right before the lift.

Teenage Lesbian Couple Found in Texas Park with Gunshot Wounds to the Head
Portland, Texas June 24, 2012

It's always the girls   (we girls)
who mistake our heartbeats for hammers –
suffer their pounding when your kindness
insists it requires no exchange, & hush
their racket when a few rounds with Captain
or Jack change your mind, training us like dogs
to flinch every time you raise a hand.

It's always the girls   (we girls)
who wake up with more Adam in our step
than Eve, who weave back & forth
with intention, or wear our hair & lashes long
for anyone that is not you; who try *Please*s, try tears, try Jesus
but still pop up in pairs along Colonial Parkway
& in Medford, our bonds made literal & eternal
in truck stop restrooms & along the Appalachian Trail.

It's always the girls   (we girls)
who assume we'll outlast your barbed wire
boundaries our bodies hurdle on the daily,
convinced our steel jaws will be found intact
when authorities, or archaeologists, unearth
each grave you chose for burying your rage
alongside our bodies, still intertwined.

DANIELLE EVENNOU (U.S.A., B. 1985)

Heretical

At ten, I learned the art of carrying two twelve packs down
three flights of steps. Coors lighting my way to the basement,
where my Grandmother sat washing and folding the laundry
used to mop up the spontaneous vomit of my childhood.

I am charged with the electricity of her electro-shock therapy,
memories of unexplained injuries. Our house was an asylum
a sanctuary from psychiatric institutions full of St. Anthony figurines
and framed photos of the Blessed Mother, cradling a blond baby Jesus.

When the dementia set in she'd ask me, "What time is it?"
Over and over again. Each time I brought her a drink,
I'd fake evening to see if she would sleep.
She'd wake at 3:00 AM and believe it was morning

make coffee and recite the rosary in the kitchen.
Hail Mary full of grace the Lord is with thee
blessed art thou among women
and blessed is the fruit

flavored wine cooler my mother holds when she says, "If…
When this happens to me, I want you to shoot me in the head
with the shotgun from the shed." It only takes one silver bullet,
and we'd laugh about it because I find levity in the mind's unraveling.

My Grandmother separated my presence from adolescent
photos of me in a dress. She mistook my high school boyfriend
for childhood playmate, Katrina. "That woman, that woman is
in the house again and she's always with her girlfriend."

It makes sense, the first time a woman puts her hands on my hips
my lips are drenched in vodka, my hand grips tightly to a sweaty beer bottle
I drink from before the kissing starts, and once it does I think
I never want to stop feeling this.

Grand Rapids, Michigan

Growing
for five years
a Chinese Peony
that's bloomed surprisingly, for the
first time.

                    Sorry,
                    there are no blue
                    peonies, the closest
                    is a lavender color called
                    lagoon.

Only
the blooms are pink.
Supposed to be blue blooms.
What can I do? Now, to have blue
flowers.

                    Many
                    gardeners expect
                    to see cerulean.
                    New peony varieties
                    come in.

          Suspect
          the nursery
          embellished the color.
          Perhaps, that's the variety
          you have.

How I Broke My Keyboard In Six Parts

Part 1: The Incident

We met on OkCupid. It was a mistake
to make me cook on our first date.
You drive me home in your Oldsmobile
flooded with State Department documents.
This is how you say, "I have to pee" in Farsi.
Pulling onto my street, you hand me pepper spray.
We don't kiss. Spend the next few years liking each other's
Facebook statuses. I think of you like
a pet hamster. Take you out of the cage when I'm lonely.
Make you spin aimlessly around the room in a plastic ball.
Play with me until I stop you, suddenly like
the blue screen of death.

You became more mammalian the night you *liked* my glasses.
Later, you send me photos from an orgy in Bogota.
I pretend like a black passport is entry to some kind
of secret sex society. What really happens at the Cosmos Club?
I get an A+ for writing an op-ed with an anti-labor, Republican
perspective, and wake up like a polar bear from an ice age.

The glacial movements become more sudden.
Conversations shift from Facebook to GChat. I download Skype.
Before I show you my pussy, I turn down the audio.
You unveil your cock through unassuming boxers. I straddle my laptop.
I can't see you ejaculate through the pixilated video quality.

I know from your face, not your sticky body. You lick every milliliter
off your fingers. I move mine inside. You watch.
Intermittently, I reach over my body to type.
Mmmmmmmmmmmmmmmm

Part 2: The Damage

My computer won't stop injecting zeros into text.
It bec000ome00s i00mpos000sib00le t0000o ty0000p000e.
I can stream video and music, but lack the capacity to search
or communicate with anything other than emoticons. ☹

Looks like I'm bloated with pimples, a digital equivalent to PMS.
00hel000lo. 00wh0a00t00 a0r0e00 yo00u w00eari00ng0?
Who wants to have Skype sex with this?
More naked than nude when stripped of wit.

I desperately purchase so many cans of compressed air
Best Buy starts checking my ID like a teen junkie.
I take my machine to work.

The uncharacteristically generous IT guy says my problem is not zero.
It's the M stuck in num lock mode.
Oh, I say. He claims he's fixed it, but as soon as I get home
the pr0000oblem r000esu000m000e00s0000000.

Part 3: The Repair

I need professional help.
The sexiest computer technicians on Yelp only work on Macs.
So, I select the guy with the most reviews by people in their seventies.
Read about how he raised a 12-year-old PC laptop from the dead,
like Lazarus. This is my guy! The shop, conveniently located
a block from my therapist's office, reeks
of screen cleaner and body odor.
Sam the computer man is barefoot
in a t-shirt that has no irony.

I explain, My laptop wouldn't stop typing zeros.
Yes, I sprayed it with three cans of condensed air.
When that didn't work, I started peeling back the letters
to clean underneath. Now, M and N are completely detached,
and it's still doing it!

Sam says, Looks like you have permanent damage.
Upon closer examination, he's blown away by the magnitude
of tiny furry creatures floating inside my machine.
I live in an artist studio. Converted warehouse, more prone to dust.

One week and $200 later, Here it is with a brand new keyboard.
But, you know, the dust and the broken keys weren't your real problem.
Oh?
Somehow, he says, you got liquid into it.
OOOOOOhhhh??? Really? I don't suppose how that could have happened.

(Oh my god, oh my god, oh my god! Does Sam know
he's been working all week to repair my cum-soaked laptop?
Do you think he tests for DNA? Calm down, calm down.)

I respond, I like Diet Coke.
No, I really really like Diet Coke. I must have been drinking it while
doing my homework and the condensation from the can
must've dripped into the keyboard.
An innocent mistake. Really.
Sam nods.
Here, take my credit card!

He rings me up with one of those old fashioned carbon paper processors.
Good luck, he says. The whole interaction takes longer than I budgeted for.
I'm late to therapy. When my therapist asks, What are you feeling?
I say, Zeros.

Part 4: The Waiting

You tell me we'll eat bandeja paisa,
basically a giant hamster,
when I visit you in Colombia.

I spend $26 on a Lonely Planet guide
that collects dust next to my bed
with the last book of the Hunger Games series.

Money better spent on Baruchkus,
but I needed something to hold onto.
Say you'll be in DC at the end of the month.

I get a new bra and panty set. White lace,
bejeweled crotch, just the right amount of see through.
My laptop's in great shape.

I'm not motivated to masturbate. Like when
I wanted a Cabbage Patch doll for Christmas,
with red hair and freckles, but got a blonde.

My parents say, they can take it back.
I say, Santa doesn't accept returns.
I will find a way to love it.

I stare at my chat list. Red, orange, and green
circles next to people I haven't seen in years,
and wonder if you're invisible.

Part 5: The Cancelation

I feel like I've been hit by a school bus in the Wendy's parking lot.
The scent of grease wafts over me on the steaming asphalt.
By the time I get home, I've eaten all the fries.
Still empty after a Baconator and chocolate frosty
like a faceless cumshot on Xtube.

Part 6: The End

The trail of cookies you leave me
leads me to videos of cream pies.
Being with you lets me touch some part
of myself, I've been too afraid to lately.

I wonder if you stream this girl in glasses,
when you fuck your hand.
I watch her for hours,
knowing you may never eat me.

I put on my headphones,
so I can't hear my bed squeak
like a hoard of hamsters mating
when I finally cum into my own.

Eye Contact

I am a litany of continents on a map written for islands, or a pinched voice, or the day the Rabbi dropped my name during blessing for the child, or the magic of a heart that drowned its patient horse. The room you walked out of became another hour that would later suspend a mountain. I am unabashedly angry at how easily I interrupt myself. I am enough. Enough. I am large enough to hoard all of my shine where I want it, right here, in this gourd of a safe house the fear gave me, in this desire to bellow with my mouth full, enough.

Keeping Men Out of Prison

- When I chose to return, I knew
that I would need to learn the language
of the seamstress
the ever-fitting
the mother
the all gone
if I were to speak of staying.

- I was 15, and he was
a crescent of what I
could fit.
I held it beneath
the feather flesh of my cheeks,
suffocated many a moon,
revived it
and still walked home
alone.

- The next day
the phone rang
too late. Mommy
swept the call up
in all her knowing,
and sent me to read
the Haggadah, the
all weathering, the
testament of the orator.

- I was 15 and I told
him of a home I could
not cultivate with my bare
hands. It was a lie I
told my belly to keep
it full. He believed it
though, took my full
belly in his hands—
made a mockery of
my calling winds.

- That summer we
hugged the block
together. We were both
15. I held
ten times his weight
in both my pockets
and sold my
heavy smile,
my messenger eyes.

I wanted to tell
over
and over again
of The Haggadah
of how I
birthed his story
every day
and never worried of going
down for it.

ADELE HAMPTON (U.S.A., B. 1988)

Salt Line Economics

There's something sexy to be said about heat lightning when your body hasn't touched foreign skin for months.

Like two girl scouts rubbing sticks against stone trying to create holy flame like their lives depend on it.... So they don't get eaten by bears or caught by their scout leader, perspiration slips down legs with enough friction to set the sky on fire. Y'all it was one of those nights you thought the world was going to end as you tried to sleep naked above the sheets and the only time I've thanked God for a lack of air condition.

You know we always say sweat when we talk about sex but no one ever mentions the salt. And maybe it's because salt crystals don't sound as sweet as sugar cubes, but baby believe me, when they come from the body there is nothing more satisfying. And trust me twice when I say I want to feel your iodine on my taste buds.

Butterflies are too gentle for this thrashing inside my bones so I try and say settle down to the grasshoppers in my stomach every time your tongue jumps my skin. Hearts are something for love to grip; loins are for passion's hands.

So come… and clench me woman with fists strong enough to grasp whole bodies. I am rock solid and ready for your palms. So take me.

But things get complicated when time turns into temporary and you realize lust is just on the tips of your shaking fingers. I won't be gentle when I pull your hair lover. I wont be gentle when I press my lips to your muscle. I won't be gentle when I claw your bones with teeth-bitten nails because I'm trying to ink my fingerprints onto your back so I can stake some claim to the only thing I've had control over in months.

We were never meant to withstand this kind of heartsick and fucking is only weak plaster to be torn from our wounded heart caves.

Lover, that's why when you asked me to come into your apartment I only went so far as the bedroom. Avoiding eye contact with your picture frames, I didn't linger long enough to learn if the scent on your pillows matched the taste of tar, carbon monoxide and bad decisions on your tongue.

Listen, I am no permanent fixture here and hold no stock in your heart. I don't pretend to know shit about economics. But I can appreciate the fact that salt lines, like money, don't stretch as far as they used to.

So for now, I'll take these sheets and walk away with your skin cells.

Bones

You told me if I spit out my gum on the ground outside I would be a murderer. But since I didn't want the title of baby bird slayer attached to my last name I asked you for a piece of paper. You pulled a CVS receipt from your backpack and I spit my gum out in the evidence of your purchase of O.B. tampons.

Now how you use an O.B. tampon is something that confuses the hell out of me but I was too afraid to ask for instructions because the topic of female hygiene makes me a little uncomfortable.

Just like how this attraction makes me want to open my ribcage and let you settle inside my chest regardless of how much it aches to set my bones by the wayside.

Your beginning was ferocious. Back handed me across the face, within ten minutes of our first conversation I wanted to know all the places you've called home. Your quiet thoughts thundered so loud when they sifted through my body that sometimes I wish my marrow had earplugs.

But I've realized my bones can sometimes be too brittle for your amplified crashing against my skin and I'm afraid I'm not strong enough to hold steady through your floods.

So I am trying to stand two feet, two hands in front of you with a windmill heart painting a Dutch sky because I want to take you there some day. Show you where my roots started to form hair triggers, peel back my skin love and you'll see I've been wrapping my heart in Kevlar. I've never been called delicate so do not tip toe around my mines.

I'm not asking you to drape your ribcage across my chairs, only that you leave enough room in between your bones and your blood for the possibility of miracles.

I would have cradled your fears in my belly and filled your bones with stardust confidence because that's how much hope I saw in your fingertips. I would have braced your fleeting eyes and told God to hold steadfast the levies because I've been running head first into mortared bricks for the glory of open hearts.

But now, I want you to talk to me about loneliness love. I want you to tell me tall tales about hearts that can't remember how to breathe through sawdust forests or lungs that have forgotten how to pump red blood cells into clouds because I'm starting to lose track of how many times I've been bent under this weight and not broken.

I'm not elastic love. Keep in mind that I have the ability to snap, buckle. I can become willowed and will forget how delicious your name tastes even though my tongue will always remember how to form the syllables.

I refuse to call myself empty even though you've left me scattered bone dust for the stars to sweep under carpets. I will not label my heart vacant or my stacked marrow bowed just yet. So show me how to walk these streets upright knowing I'm not fit enough to chase after the ground.

These are not easy words gasping for air between the gaps of my teeth because I never wanted to write this poem again.

So I preach to you caution from the pulpit because I know how good I am at this pen to paper, feet to pavement. Know that I'm not one to repeat myself so please open your beating drum heart to my gospel. I will walk away from your smile and feel good about not looking back.

Now the least you could do is pretend you know how to pray.

JOANNA HOFFMAN (U.S.A., B.1982)

ON LEARNING TO OPEN MY EYES DURING SEX

The brightest sky is a blindfold stitched
with black rain. I think of the dog pacing
by the back door. *Control* clocks the moan
sprinting past the flinch, how her teeth
make me dream of doorbells crashing screams
into a quiet house. I once trained myself
to tiptoe; to gag the *yes* tapping underneath
the ice; to vault the rip-roar tripping from
my tongue— a parade of magician's scarves
I want to keep pulling, pulling.

I am a master of Exit. Show me a body,
I'll show you an escape route. Follow the thrash
to Oz, to 1998, to a woman too ghost
to ever raise the alarms.

The first time I opened my eyes, I thought
of surfacing from chlorine. O, the sting
and the entire hive swarming into the
swimming pool outline of me. I look into
her eyes when the honey begins to drip
from her lips. She swallows my windows
whole. There is nowhere left to go but inside.

The summer I turned 15, my grandmother got me
totally smashed at a wedding in New Jersey.
Somewhere between the third ABBA song
and the fourth glass of champagne, she told me,
You know, someday you'll have a wedding just like this.
And when you do, please don't let them play any disco.

I didn't know how to tell her that I probably
wouldn't be having any wedding at all. That I
wore these bones like a voiceover when really,
I was in love with my best friend Kathleen.
I thought just maybe, if I held this itch
underwater long enough, it would float up blue.

I tried to claw the dripping want from my voice
whenever Kathleen asked me what I thought of
her boyfriend, snuffing out my drive-in imagination
and burning every lamp in my throat watching her.

I learned what shame feels like. I coated my skin
with postcard gleam, as if the best I could ever
hope for was to reflect someone else's shine;
as if some parts of me were better off drowned
in a swimming pool of white-out.

But it is not in our nature to cower
before the mirror like this.

A person born blind will tilt his head back
and extend his arms when he feels proud.

It is in our blood not to bake shame into our
bones, but to live boldly.

And so now, all these years later, here is
my pride—

for every time I refused to allow the wet
blanket stare of strangers on the subway
smother this burn to hold her hand;

for every time someone told me, *Wow,*
you don't look gay, and I didn't say, *Thank you;*

for not letting my heart be strip-searched
by those who want to know if my love is
pure enough;

because I have committed hate crimes against
myself for years and I already know all of
the tricks.

So, when my friend asks me why there is no
Straight Pride Parade, I tell her, *You can't
be proud of something you've never had to fight for.*

This is for every wedding I watched from
the sidelines; every fairy tale with stipulations;
every *it's a choice, it's a phase, you're disgusting;*
every swollen choke of shame I learned to
coat my throat with; every gay kid who
believed nothing would ever make this better
because *home* meant *break the parts of you that
don't fit into the plaster of who you're supposed to be.*

We already are exactly who
we are supposed to be.

Just last month, I woke up living in a city
where I could actually get married one day.

I think back to that wedding in New Jersey
all those years ago—

how I was the last one to leave the dance floor,
makeup smeared and beaming; how my
grandmother grabbed my hand and said,
I'm proud of you, with no *if onlys* or *buts*
clinging to the underside of her voice,

how finally, after all these years,
I am able to say the same
to myself.

MY DAD GOES TO MEETINGS FOR PARENTS AND FRIENDS OF LESBIANS AND GAYS

When the facilitator asks them to share,

he tells the group,

I think it's a choice. But it doesn't matter. I love my daughter.

The other parents sputter and spit

hot oil. He sits, arms crossed,

and closes his eyes.

On the drive home,

he says nothing. The sky

fades from postcard blue

to greyscape

threatening to collapse

in splintering curtains.

When it does, it is not

any less beautiful,

any less sky.

DAVID KEALI'I (U.S.A., B. 1982)

Advice To Men

When standing at the urinal:

feel free to look up,
down at what is being
voided, or off to the side
if no one is there.

       If another man is
       to your left or right

avoid
            all
                   contact.

Feel free to be as
           awkward

as possible.

Avoid all eye contact.
Try to keep at least one
urinal between you and
any other man in the restroom.
When finished:
shuffle away,
       gaze,
       downcast.

Of course,
if you're too nervous
use the sit-down toilet.

Don't let them think
you want to see their
penis, even if you don't,
but especially if you do.

You know better
than allowing yourself
to become the

punch line

scrawled in some dirty stall

Quilt Poem

Mahealani's hands
know quilting easy as freedom.
Push the needle,
tug the thread
Push.
Tug.

Mahealani learned this art
from her mother and grandmother
who had learned it from
missionary women who came
to Hawai`i from New England.
Those pious ladies had no idea
that Hawaiian women were already
masters of fabric.

Mahealani's grandmother would make
tapa, Hawaiian bark cloth by pounding
the pulp of the mulberry tree
into sheets used for clothing and bedding.

Like so many other Hawaiian women
she knew the skill of dye and prints,
added her own personal touch.

Mahealani continues the this tradition by
quilting for those rare nights
when the island's temperature dips below 70 degrees.
She makes designs based on local flora,
bright colors, ocean views or patriotism.

Her masterpiece is always on her bed.
This quilt shows deftness of skill and
attention to the different changes around her.

Her masterpiece is a quilt whose borders
consist of four Hawaiian flags.
In the mast corner, the Union Jack.
Then, eight stripes of white, red and blue
for each of the major islands.

When you look down at Mahealani's bed
you see the flags flying upside down
the international signal for a country in distress.
On the white center field of the quilt
the crest of her Nation,
embroidered with diligence, absolute care.

Closing in on the crest are four white stars,
symbol of a foreign nation,
their edges sharpened by manifest destiny.
At night Mahealani snuggles herself beneath her quilt.
She looks down at the flag opposite her head
sees it flying as it should:
Unbound, not dominated by unwelcome alliances.
During the day Mahealani's hands
know quilting and resistance easy as freedom.
Push the needle,
tug the thread
Push.
Tug.

SUTY KOMSONKEO (U.S.A., B. 1993)

Confessions of a Lanky Asian Dancer

One
I can't touch my toes

Two
I find it fascinating
How every time a person finds out I can dance
The first thing they say is
"Do a dance move right now."
I don't think they understand how
Awkward dancing looks without music
It's like saying,
"Oh, you play the piano?
Play a piece right now.
No piano? Well, that sucks."

Three
I'm a nerd
And not those nerds who wear jeans
That cause calves to scream suffocation
Or do the jerk in the streets
As much as they do it in their own beds
No
I'm the nerd that can translate the "Aeneid"
From Latin to English without "Google Translate"
And no, my ability to integrate or differentiate
Does not affect my ability to dance
The fact that I like math
Does not subtract the rhythm of my body
Don't believe me?
Well, I love proving stereotypes wrong

Four
I also hate proving stereotypes right
Yes, I'm Asian
No, that's not the reason I can dance
Yes, I'm gay
That also isn't the reason I can dance
Neither Buddha nor Lady Gaga
Came from the heavens
Or a giant egg
And bestowed upon me this talent

Five
To the people who say they can't dance
You might as well say you can't breathe
Because dancing is in our blood
Our ancestors told stories with their movements
To try and keep our roots from shriveling up and dying
The first time you danced
Was in the comfort of your studio crib
Your limbs raised themselves to the mobile that spun
Hypnotic carousel above you
The notes floated amongst your fingertips
And you swam
Playful innocence flailing in the magic of the music
We comprehend rhythm from the boom box in our chest
Have you noticed that when the speakers are blazing
At eardrum bursting blast
Your heart is pounding in time
With the beat of the song's pulse
It's fighting you to move
Out of that rigid statue staring sadness
You call a body
It wants you to feel what you were always meant to feel
You are a dancer
From nodding your head in the car
To initiating a head spin on the sidewalk
You are a dancer

Six
I hate dance battles
Not because I'm afraid
And no disrespect to those that do battle
But I hold true to the quote
That one dances to express
Not to impress
So don't call me chicken
When I'm being compelled
To reveal the intimacy
Of my body making love to music
To those who want to see
If their bodies can do it better

Seven
Never tell me to stop dancing
My arms are the tips of calligraphers' paintbrushes
My chest is the kick drum of a rock band
And the arpeggio of a pianist
My legs and feet are the explosion
Of firecrackers the day before the fourth of July
My hips are the rise and fall of buoys
On a calm midnight summer ocean
As the sea softly kisses the lips of the shore
Dancing is my life
And the day I stop
Is the day the boom box in my chest
Plays its final song

Finding Culture

"Sa bai di"
"What language is that?"
"Hello in Laos"
"I don't know what that is..."

I then smile at the chance to
Give them a taste of my ancestors' culture,
An image of my father's land,
A pin drop resonance of my very existence,
But as more and more people ask me
The less and less I smile
Because nobody knows
Where this fucking place is
And it becomes insulting
When the only people who
Have heard of my heritage
Heard it from "King of the Hill"
And no, I do not "Lay in the ocean"
However, I do lie in an ocean of failed expectations
Drifting somewhere between Asian history
And American culture
Currents drag me towards my current interest
But I'll never reach land
Because it's difficult accepting a country that
Contradicts its own definitions and
It sucks realizing that history books
Know more about your roots than you do.

I get excited when filling out
Home surveys and they ask me
"Language spoken at home"
Yeah, I get excited pretty easily
I take pride in known words foreign to this country
Unfortunately also foreign to my lips
It's as if my eardrums have been accustomed
To the rhythms of Laotian verse
Capably playing along to its beat
Without any sheet music
But my vocal chords struggle
Incompetently strumming harsh tones
In places where there should be captivating choruses
Why are my lips forbidden from
Properly kissing the hands of my maiden language?

I hate it when people
Seek profanity in as many
Different languages as they can
Fit in their hollow heads
Like when they ask,
"How do you say 'asshole' in Laos?"
Now tell me why would you want to
Find another way to describe yourself?
But I stutter when asked,
"How do you say 'I'm going to the store' in Laotian?"
"...I forgot."
I always seem to be forgetting
But when does forgetting
Start to become plain negligence.

I must admit I'm stereotypically Asian
Eating noodles with chopsticks
And pulling out the peace sign
Whenever I see a camera.
But these cameras and these luxuries
Have been taking pieces of my soul ever since I was born
I feel like I've been poisoned
By soil unnatural to the feet of my parents
Having slowly been eaten from the inside out
To the point where I can't
Even identify with myself anymore
Labeled as an Asian American
But feeling more and more everyday
Like an imposter in an Asian mask
A person rejected by his father's land
And having difficulty accepting his own

"Sa bai di"
Hello
"Koey pai tha lath"
I am going to the store
"Koey bo yahk boeun doy leut eng."
I want my skin not to sting when my blood touches it.

You Can't Be Gay

You can't be gay
Considered savior to your siblings
And mentor by your peers
What will they think of you now?

You can't be gay
Society will tag you
Right ear inferior
Strive to keep track of those
Who are different
Rumor will then fly
Drag out surprised gasps
From people's throats
And spotlight you outcast

You can't be gay
Your friends will diminish you uncomfortable
Make the presence around you less
Simply because they're not "used to it"
The male race will tattoo "leper"
On the bell of your left lung
Think you're breathing some disease
That being gay is an illness
You will paint disappointment
On the fingernails of women
Who longed to crochet their hands into yours
They will call you liar
Think your kindness was flirtatious
They will make you the reason for their heartbreak
Complete strangers will set fire to your worth
Carve suicide in your forearms
With every casual use of the words
"Faggot, homo, gay"
You
Almost every religion in the world
Has considered you a sin
No options for salvation
Just ultimatums
Live in the falseness of your conversion
Or the baptism of ignorant fists

You can't be gay
Your parents have trudged through mud
For by the tears of their fallen dreams
And the soil of a foreign land
They did not give up their hopes
So you could destroy the very few they had for you
To grow up in a country
Where the government won't sacrifice
Your rights at the altar
And to raise a family of your own
You dreamed of being father
Hold your infant in the smile of your arm
Your hand blanket to his face

He will never be now
Because of you
You society inferior
Friend uncomfortable
Male-race leper
Unintentional heartbreaker
Faggot, homo, gay
Product of the devil
Family dishonorable
Never to be father
You
I hate you
You can't be gay

And as the bathroom
Echoed the blood of my words
I could hear my reflection say
"But I am
The world is not as hopeless
As you make it out to be
Some may call you words
But do not let them define you
Physics calls us earthbound
But we soar beyond all expectations
Learn to accept who you see in the mirror
And one day you'll find
It's okay to be gay."

SAM LAROCHE (U.S.A., B. 1985)

Abandoned

You left her unattended
Left this little cabin all misty-eyed on the prairie
Your wife sure did taste good
We rode in like the cowboys we are not
It was just two of us
More than enough for the wife and two small children you left behind
I beat your son until his ears bled
Bruised your daughter in all the right places
I knew she was young but these lands show no remorse
You should have known better
Where did you go off to?
Your wife did not know
Trust I tried to be a gentlemen
I knocked, asked politely for some water and food
She obliged
Sat us down, took our hats
Asked where us gentlemen were headed
Said "My husband ought to be getting back any minute now"
When she realized we wasn't leavin
We'd been traveling awhile since the last abandoned home
We are not cowboys
No gun slinging, saloon brawling, tobacco spitting motherfucker
But I am the mother fucker
You left her unattended, went out to a town about 20 miles from here
We passed it on our way in
Bought a hooker and horse feed
Saw a young man just like you
Weary in the face, looked like he was in a hurry
Had to be somewhere, get to somewhere
Him and I bumped shoulders
"Pardon"
He could of been you, matter fact he was you
I wasn't mad about our little run in
Naw don't think this personal at all, please
That will offend me
This, this is just what it is
See some people got to die
Now if someone ever discovers this here home
All that'll be left is the tear of your clothes and bones
You will decay quicker out here faster than in the ground
Or the wild will get to you, bears and wolves and shit like that
See people will call this the devil's work
Hell on earth
When what they don't realize, this is all God
God's mighty hand
He put the knife in my hand
Made us men, made us prey and predator
Made us savage

If God didn't want us to kill like this
He would have given us sharper teeth and claws
Naw he gave us hands and tools and a brain
Now some years from now they will psychoanalyze a man like me
Assume things about his childhood
Say that some parts of his brain are defected
Or some will say he just had a bad soul, or no soul at all
If you ask most people if they believe in God they will say yes
When they really mean only a bad day
Well today the Lord is calling your name
He gave me a steady hand, I make the unsuspecting tremble
Make you cry out for your maker
Rejoice, your children only agonized in this hell for a few hours
Compare that to eternity
And you will thank me
Right now, they will hunt me down
But they will need some renegade Indian fuck to scout me out
I'll be waiting with my blade follow them home
Or I will be long gone
Get back home to the wife and children I left behind
Our daughters are about the same age, you know that
Your wife begged me not to hurt your children
So I nailed her tongue to the floor
I was going to leave as is
But I thought they would make better ceiling decorations
My partner had enough of me so he went out back
Slaughtered your chickens
We ate them for dinner
It was around about dusk when you got home
You know you can never tell if something's wrong
when the dogs are barking or when they're not barking?
I was going to be on me way before you got home
But instead I waited behind the door
Just to see the look on your face as you walked in and saw them hanging
Right before I cut your throat, your neck bled like hot rain
Being a family man myself I knew you couldn't live like this
The guilt, I know
I still am human
Consider this a favor
Nothing personal we was just passing through
And by the way you have a very lovely home

DAN LAU (U.S.A., B. 1985)

You are not a girl you are a boy

is what they tell me when I play with dolls or bake a cake that everyone wants a piece of or when I don't want to play softball or light cats' tails on fire with a lighter found on the playground next to the swing set where all those soggy condoms are layered one over the other like fallen leaves behind the bushes left by boys called men or men that should be called boys since some of them still sell peeks at their naked sisters through the cracked bathroom door to boys who don't know what a vagina looks like and when they're trading baseball cards or smoking basil they were told was pot they tell me *you are not a boy you are a faggot* which is worse than a girl because girls don't really choose and I, myself, get a little confused at what is happening since I can't focus the batch of fucking cookies in the oven and so my mind wanders to fabric swatches of silk damask my mom asked me an opinion on for the new curtains she wants to put in and then to the boys they call soldiers and girls they call sluts and my mom who they call a warped bitch because she's mean to them when they call me faggot and because I am a faggot and sometimes when I take a shower I don't clean the mirror when I brush my teeth because the fog is better.

Pruning

Cut it   *off*
she said,
                        looking through
the mirror at her two daughters

standing in the hallway.
The daughters' eyes, thrown open
like shutters in a gale, fixed

on hair   dyed
to cover the rogue grays kinking
down the trellis of her back.

Hair their fingers ran through
as they sat on her lap and named

flower   animal   joy

on spring evenings, pulled back,
fastened like a noose, bundled
like corn stalks in the end of summer.

Bring me   *the shears*
her tone leveled
through the cadence so the words
glided one after the other

to her daughters.

Your father   *is dead.*
I don't need the hassle.

It's One AM and I'm Not Drunk

And I'm sitting at the kitchen table
reading poetry aloud in my father's voice

or what I can get of it with my sharp tongue rounding
the mouth back and forth. My tongue clapping

the hard palate like rain boots in mud. My mouth
relaxing, gaining slack like releasing the pegs

of a violin we were too poor to buy. I sit here
in San Francisco trying to shove Henry Street

down my throat working and unworking the curves
and kinks in the words we both know differently.

Iron. Eye-uhn. Through. True. That. Dat.
If I could, I'd lay my tongue over his to see

where the tension is held. I'd cast a mold
to catch the forms that soft muscle makes.

I'd hold the timed release of his exhalation
in my chest the way he used to say to smoke,

the way he'd sigh before he punished us
with a ruler and the words *which hand did it?*

Tell me, how does he say *I love   .*
I miss   . Come home.

Because I already know how he holds
his breath and grits his teeth.

I already know how he says
D'ya wanna tawk to mom?

And even through the phone I can hear
the corners of his mouth pull back,

lips tightening against his gums trying
to conceptualize the word answer.

ADAM LOWE (U.K., B. 1985)

TRYST WITH THE DEVIL

Come. Let me show you dewy wonders
here in the grass. Let me feel the flicker
of your tongue in my arse. Come

slide over me, muscular river,
rockstar-pornstar in the shape of an asp.
Now. Splash your coat of stars across me.

Wrap me in your night. Prophet
of rebels, let me taste your dissent;
wet me with your meteorites; with tongue

I'll trace your proud descent. King of things
that scrabble in the dirt, raise
your fallen army—drive it through me.

FRUIT

You call me a fruit,
and I agree,
say

a fruit is ripe,
promising seeds,
bursting with juice.

You call me a fruit,
as though a vegetable
while I recite a litany
of fresh attributes:

a fruit is rich,
remembers its roots,
nourishes, quenches,
makes a display of any table.

I say,
I am the apple
that announces the gravity
of a given situation;
I am the pomegranate
whose gemstones teach
of the burden of possession;
I am the fig
our ancestors couldn't resist.

You call me a fruit
and I agree:
soft, round and sweet.
Peel back my layers,
take a look at my pips.
Full as a melon,
sharp as a lime,
come over here
and bite me.

J MASE III (U.S.A., B. 1984)

Neighbor

To the woman who frequents my girlfriend's apartment complex
with the **stank face** that always reads
Here come that gay bitch again
I want you to know that *I get **it***
You are not used to gay people
They've been the stuffing that jokes whispered on sidewalks
and behind the backs of strangers are made of
Not real
Not very tangible
Not even very human
As a teenager my father (*or the way I imagined him*)
Would tell me that **we're all the same**
and anyone that didn't like me 'cause I was gay
was simply just ignorant of that fact
Black
White
Gay
Straight
We're all the same
like a **handholding**
multiracial
'We are the World'
sexually indifferent
block party
My father was pretty *corny* like that
And you my friend
are more right than my father ever was (*even his imaginary parts*)
There is a ***very distinct difference*** between gay people and straight people
that is sooo slight
I'm glad *and a bit surprised* you've noticed it
Gay people just fuck better
And I know you know that
because you live next door

And the particular **intensity of anger you are expressing** comes from a focused type of sexual frustration
that can lead to ailments such as **delusions of heterosexual grandeur**
snarled lips
and ***rampant unchecked homophobia***
that leaks out into cultural norms *as **emotional and physical transgressions***
from a lack of clitoral release
If I were you *I'd hate gay people too*
Because we have been interrupting
quiet nights at home with your cat
and repeat episodes of Meet the Browns
America's Next Top Model
and The Housewives of Orange County
That is some important shit!

I only can offer you an explanation
and hope that with my sincerest of apologies we can be friends
or in the least civil neighbors
I understand the other day you asked my girlfriend
Why you gay anyway?
You too pretty for that
And you're right she's very pretty
Gorgeous in fact
And I find her attractive in a way that
makes me frankly a little sad that you're not getting the same attention at home
I mean
We're insensitively cranking up the noise day by day
And I haven't heard so much as a mouse squeaking through the
Walls of your place since I got here
Is everything okay?

Most of us gays double as therapists and are experts on talking about our feelings
So you shouldn't feel ashamed
Just let it out
I'm here for you
Men and women together is just unnatural
I mean
A better question
is not why are you gay
but rather
Why do y'all fuck so much and so good when I'm trying to sleep
or in the four corners of my mind?
See I added that last part because every time you say the word gay
Behind those eyes I can see your perverted ass is only thinking about sex
(To the point I often wonder if my butt looks good in your preoccupied heterosexual fantasies)
So let me answer both of those questions for the two of us
Of course it does and
I don't fuck more
I fuck harder
I fuck harder
For when my mother slapped me across the face at Christmas for looking
like a boy
I fuck harder
For the boy who thought he could fuck the gay out of me
I fuck harder
For the 13 year old trans girl turned prostitute
because her parents forced her to sleep on the streets

I fuck harder
Because Ugandan activists like David Kato
don't deserve to die at the hands of American Evangelism
I fuck harder
Because my government thought it was more important
for me to be able to die for my country
than to live in holy matrimony
or with equal job and housing protections
I fuck harder
Because the trans life expectancy in this country is only 37

So don't blink
I might not be here much longer
I fuck harder
To prevent forgetting
that the ability to come into the warmth of your partner
from the cold of outside
is a luxury not everyone is allotted
so
I fuck harder
To let her know
that **this** very *moment* is sacred
and
I fuck harder
Because every time a post-dyke transfag thrusts
A faerie gets its wings~
So that being said
If you have any more questions
you can feel free to **give a knock on the door**
of apartment 305**B**
and I'd be happy to answer them for you
I hope you have a good night
*I'd say **good night's sleep***
but between **you** and **me**
I just got back from a ***looong*** trip
and the way my girl looked today
I don't think anyone in this building is going to get any rest
for the next **week**
And don't worry—the stereotypes aren't **all** true
I mean gay people **don't just fuck**
For instance
yesterday *I had time to get a fair trade coffee at the co-op*
Which means I may just have enough time later
to take some notes **for your boyfriend there**
So leave your light on
So we can chat again

Neighbor

Gender Bunny

Subtitled:
Because a man on the train thinks it's appropriate to start conversations
with "Oh, I thought you were a guy at first!"

I am the gender bunny
And I know you've never heard of me
It's a newer position really
See there's the Playboy bunny
that chocolate Easter bunny hack
and then there's me
The heartbreaker
The deceiver
The trickster of all things gender specific
In the distance
there!
Think you just found a bio boy on whom to place your
Heteronormative affections
Ah-Ha!
You've been gender bunnied!!
And you should know that I deal exclusively with pants
I know you like pants
Who doesn't?!?
Long pants
Short pants
Corduroys
Clam diggers
Bell bottoms
Skinny jeans
Leather
Pleather
Pleated
Business
Black
Red
Purple feather embossed
It seems my entire life
you have been obsessed with pants
And you want to know what's in 'em
You want to know if it's long
Strong
Innie
Outie

Georgia O'Keefe
Or George Michael
Plastic bombastic
Flesh or silicone
You don't care
You just want to know all about it
And that's what gender bunnies are for
That's why you ask about my pants
when I'm dropping trout in the restroom
Sometimes with a gasp and a clutch of pearls
You ask when I'm catching the bus on my way to my gender bunny

assignments for the day
Sometimes when I'm just sitting around eating a carrot on my mid-day lunch break
Or making perfect little pink or blue-ribboned gender baskets for someone's more easily identifiable
binary appropriate offspring
Pants are very important to you
It's almost like you made them yourself
Like every fashion choice I make
was somehow constructed by you personally
So you want to make sure everything is working appropriately
I appreciate that
Sometimes I pretend I don't hear you wondering about my pants
when you're yelling at me down a street corner
or are asking what my "real" name is
I'm just playing hard to get
And the more angry you get
the closer you are to finding out
See tooth fairies are fueled by the dreams of children
but gender bunnies
are fueled by the incessant anger of strangers
Yeah, it's true
It's how we know that you believe
In our gender bunny
gender non-conforming powers
of genital transformation and gender relocation
Sometimes it's even better if you guess
If you guess right the first time
we'll grant you 3 wishes
And I'll even hand over my social security card
and IRS statement just to make sure you are tracking down the exact right
gender bunny
to fulfill all your "reasonable" gendered commands

Don't worry if I ever seem like I am being a little short
or curt
when you're asking about the detailed definitions of my genitalia's makeup
I could never be offended
Because I know you'd do the same for me
In fact
I think we should stop even greeting each other with simple hellos anymore
I mean we have just simply evolved beyond that
Whenever we meet a new person we should be exchanging Polaroid pictures of our genitals
just to make sure we know who we're really talking to
And see it's ideas like that
that got me promoted to gender bunny
status
I have just so many more racing through up here
that just need more believers like you
So if you believe in the gender bunnies
of the world
Keep asking inappropriate questions at inopportune times
Keep mispronouncing
And be prepared
to expose
your genitals

Hello
(For Kyra and every other transwoman forced to be afraid)

Hello is a greeting
Used to acknowledge the presence of another on the street
Two strangers meet
and Hello joins them
In a look
A conversation
Hello is a word that communities
Use to mean we're the same
You and I are the same
Except that Hellos haven't meant Hello to me for a long time
Not the ones I've received
between two strangers
Hello has always been a complicated word that we use all the time
usually with a *how are you?*
A simple greeting that
Could mean Hello
Or it could mean that a store clerk saw you walk in
and his eyes on your maple sweet skin
means you better not touch shit
Because they've counted it
and if anything is missing
You are suspect number 1
Hellos could mean Hello
And aren't always followed by how are you
But may have the distinct ring of **what the fuck are you**
Sometimes *it's a game played* by two strangers on a street
trying to detect a pitch of your voice
trying to place you
while staring at your chest
to make out the shape of pectoral muscles
or breasts
Displeased when their scientific measurements
don't add up to the direct answers they were looking for
Hellos are sometimes angry
Sometimes Hellos
often followed by how are yous
are warnings
from strangers on a street
to a stranger
That *this is not where you should be*
At this time of night
Looking like that
I'm sure you
Said Hello
I'm sure you said hello
When you saw her
How could you not
I'm sure she said it first
Greeting a stranger on her block
With *how are you*

I'm sure she felt safe
Walking down the street
near her house
You couldn't let her have that
Hellos sometimes mean *home*
That this was her home
And her piece of night
to do with what she could
These were her stars
Hello joined constellations
on her walk home
and made graffiti
into the velvet curtain
of a stage
Hey
Hey *you*
A derivative of hello
that could denote
familiarity
Hey
Hello
You
Could mean ~~danger~~
Could mean
Stranger
Could mean
Hello
To a *Beautiful woman*
To a *transwoman*
Could mean that you were pissed off
That she existed
Despite your belief that unicorns aren't real
and you found her attractive
Hello
Means
Hey
Sexy
Means
Can I take you home?
Means
I'd love to make you my baby's momma
and my mother's daughter
Hello
Means
You didn't know
Until she walked by
Until she said Hello
Means
You didn't see her
You didn't believe in the ability of her
to be
Means
that you shot her
because
you didn't have the decency

Means
you were too much of a coward
to go beyond the cold hearted compassion of
hello

COLIN MCGUIRE (U.K., B. 1982)

Fruits of Labour

Jam loved Honey
Honey loved Sugar
Sugar loved Strawberry
Strawberry loved Lemon
Lemon loved Salt
Salt called them all:
FAGHAPPYFOOLS!
Got drunk
Peppered their eyes
And never returned.
'Bitches!' he salted.

As Adam Early in the Morning:

Adam: Men make such strange women….
The hair on your ass is not Shakespearean
and there is much that the world feels wrong.
But the universal whiteness of our bones is enough
to let us know God loves more than words confound...
And your touch is wholly more than sound...
Your body with my body is so clearly true...
And together we learn to come clean
Realise tender to warmth, so this is
what made worlds grow and love kindle.

KATHERINE MCMAHON (U.K., B. 1988)

Blackberries

We ate blackberries,
staining our fingers and our mouths purple,
dark and beautiful.
She gave a berry to a child who passed—
he had never seen one before
and, wide-eyed, he put it in his pocket
for safekeeping.

Our bikes were strong and old,
and the sun warmed the new fruit.
I felt like we were children
from a long time ago
blackberrying in the school holidays,

and then
she kissed me—
long and soft and warm, sweet with juice,
and suddenly it was now and I was grown.

But still, she said, she was sure
that there were plenty of secret kisses
shared by olden days schoolgirls
in blackberry vines.

Her dimples corroborated.

New and old mingled in the vines around us,
dripping with dark juice
and shared secrets.
We picked all the berries we could,
not wanting to miss a thing.

Gold

My ex-girlfriend—
she of the best breakup ever,
of the old bikes and blackberries;
she of the loving of my underarm hair,
and of the barrier-busting honesty;
she of the sock giving,
and the fierce compassion
for old drunk men falling on the street;
she of the sixteen pencil hearts
hidden in my room for me to find,
and of the making out in the drunken dark
under Arthur's Seat—

my ex-girlfriend
sent me a picture of a cracked pot
with fat, sparkling veins,
and a legend that said something like:
When the Japanese mend objects
they aggrandize the damage
by filling the cracks with gold,
because they believe that there is treasure
in the history of things.

She said she thought that,
culturally, that was a load of balls,
but she liked the idea.

We had been talking about love.
I quoted Woody Allen (after Groucho Marx)—
you know, the one about
not wanting to belong to any club
that would accept me as a member—
and then, of course, I brought out some poetry.

She told me that a heart that doesn't ache
or isn't squeezed
sometimes doesn't throb at all.
I thought of electric shocks in CPR
and then, somewhat less violently, of exercise—
the way that muscle only gains
in strength when something tears,
when there is rupture
to be repaired with stronger cells.

Fact: There are plants
that can only germinate after forest fires,
when the ground forgives the burning trees
with fertile ashes.

But
defensiveness has reasons—
running from the heat
lungs closed with the smoke
of days of breathless needing,
and feeling suffocated.

The world is full of struggle,
and sometimes dealing with it
looks a lot like being a dick.

Sometimes it's hard to believe
in green shoots,
and coming back.

But there are times
when eye contact through the haze
has saved me—
irises reaching out like flowers
given for no reason except that
someone found them on the ground
and thought they might do better in my hands.

Give me something to remind me
to keep feeling like this—
a taste or smell to fire synapses
like the way a certain kind of perfume
takes me back in time,
carried like a cartoon
floating on pie-steam from an open window,
to a different love, into a past where
we baked ourselves a home
made of gingerbread, with icing for cement
and boiled sweets melted
into sticky stained glass.

By the time we had finished,
we were too drunk and full of laughter
to care that it collapsed.

Nothing holds together solely with sweetness.
We should've known that.

Give me something bitter
to make it stick—
give me gin and lime,
give me understanding why
you drink so much,
give me anger at the things
that make us curl our tongues 'round words
that scour our mouths,
because we can't afford the good stuff,
because sometimes we count the cost
of being kind.

Maybe
maybe love is just formless lumps of feeling
like wet clay, until it's fired,
until heat from burning binds it
into shapes that can hold water,
like an argument,
until its strength is tested
with nights of wine
and things we never should have said,
until it's whole enough to hold
cracks to fill with gold—
history to treasure.

Like the best breakup ever
turning into friendship
where we muse on love's mechanics,
where we know each others' fault lines
and have declared them fine,
and filigreed our veins with time.

Afforestation

It feels like you're sauntering
across the field of my back,
trails of vines unfurling in your wake
and bursting into shivering bloom,
ricocheting down
the tap-root of my spine.

The bed is warm
like leaf litter in the summertime,
full of dens for hiding—
pockets of soft
and pungent air
edged by the inside curve of your hip
where I want to lay my head.

We are full
of veins and canopies,
full of wanting life—
like the forest
you are hardly ever quiet,
so when you still
and bite your lip,
I take care not to rustle—
an explorer, bated breath
to catch that rare and tender sound
that you barely know is there

and the glitter in your eyes,
like an unexplained reflection,
pulls my gaze
and holds it tight—

why are you smiling?
you say.

Because kissing you
makes me happy,
I reply—

and you say
kiss me again

kiss me where the shoots grow green
kiss me where the forests tumble vines,
and tell me that the roar
in my ears is a waterfall;
I have always loved those
deep and swirling pools—
they just invite a swim,
and I can never help
but dive in.

SEAN PATRICK MULROY (U.S.A., 1983)

on the day you caught the plague

policemen circled your block,
searching for the kind of criminals
who exist only in books.

picture them, watching and waiting
for men in black masks with greedy smiles
and sacks of money, clearly marked, hoisted
above their shoulders.

how they longed to sink their bullets, deep,
deep within the tender flesh of bank robbers.

elsewhere, men in golden hats climbed ladders,
thrust their long hoses into buildings set ablaze
by teenage boredom.

imagine the men sweating with their secret fear,
inside their rubber suits.

while you lay on your back, wailing, *yes yes yes*
the birds outside your window pecked at worms
along the sidewalks. fought over their sweet meat,
tore them violently to death.

thirst

At the goodbye party for the British exchange students,
while everyone else is inside getting drunk, or outside,
puking in the bushes, David, who comes from London,
and I are listening to music in my car. We're parked
in the woods, and the sky, half-moon sparkling with stars,
is the same deep navy as the leather seats. Just a half hour
before, I was trying *not* to watch him play the drums—
covered in sweat, smelling like alcohol or pot.
I don't know what the boy in the leather jacket wants with me.

But I'm glad to have him to myself.
We laugh about the last week, his big trip to America,
and our silly friends, smoking cigars and climbing trees
He tells me that he's going to join the British army,
says he's not afraid to die. I don't ask him why not,
and I don't ask him why he keeps looking at me like
there's something written on my forehead.

I keep listening to the music
of his voice. I like how it sounds when he says my name,
love the conspiratorial promise in the rapid rise and fall
of his eyebrows. He pulls a bottle from inside his jacket.
shrouded in a brown paper bag, so that anything imaginable
could be inside. He keeps tilting it toward my lips, saying
"drink, Sean. drink,"
but I won't.

without words

his friend the fag said,
"please," and so my brother,
being my brother,
let him suck it
in the closet
of a basement
at a house party.

Sure he liked it. They were
high school friends, and
nobody really knew the fag
was a fag yet and anyway
who doesn't love a mouth
without words?

Is it strange that I believe
my brother when he says
he didn't feel anything, or
that it doesn't strike me
as brutal, the boy on his
knees for what little is given
with the swallowing of flesh,
a long kiss unrequited,
in the absence of a whisper,
or a thank you, or a name?

I guess it became a regular
thing between the two of them,
for a while at least, until quiet
Curtis entered without knocking,
saw the ripped jeans wrapped
around a pair of ankles,
the torn Metallica t-shirt pushed
up and over a heaving belly
by a desperate hand below
the belt. An awkward moment,
a shuffle and zip, and that was all.
"Curt was cool, though"
my brother says to me,
maybe 25 years later.
"He never said a thing,
to anyone, never even
brought it up. He just
turned around, and
closed the door."

ALESSANDRA NACCARATO (CANADA, B. 1984)

Hallelujah

There is a grace to skeletons
we cannot read in each other's bodies.

Look at the dinosaurs, their clumsiness extinct.

One can almost taste the wind
under pterodactyl wings.

The spaces god once fit, fingers
poking out the ribs like a schoolyard bully.

The first time I watched a woman sleep
I saw the ape we each hold in our bodies.

Fists like hot corn kernels, unwilling to open.
The fits, shivers and slack bellies.

There is so little we decide, all this time spent sleeping.
Trimming nails and grooming each other.

It's not our own beauty.

We are here to write gospel
in the hallelujahs of our bodies.

No asteroid sees its own rock burn.

Sing

I liked him but   *I wasn't sure*
I had one, I had one   *too many*
I was one, I was one   *too gone*

Open your mouth wider, girl.
That song needs a window to weep from.
Open your mouth wider, girl
because they expect an ocean of silence.

First it was November 1996
when he, young boy
forced you, young girl

into a brick corner seamed with urine.
His course tongue like an untrained cat
violent and hungry   *your first kiss.*

The principal mistook your blush
for complicity. *Oh young love, young love*

how sweet.

The next time, you were silent.
In a parked car, you were silent.

On the one-fifteen, a stranger fell into
fistfuls of your breasts and you were—

Until your breath could not quiet a candle.

Open your mouth wider, girl.
Let love be a form of resistance.

Love for your grandmother who crossed an ocean
to marry a stranger.
Love for your mother who wrung tears from the bed sheets
with a bracelet of bruises.
Love for your daughter who woke at Penn station,
penniless and hip sore.

Open your mouth wider, girl.
Let us know your weeps and bellows.
Let us hear your song.

If it be familiar:

I liked him but   *I wasn't sure*
I had one, I had one   *too many*
I was one, I was one   *too gone*

If it be in the family:
Lover. Brother. Father.   Fist.

Or in the audience of alleyways
where calls are lost on dark doorways,
a scream mistaken for a siren
if there is anyone to listen.

Is there anyone to listen?

Sing even into that silence.
There is an ocean of weeps and bellows
you summon to your teeth.
The orchestra not absent
where there remains the will to speak.

Open your ears wider   boy.
This song is your song   too.

DAN NOWAK (U.S.A, B. 1986)

Mantra

I find myself chanting "This too
is temporary" This too
is not meant for us.
For now, we have to stand
against the wind because
the corn has fallen. There are
no windbreaks on the prairie.
There are no phones or phone
booths to carry us away,
the robins are far too small.
Tonight we shall sleep too long
and imagine ourselves not
as the bones we are becoming.

Atlases of Old Lovers

There's a hurt in my throat
like I've smoked one too many
cigarettes and passed on too
many shots of whiskey.
Somewhere a DJ is playing Gaga
and I've yet to dance alone.
Pity.
Dancing alone is where I
find myself singing Radio Gaga
with entire packs of whiskey
and shots of cigarettes.
I burn my throat one too many
times, pointing out my hurt, there.

you hated me on my birthday

because I refused to dress up
or because I wanted to drink in
dive bars while wearing too
short shorts. you rolled your eyes
at me and I couldn't help but
drink more gin even though I
really hate gin. you didn't even
notice that one, but you did
see whenever the bartender leaned
over a bit too far and touched
my cheek like I was a walleye.
you hated me and sent texts
to your new man about how much
you hated me. if you ever look
back and wonder why I got sloppy
that night think about how many
times I watched you and thought
about how beautiful you were then.

Bad Clowns and Pizza Parties

OMG you're a poet? Like, I've got something you can write about:
Because you think a friend getting older, getting a little closer to
hip replacement surgery isn't enough to write about? As if
listening to Michael Jackson's entire singles collection crammed
in between Wreckx-N-Effect and Nickleback and Ani DiFranco
is missing some sort of merit. I know we're dancing—well I'm
dancing, you're doing your best white-girl-does-Tina Turner-
in-skinny-jeans-and-chunky bangles—but this bar is shrinking
in more and more awkward ways. *Do you know Pizza Planet?*
Well once I got frisked there. And I can't help but wonder why
this is interesting. Maybe being blatantly middle class in a late-night
pizza place requires a weapons check. I'll just politely nod,
drink my stolen drink, and think you're beyond spectacular again.
Isn't that wild? All I can agree to is the rhythm of the bar moving us.

ANDRE PREFONTAINE (CANADA, B. 1990)

If I should die tonight
do not bury me.

Cause the last memory you'll have of me
is being laid to rest,
covered with all the dirt that will spill
from me no longer guarding the skeletons in my closet.
Instead,
have me cremated
and fill the insides of fireworks with my ashes.
gather on top of the highest hill
feel the breeze dance around like a Kabuki clown
as I say my final goodbye.

If I should die tonight.
Open my safe,
the contents of which,
my birth certificate
I.D. cards
passport
and other paper trail paraphernalia.

Draw on them.
With snazzy names like Captain Obvious or Maurice.
As those names seem more representative of my identity,
than the name I keep locked up in a safe.

Better yet,
steal my identity.

Grow a scraggly beard
wear a bad wig
so my photo I.D.s look legit with you.
Then get credit cards,
buy a car,
ride off into a random sunset
with the road map fluttering behind your speeding wheels.
But no matter where you go,
don't go overboard
as there are people I don't know of
that love you more,
more than you will ever know.
And you don't need to destroy yourself to try and prove it,
trust me.

If the car breaks down and you feel lost, don't worry
you can place a globe as my memorial,
spin it like a basketball until it falls on its axis
hopefully then I can teach you that direction is unnecessary.
Most times all it takes is leaving the house
and shaking your world up to figure out
where you really need to be.
So be adventurous.

Never diminish the beat of your own drum.
Simply shape it
strengthen the presence in which you present it
so that others may dance freely
comfortably alongside you.
Know that you,
as a freewheeling agent of the universe,
are capable of many wonderful things.
Love being the greatest of which.
So dance,
just dance.
Know that you are only bound by the expectations you have
and the doubts you place on yourself.
So cut your shackles, babe
and believe in everything you do
sounds cliche,
but it's true.

If I should die tonight
know I'm writing this to refresh my memory on the precious intricacies
of a ladybug crawling up the dewy stem of a flower,
and how we're equally as fragile.
How I am the sum of my experiences
yet what defines me is not my past,
but my heart.
Much like yours does,
too.

So if I should die tonight
Find a lover,
grab hands
and after ditching the car you bought with my name,
run to the highest hill
where there will be a jukebox.
Place your quarter in it
so that you can listen to Meatloaf's "Bat Out of Hell"
as my ashes get shot in a fireworks display that spells out "L.O.V.E."
with a cheesy heart surrounding it,
As that's the greatest lesson I've ever learned,
And if it's the last thing I do,
I want you to feel the same way, too.

Dear Edith Piaf,

When you were born in the doorway outside some boarded up shop,
you mother screamed in agony while the pavement was the first thing to hold you.
From that moment,
you were born a Molotov cocktail in a champagne bottle.

Your soul, the bull,
your body, the china shop.
Blinded as a child then miraculously cured
you were abandoned into the hands of your grandmother's brothel
the women sold their bodies in ways that made the devil wince.
You cried to the heavens inside a lonely crib,
the angels listened but did nothing,
as your voice was that beautiful and God's ways just that mysterious.
And you grew a love for the downtrodden,
the rejected,
the hurt
because that pain was from whence you came.

You learned to sing,
serenading the tragic parade that was your life.
For the lovers who were ripped from your arms
and for the ones who ripped the heart right off your sleeve and ran away.
Three car crashes that left you increasingly crippled
substance abuse left your pain in limbo
yet with the force of a thousand brass bells,
you sang.

on cold winter nights when lonesome bodies went to bed alone
and on dreary days when Hitler invaded France
when there was nothing left for you or your country.
You sang
because you held out hope.

So,
Madame Piaf,
How did you do it?
I ask because I'm stuck with bark that's grown over my heart
carved with initials I can't erase.
I'm perpetually lonely
and left awake from nightmares of a small boy locked in a bedroom
with tin foiled windows and a wet bed
and a heavy handed shadow man waiting to play patty-cake with his belt.
Cat's always got my tongue when I'm the cowardly lion
writing the same "I wish you were here" postcards
out of apology letters thrown into a burning bridge
and calling it a smoke signal cry for help
because they got close, and I got scared
and I can't handle being hurt anymore.
Madame Piaf.
That is just one of those nights when lighting strikes twice out of spite
and I'm left withdrawing into that nervous alien wearing my skin.

Madame Piaf,
one of those nights where I'm fumbling to pick up the pieces
like fall leaves on the sidewalk with hands so out of touch
Madame Piaf
this is one of those nights when you would have sung the loudest.

One of those nights where you would have damned your fears
and all those who hurt and doubted
and you would have sung
with the force of a thousand brass bells
because what else is there to do
when you have no say in what this life has in store for you.
But develop a voice that sings of hope
and inspire the world to do the same.
You were barely five foot-two
life never once took you into consideration
so you took the name of a sparrow
with a song just as sweet
because on nights like these it's nice
to have a little bird tell me to keep my chin up.
And that's what I needed most.
Merci, Madame Piaf.
Merci.

SAM SAX (U.S.A., B. 1986)

the digital harvest.
   or my introduction to internet cruising

ohio winter's a dead rock growl. the ground
water's lake erie slick. means it can catch fire.
nights with only computer light for warmth.

my boyfriend at the time showed me men
planted in terminal rows, all seeking grow.
they were seeds cast off by turncoat birds
all died flying north come winter. means lonely.
these plants grew dollar bill leaves for us.
i was young then and the price for unripe
peanuts is still going up. learned to pluck
the least sickly clean from dirt. to wash them
in the sink. i cut their roots. they held me
like a wicked son. each week, a new slash
and burn. my name became a greenhouse
with melted windows. a windmill of pulp
photographs, script written in herbicide
and impulse. my blood a red letter.

by the end
i had collected a silo of men.
a web of dead stalks to burn.

it was no accident i left the farm then,
when the fields thawed open.

it is no accident that a bird wrapped
my heart in it's metal claw and flew west.
that it dropped me in this asphalt garden.

in my city people don't know winter.
      means the harvest is all year long.

first will and testament.

will work for dollars   for cents
for scratch bones pounds pence penance
sense shekels sentence shelter bread.

four times two bucks an hour
four hours a day   four days a week
for the rest of my life

will sell knives   will pyramid scheme   will dress nice
will call during dinner   will door to door   will carry a knife

will work for peanuts   for pine nuts   for pineapple and cashew

will work for you for less than you pay others to do
will work force   will force out   will overseas

will nonprofit   will not profit
won't trade but will eat for free

will burroughs   will suck for skrill
will test pills   will fuck for money

will call   good will   will drink on job
will of drunk god   will lift for tips   will pay check

won't background check   will shakespeare
will faulkner   won't dress appropriate
won't pass on purpose   will laundry and transit
will work for store credit   for college credit
    for credit card necklaces
            will you have anything else with that sir?

will work for a laugh a smile a blow job
            an hour an asshole an alibi

will work for change
willblakewillpoemwillspokewillyeats
willsmokewillcoldwillbankswillbroke

will fold the will of a drunk god into my bones
though none of it
will work
for me

reuptake inhibitors.

a.

the first time i did cocaine liz let me borrow her rollerblades
my feet carved sharp wax grooves into the pavement.

i wore a headphone helmet. the wire dangling behind me like a giant
iguana tongue as the rhythm of the night thumped against my skull.

this is the rhythm of the night. night. night. night.
    [oh yea.]

each street lamp had a song burning in its eyes
the roads in rural ohio are rough
my legs vibrated a numbed baseline

each star was a pill in a rich lady's medicine cabinet
the sky   a pharmacy begging to be robbed

i skated so fast
i outran all my baggage

collapsed into a field of sheet music
i have yet to emerge from. my friends
wrapped me in a blanket of sweat
walked us home toward our warm beds

                                                              z.

                              the last time i did cocaine
                               is a different story altogether

               it was denver pride as a strange man cut lines with a razor blade
               that had developed a taste for his sad forearm. the port–a–potty

                       stank in time with the rumbling bass outside
                       his trousers smile opened into a scarecrow grin
                       my skull tried to free itself from its skin sarcophagus.

                               buried alive in that filth stink sauna
                               there were no wheels to run away on
                               no bed to wrap my bleeding heart in gauze
                               no air to calm these snakes twisting through hair
                               and no corona song to quiet the monster
                               rattling in my stomach

NATHAN SAY (U.S.A., B. 1983)

God Take Me Willing

There is grit and grime on the sidewalks I roll on:
I recognize it, wedged underneath my finger nails,
Etched between blocks of graffiti in the Men's room,
On the homeless woman, who sleeps in an abandoned storefront
On University Avenue.

I see her life in my third eye:
Her husband leaving without a note,
Vanished somewhere between her scalp
And the baby's amniotic fluid.
Her four year old son, eating his last box
Of cereal, drinking his last carton of milk,
The night before the planned CPS pickup,
After which, she would be living on the street.
This rapture is the only thing she has going for her.

Met her on Friday with the biggest smile
You would ever see on a homeless woman who sleeps
In an abandoned storefront on University.
Hands turned upright, eyes glazed towards the sky,
She says:
"God, take me willing,"
"God, take me willing,"
"God, take me willing,"
The billboard above her and to the right
Reminds everyone that tomorrow is the day.

That night, she dreams easy with false promises glued to her ribcage.
Tricks herself into thinking she can drink scripture verse
and eat church hymns, to ease the burn of hunger.
Her body is quickly becoming a shrine to you, Harold Camping.

Family Radio fills her eardrums, her mouth drips the Lord's Prayer.
She wakes up Saturday morning, she is dancing down University.
Uses her last $25 on a Bible and a cup of coffee, because she wants to
Be perky and attentive for that rapture. "God, take me willing" is vibrating
Throughout her soul, her smile wider than the night he proposed to her.
Uses her last coins on a long distance call to her sister in New York,
Explains "God, take me willing," and hangs up.

She goes back to her store front, eyes bursting with heaven,
The angels dancing on her breath. She thinks she feels The Earthquake
At 6:00 pm, thinks she feels the sweeping upwards, but realizes though, it's
An ambulance and a fire truck. A cold wind blows grit in her hair again,
And now it is 6:15 pm.

I am knocking on your door, Harold.
Your neighbors tell me you're home,
I imagine the nursemaid caring for you,
Feeding you soup out of a terrine, the plate
Etched in silver, fire burning brightly in the fireplace.
Could you give this woman, your human shrine,
A couple thousand bucks, Harold, give her space in your garage,
Because the fire for God in her eyes is turning to embers.
She is pissing scripture verse, shitting church hymns.
Soon, she will remember she is hungry, forget to believe in angels.
Question God's love for her again. Nothing is a surety.
She didn't recognize me tonight at 8:30 pm. Her body held a shell
But, no one was home. There is grit and grime on the sidewalks I roll on.
The empty dust of your lies.

After Brain Injury
Dedicated to Our Troops

When you awake like a matted bird,
Bent to the Earth,
If someone says
"You are looking good"
This is not a compliment,
It is a simple kindness.

When you notice your room
Littered with cigarette butts,
An unused bong,
A joint in the corner,
Be grateful if your mother says nothing at all.
Rejoice in your hoarded joy.
Gather all these things in a circle around you.

Remember the days when your grandfather was still living
When the muscles in your mouth remembered how to smile
This is not a luxury anymore.

Do not empty your catheter onto the floor
It will piss stain the carpet permanently.

When the echoes of "you, you, you, you" ring valiantly in your ears
Do not try to remember who said them,
This is a futile attempt that will end in an infinite migraine.
Do not try to remember everything you did last week.
It will make your beating heart a thick heavy purple.
Remember, your life will consist of no more than repetitive noises from now on.
Pick your favorite, and masturbate to that rhythm. You need to learn how to use your
Hands again, and this is a perfect way.
Touching your dick with the end of a cigarette is more stimulation than you will get for
Years to come.
You are a sexless orb of a man. Your masculine identity exists only in phantom thoughts.
When your mother's tears stain your beard the first time she shaves you,
You will look at each other with an equal amount of resentment;
After all, she only got to live half of an adult life.
You only got to live half a childhood.

The cards, and the friends, will stop coming soon. The drool down your face will make
Them cringe like a freak show advertisement would.

You always wanted more reasons to resent your parents,
Pick three! Slide down in the bed further.
See, the activists would never tell you this part.
They forget about the day you come home, like the backside of a carousel.

LISA SLATER (U.S.A., B. 1983)

An Unsent Letter from a Mother to her Two Queer Daughters

My darlings,
I am so worried for you.
The world is full of people
who will hate you for
your love.

When I was growing up,
it would have meant that
girls would whisper behind your back and
boys would treat your body like
a crooked thing that needed to be
banged back into
the right shape.

Maybe this is why I can't seem
to fit the word 'girlfriend'
in my mouth. Why I only say
'Sarah' to relatives who ask about
your new apartment.
The quiet girl you share it with.

Sometimes I wonder
what it would have been like to
kiss that girl who gave me
butterfly windstorms in my belly.

My darlings,
I don't think that I will ever be able
to tell you her name.
It's been so many years that
her face looks like every
pretty brown-haired girl on the subway,

but I think of her
every time someone mentions
the Moon, or
Neil Armstrong.
I remember her smile
every time the radio is playing
Nina Simone.

I will never know what her kiss would have
tasted like. How my hand might have
cupped her cheek or found anchor on
her hip. How I might have stammered an
apology. How she might have kissed me
back. How we might have held hands
in secret and made up boyfriends. What
my mother would have said if she came home
early. The colour of my skin when my mother
was done with me. I will never know
which friends would have still invited me to
their parties. Whose parents might have
taken me in and taken pity on me. How
I would have paid for college. Would I
have ever had children?

My darlings,
I do not know any of this.

I am sorry for this crooked love I left
living inside you.
I am so worried for the way
your love might never fit properly
in my mouth.

Having a Nervous Breakdown: A How-To Guide

First, let someone matter to you.
When she tells you she loves you, cry.
Then yell.
Call your mom.
Yell at her, too.
After you hang up,
Open the fridge.
Finish a bottle of Australian Chardonnay, a block of cheese, and a roll of Pillsbury cookie dough.
Throw up.
Rest your head on the triangle of your crooked elbow as it rests on the edge of the bathtub.
Ignore the ringing phone. It's probably your mother.
Fall asleep on the bathroom floor with a bit of vomit at the corner of your mouth.
Wake up eleven minutes before you have to be at work.
Swear, shower, throw up.

Next,
Snap at your boss when she asks you why you're late.
Get nervous and spill coffee all over your shirt.
Swear. Apologize.
On the way home,
Call the ex-boyfriend you never got over,
ask him if he'd like to get a drink later.
Wear something low-cut and too much eyeliner.
When he asks how your new girlfriend is,
Fuck him.
Come hard against his fingers in the men's room,
Go home before he sees you cry.

In the morning, tell regret to go fuck itself,
Retch up what's left of your dignity,
Then call in sick to work.
Text your girlfriend to tell her that you're sorry and you miss her.
Facebook chat your ex,
"thanks for last night"
and then untag all of the unattractive photos of yourself.

Drink vodka until the sun sets,
Call your mother and ask her why this all has to be so difficult.
When she asks what "this" is,
Tell her she never understood you,
And ask to speak to your father.
Talk for an hour about American politics.
Let the dishes pile up.
Forget to do the laundry.
Turn your underwear inside out and wear them anyways.
Repeat all of these steps as necessary.

Finally, wake up amidst the rubble. Smile.
Find God.

DANEZ SMITH (U.S.A., B. 1989)

Baldwin to his white lover

I

Most days, after I am amazed the sun persists,
your skin is there all at once. My eyes dart
from the blotchy hair on your limbs
to the obvious sin on this bed. Quite a mess, isn't it?
Your pale skin draped all over my room
I admire how it looks like cotton seduced through the best gin.
I think of cotton. I think of the South. You
make every morning's prayer a little harder,

but when you stir from sleep, oh, if you could see your eyes.
You look at me like my body is fire confessing it's God.
In this tiny room, which our mouths decided is holy
I have nothing to offer you but coffee and myself
you like everything dark. Here, right here, your body
is not secret nor ocean nor Mars nor creation. Here,
right here, your body is a weathered bible, a broken watch
a stained shirt I refuse of wash.

II

When we are strangely untangled,
when your eyes aren't the only eyes on my spine,
when I suggest servant, not your dear,
when skin becomes barrier again,
I remember the truth on my body. Your body.

Love, you have my heart, my hand
not my pigment.
My world is a fist. Yours is flat   an open palm
awaiting dreams. They let you dream.
One time I dreamt
the world woke up in flames.
They called me Turner's boy then.
I haven't slept since.
I never meant to sleep
with you, but your body
may be the closest I've come to dreaming
in so long.

III

You came to bed tonight. My body chilled.
You said we should role play. My body chilled.
You said we should play "Roots." My body chilled.

You rooted teeth in my heart. I stabbed yours.
You licked every inch of my back. I choked you.
Your hands were no caress, all take. I fired fire, spear

cannon, prayer, bullet, march, song, poison,
you still ended up on top. I couldn't fight
my moan, the song you rise in me.
When I say your name, you say mine
When I say *conquer*, you say *resist*

Brother's Bar and Grill, Game 3, NBA Finals 2011

'I like no interruption when the game's on.' –Kurtis Blow

He look at me	like	What kind of balls this nigga come for?
I look at him	like	Nigga, I will fuck you
		up on the court.
He look at me	like	Why your pants so bright
		and tight like a sun with stretch marks?
I look at him	like	You mad cause you can see my dick
		bigger?

...and winning is a huge thing for me.
LeBron James

He look at me	like	See! that's how gay niggas do!
		Be bringing up dick all sly and shit!
		Like a trap!
I look at him	like	Homie, the trap only snatch
		if you wander in jungle.

I've been around for a while, I know a few things.
Larry Bird

He look at me	like	You come here to play?
I look at him	like	I come here to watch.
He look at me	like	I know you know.
I look at him	like	I come here to watch.
He wink		
I look at him	like	I come here to watch.
He move closer		
I look at him	like	I come here to watch.

Some people want it to happen, some wish
it would happen, others make it happen.

Michael Jordan

He reach his hand on my knee under the bar cause we the only two people in here, besides the man making drinks.

I think   Not tonight please.

He tell me his name James.

He tell me he got kids, got 2 many drinks in him, got a woman who love him so much.

He still got his hand on my knee.

I look at him   like   Not tonight please.

He order me gin.

He watch me drink it.

He talk about the game and stats and all them things men talk about.

We watch the game until buzzer, until last call.

He say he like my pants,

He say he like that I look faggy and talk like a man

He say he like that.

He ask 'Why did you come to the bar tonight?

I look at him   like   to watch.

Blasphemy
after hearing a sermon on how is wrong to call on the Lord during sex

I've never known an orgasm
not to be holy. You try to siphon
a sweet name from your blood
and not thank the lord
for endless rows of skin
begging someone to run, to seed, to harvest
a tithe of teeth. The body is a temple
filled with Holy Ghost thick as good crème
filled with people who've risen from the pews
dancing far too close, far too slow
might not be dancing at all
but the music? The steady headboard
like a thousand believers rejoicing
raising the dust, to raise the spirit
until someone has no choice
but to submit, bend body and mouth
to something inside that demands out.
You ain't lived until you been made gale
out-thundered the storm at the window
until lightning takes shelter in your bones
until sweet execution, shock of stubble
and fine hairs on honeyed thigh
paradise lost, now found in the back of the throat.
I shout '*Oh, my fucking God*' for a reason.
When my glory comes, my mouth snatch
to name something greater than my bed
to lure me back to body. For me, that's heaven
doesn't have to be God for you
could be '*oh, global warming*'
or '*ahhh, shit, coupons*'
or '*holy veganism*'
when each cell is a war
suddenly at peace. When you
are dizzy and drenched in his sweat,
when you mouth is filled and his mouth is filled
and what needed to be drained is drained

let the first word after be praise
for the possibility of skin
the promise of nails sunk into back fat
the gospel of nipples and earlobes.
I dare you to watch a really boring movie
with your lover, get tired, lie you head in his lap

fall asleep to the loyal churns of belly and heart.

Mail

Dear Mrs. Thompson,
Sorry if you ever tasted the salt of me
when you kissed your husband good morning.
I hope it didn't taint your coffee
or make bloody murder of your lipstick.
I killed your marriage, and you
deserve to know that
he is not everything you prayed for,
but maybe his sweet kiss morning
is enough.

Dear Mrs. Thompson,
Your ATM code is 9976.
Your family owns one Honda, one Ford,
all 3 of your children have bikes.
You have a fireplace,
3 copies of People magazine,
at the top of the stairs your children's room is to the left,
the guest bed to the right,
your room straight ahead,
all your walls are white
like lies,
everything smells like lavender,
you have really nice sheets.

Dear Mrs. Thompson,
Your husband pays me 50 extra dollars
when I bust on his face,
25 more when I kiss him after.
I have never seen a man scrub so hard,
his skin red like the sin he's trying to exfoliate.
He never brushes his teeth.
Can you taste his shame?
Did I bitter the back of your tongue?

Dear Mrs. The Bitch (as he calls you),
I imagine your scalp
adorned with 300 grey follicles,
one for every dead president
your man slaps on my chest,
his hand dragging until on the pillar he prays to.
I'm sorry for being holy to him

Dear Mrs. Clueless
Sorry if I ever took food out of your children's mouths.
If they have ever gone hungry
because your hubby feasted on me,
let me offer them the groceries I bought with his sacrifice.

Dear woman,
Have you ever wondered
why it takes him long to get dressed?
His outfit must be perfect and able to disguise.
He can't leave the closet
until he can't recognize himself.

To Whom This May Concern,
Have you ever fucked your husband
from behind?
I have, when he's been a bad boy
cause it hurts him more,
but most of the time he is on his back,
he likes to rub my chest
while I gut him.
I wonder does he rub yours
when you are laying and open
and lied to.

Dear Mrs.,
When your husband tells you the bruises on his neck
are from bar fights, that's my fault.
I have choked him twice.
Once because he asked me to.
The second time, he called me his nigger child
and I choked him.
Yes, I still came.
Yes, he came harder.
Yes, he paid me extra to apologize.

Dear Ma'am,
You look lovely
in the pictures next to the bed
he turns face down.
Your smile bright as starry country night,
never let him cloud it.

Dear, Dear, Dear Sweet Woman,
I feel like we are family now.
I say this because I love you:
Caution the way his hips grind
and teeth part in his sleep.

Dear Mrs. Thompson,
I fuck your husband twice a week.
He pays me.
He is lying   next to you.
                                     Dear you,
                                     He called me your name once, Ann.
                                     I just thought you should know.

MAX WALLIS (U.K., B. 1989)

Different Versions of the Same Thing

As for death, my love, let's not talk of beauty.
The last time I saw your face about to plummet on a fair ride,
your eyes spinning like slot machine reels.
Today your name is just newsprint. Those thoughts
yours alone except in CCTV as you zoomed, then toppled,
over the Victoria Line track. Your phone without signal
as I called you to stop. Your hand, that minor twist,
like a turn in a line, or a key change;
was it grasping for the platform's edge, or air,
knowing it wouldn't latch?

*

As for death, my love, let's not talk of beauty.
The last time I saw your face about to plummet on a fair ride,
your eyes spinning like slot machine reels.
Today your name is just newsprint. Those thoughts
yours alone except in CCTV as you zoomed, then toppled,
over the Victoria Line track. Your phone without signal
as I called you to stop. Your hand, that minor twist,
like a turn in a line, or a key change;
was it grasping for the platform's edge, or air,
knowing it wouldn't latch?

*

As for death, my love, let's not talk of beauty.
The last time I saw your face about to plummet on a fair ride,
your eyes spinning like slot machine reels.
Today your name is just newsprint. Those thoughts
yours alone except in CCTV as you zoomed, then toppled,
over the Victoria Line track. Your phone without signal

19 Kirton Gardens

I like it when no one is in the house and I can pretend to be the best poet that ever existed. It's all about surprise and turning left, taking the ulterior argument, giving less than you should. I mean whoever thought of a light bulb in a frying pan and said it was the birth of an idea was a genius, right? I catch myself in the mirror sometimes, that's when I realise that all of this is just shokuhin sample food in Japanese restaurant windows, bought for over seventy US dollars they look like a perfect imitation of food but lack substance. In the morning I run downstairs with my cock waggling about as I jump down to the lower floor of the mezzanine flat, in search of coffee. Sometimes I think about the Asian children across the road in the tower block who hang out on the balcony and think what if they see me? Is it paedophilia if they are the ones who get the camera and take photos of me? My partner tells me that I should wear boxers. He tells me this while only wearing a towel.

SOPHIA WALKER (U.K., B. 1985)

After Words

When I moved to Vietnam you took a Sharpie
and wrote 'Mine' on my breasts. You signed it.
That was two years ago but some nights I swear
I can still see those letters spelling you into my skin
With new lovers blindly tracing the map you laid on
My body I think, 'For your next girl, write it in braille'

See, this is not a missive
Me standing in a room you aren't in
Begging 'Take me back.'
I have no desire to go back.
This is for the loves that
Don't get to last, that
Flash of glory in our failed pasts
Baby we were great together
Some days.
All those times you didn't want to kill me?
Those were awesome

Remember Italy?
We'd curl up together on the David steps,
Florence lighting up the dusk below, it
Would've been so romantic – if the two
Euro bottle of red wine hadn't been picked by me.
It had even turned fizzy.

I wrote you a love poem once,
Describing you as voluptuous,
Showed it to you when it got published,
You thought I'd called you chubby in public
We spoke in different languages
I thought I got it without understanding
This, not uncommunicative just
Speaking in dissimilar dialects

We were the almost made-its
So perfect on some occasions

Those arms carried me through two years of broken sleep
Nightmares screamed me awake from traumatic dreams
And on the rare nights I wake nowadays I confess
I miss the safety I found in your embrace;
Baby, some nights those arms saved me

This is not a missive
This is me standing in a room you aren't in saying
'Thank You' and 'Have an amazing life full of
Everything you ever dreamed of cause you deserve it'
Hoping that one day, somewhere, you might hear this
And maybe, buried deep in the layers of your skin
You carry a fading signature that says:
I loved this girl, and it was beautiful.
And you should too. But this piece of
Skin, this small patch is taken
It carries the memories we created
And it says 'Thank You'
Traced in the letters of my name.

Dyke

To the man who repeatedly punched me
Stole all my money and spat 'Dyke'
In my face with such vitriolic hatred
Like it excused his behaviour

Let's think about this for a second
What is a dyke?
A sea wall
A mere combination of stone and bonding agent
Creating a haven against the forces of nature
A few thousand meters
Protects millions of people

As if my arms could stretch with strength in
Defence of all those who meant something to me
Could prevent them from drowning
When misfortune surrounds them,
A veritable life raft in the face of
Floods of days that shake us
As if I *were* safety, never breaking
In the wake of waves of hatred
I have stood the test of centuries pushing back at me
Shaped strength against adversity,
Made nations retract bigotry
Please accuse me of holding back the sea

With each punch he landed his hate grew more candid
'Till my mere act of standing proved too much for his handling
As he walked away with my money and his bruised knuckles
I chuckled—
I'd learned I am more fearless than Perseus
A lesson not lost on both of us
His blasphemy had deemed me
More powerful than Neptune
Cleverer than King Canute

Go on. Please.
Call me a dyke.

Deserted Storm

Jay came back from Basrah with a video
His very own snuff-film horror show, he
Showed up back home with six months
To go on his third tour in a row
A PTSD-shattered former human being,
One man fighting machine reduced
To scattered tantrums and bad dreams

Initially all we could see was the mate
We'd always known him to be:
Quietly sucking on a 40,
Ignoring the hordes of imploring gazes
And invasive questions from his naïve mates
Questions like

"So did you shoot anybody?"

and

"How many of them hajis did you kill?"

I want to show you something.
Rising from his seat, Jay approached the TV
Filmed from his perch in the tank's gun turret
The DVD captured the first week's incursion
Day One showed homes bombed down like dominoes,
Cars exploded, everything destroyed in the tank's forward roll
Day Two showed dismembered torsos, pulps of skin
And shattered bone, overturned cars were funeral homes
Rubble piles with lives inside became burning pyres

By this point, the drinks had been put away
Even the Backwoods blunts were stubbed out
The room was totally silent
Save the screams of agony and ammunition
Thundering from the audio
No one asked any more questions

Somebody switched the film off
But it was clear to all of us that
Jay was still watching

Lassie's Response

(Each Burn's Night, a male poet is asked to write and deliver an Address to the Lassies. Since the 1940's, a woman has been asked to write a response)

I don't know what I'd do without my boyfriend
On him I do so deeply depend,
For what use is the kitchen if not to feed him?
And I've never used any other room in this house

He would be the perfect spouse:
A man's man, excelling in doing –
Nowt
All my dreaming's of cooking and cleaning
These are what give a real woman meaning

A life in his service 'till his wrecking my cervix
Brings kids to increase my servantly purpose
Oh how I yearn for it, these years ahead
When all the hair lost from his head
Is well represented by those
Nose and back tufts instead

His former six pack's been
Upgraded to 'keg'
Oh god I'll want him to take me to bed
Speak to me of the Premier League,
Whisper sweet cricket scores in my ear
Oh, baby
I will make you roast dinners like
Your mother used to, I will
Separate your whites faithfully
Just promise me you will only
Ever scratch your testes
In my presence.

You sexy, sexy man

I beg of you:
Come home completely blotto
And pee all over the toilet seat
It means so much to me that
This time you actually used
The bathroom

And when you give me
Crisps and a ten pack of
Ciggies for our anniversary –
It means everything that you
Would drive around at 4 am
Looking for an all-night gas station
The day after our anniversary
That's so romantic

You know what is romantic?
He knew my day had been shit
I walked in to find each candle lit
He'd freshly cooked my favourite dish –

When tasked to write on men
From the irreverent side
I had no choice but to generalize,
I was forced to rely on stereotype
'Cause the men in my life
Are dignified.

JULY WESTHALE (U.S.A., 1986)

Monsoon Tea

My first memory of my momma
            is on her Arizona bed, eating cereal
                        from her bowl, asking *am I a boy?*

Her, staring out the window dislocating
            her smile behind her hand, spoon shaking
                        with laughter. She drew me a picture

of a frog, said *you are an amphibian, you*
            swam in my stomach, you will one day learn
                        how to walk on land.

We moved to the back porch to bring the sun
            tea out of the red dirt, rings of wet
                        on the ground where the container sat.

Baby J, you don't love women just because they are women
            or hate men because there are men.
                        I said, yes—sometimes there are frogs,

billowing in the parts of you that don't
            know. There are many times when we don't.

we say we know we are at odds
            with things that swim, things that fly.
                        Years later, I thought *you do love women*

not because they are women,
            but you love them when their legs
                        move through the water, when they give

you tadpoles, when the sand beneath them moves
            in clouds of wet dust, when turtles slink
                        respectfully near their slick bodies

and I thought, there is nothing,
            nothing like my momma's hands in the backyard
                        showing me how to dig up clay in pearls like we were rich men.

Do I want her dress on me or on the floor?

Somewhere between Avenida, Portugal and purgatory the sun goes running through buildings taking blue with it, how can we ever talk about blue, how can we ever see cement sacrificial and prostrate next to medians gone green, a grid, borders of carts of sopaipillas sold like tickets to the hourly motel Santa Victoria, how can we ever smell the moment luck changes, now it is just called *getting shit on by a pigeon*, in Bella Vista the sky is _____, the sky is us, the sky is lapis lazuli, more precious for having known Afghanistan & Chile. How can we ever dance at multilevel discotheques fire spitting around each other like angry butts out a car window, telling each other false memoirs, lonesome highway rippling between us in heat waves, pickup sticks in our bible belts. How can we ever know brutal heaven.

After Time Has Rumpled the Sheets of Your Mouth

When I am winter, shutting privately down in my own deep snow,
allow me solace in stinking rooms of books, typewriters cold and dressed
for procession. Great old ghosts grousing on stairwells, tumblers in cuff

and not a kind word on paper lips. Allow me mercy in a frozen thicket,
where parties will have come to call and left to hibernate, leaving
behind them small tracks of silent pears, tepid angels in wakeful repose.

Allow me comforts—sliced membrillo, an avocado churned by spoon,
port in crystal tasting of exquisite girls, black cherries, a photograph
smoldering magenta. Leave me hopeful for another. Waiter! *Another.*

KIT YAN (U.S.A., B. 1984)

Man Boobs

Draft One
Bottom lip to unswept pavement, she stares at me
unfortunate monster.
Stranger to Stranger,
this is our exchange.

I am not a public installation,
my hands are in errand,
my eyes still sleepy.
Pre-noon a blur, uninterrupted and slow.

The splattered disgust on her tongue I ignore, but
here I am,
weaker than I thought,
replaying, revisiting, rewriting—

~~So you've never seen a man with boobs?~~
No.
~~So you've never seen a transman?~~
No.
~~So you've never seen a trans person?~~
No.
~~So you've never seen this body?~~

Most days I settle for,

What the fuck are you looking at?
You got a problem?
What?

The tender comfort of deep night,
Replaced by a slow peel of daylight,
From head to soul,
I cover.

My torn skin aches to scorch under the common sun,
To walk—
Down this piss soaked stoop's—
Flaming red carpet.

Draft 2
Even in my dreams I am queer!
Last night,
David Hasselhoff was my top surgeon,
Only doing half the job,
Sculpting my breasts into two dorsal fins,
Leaving me to wonder,
Is God telling me that I'm trans, but I'm a dolphin?

If so, I'mna need a couple of fins bigger than A cups to swim,
So say a prayer for me,
'Cause even in my dreams I keep getting fucked, and not even in a good way!

On Monday, I went to a clothing optional beach,
I was scared, but I still stripped,
Longing to feel the sun against my skin,
Washing over tan lines, college binding scars that freckled and faded, and
Life-long stretch marks I edit my chapters on.
I thought it's now or never.

We picked the side populated by gay men,
They only briefly stared, before flagging us as lesbians,
And then it was over.

Until we started walking towards the showers.
He makes loud remarks and bayonets laughter
Into me with his buddies talking about my breasts,
Like the last time, I am frozen,
A group of grown men, I imagine putting the pieces together,
Before I am left picking up the pieces,
Another recurring nightmare.

On these days, I want to replace David Hasselhoff with
Daniel Dae Kim,
And ask him to finish the job
With anything that can be sharpened,
Stone, spear, broken shell, make me flat!

I love my chest,
The soft curves of pleasure
Are mine.
This binding is a patchwork of armour,
A secret uniform for the brave,
An accessory made for beauty and pride,

something simple, to take the trash out shirtless when it's hot,
Boxers on my hip bones,
Tan nude alone with a book and my cock out,
My body pressed against sand in an imprint that
Travels further than this white washed shoreline.

Not Girls Like You

I did love her,
To those who say she died barely breathing,
Pinched under my chest,
You will never know this woman
Who had to leave because I could no longer
Look at her,

It was the mirror I hated,
The look of a girl so scared that she became stone,
Couldn't chip if I wanted to,
When I started to love another,
Things got ugly,
I didn't want to see myself go,
Where was the one who used to run into the rain, savoring the summer sky on her tongue,
Open-mouthed to take the long way home,

I was alone, even when I was with her,
All you could see was a blonde girl and a shadow,
A half-step behind her like the second blade on a dull razor,
Scraping away at what was already bloody,
I gave her my body,
Unbound myself in the darkness,
The weight of my flesh forcing me to sink deeper into the dorm room sheets,
Falling into a lost love without direction,
I can't believe I let her fuck me,
I mean her,
Let her fuck her,

The night she began to leave me,
Dinner was silenced,
The waiter carrying our conversation,
From dish to dish,
We almost finished our break up a week later,
My body slumped in Maine,
Her hands loosely dangling the cell phone in Boston,
I drove in as soon as I could,
Didn't want this bad thing to end,
Saw her at the spot we first met, didn't even plan it,

I was dumped on the sidewalk,
Without even a door to hit me,
Heard her say,

*I like girls—but not— not girls like you, So Kit don't ask me why I chased, locked you in place through
skin, and sex, and the words that never meant to leave my lips, I'm sorry I started this, And I like girls, but
I like girls, So pack your bags ok? Butches can take care of themselves right?*

Open your own doors,
Carry yourselves home?
Tuck yourself into bed,
Make a house out of cigarettes and forties.
She ran *into* the rain that night,
Asked the sky to make a man out of her,

I never wrote about her after that,
Either of her,
They were dead to me while I
Found myself stubbled and hard,

But after all these years, I still wear her,
Bundle those collared shirts in my arms, and
Breathe in the burden she carried into the night,
Wrap my chest tight and ask her to come back if she'll forgive me,
I fear that she'll never forgive me,
The mirror will crack if I ask her to
Come home.

Someday Soon

He gave me drink,
Diamond clear water taking my thirst,
When I had given up hope of tasting sweetness again in the desert,
The road was rough, curves sharp,
Making my spirit an ugly clay mass,
That only beats when broken, and

I've been broken,
Chipping on all sides even when there is fire,
But the cool of his hands running on my back,
Smoothing over my chest,
Holding me like the wings of a hundred thousand humming birds,
Gently singing while I float away in him,
Towards the horizon.

My heart was a chest at the bottom of the ocean,
Its flesh encased in time,
Piling debris on for protection,
Even my key hole was lost.

But he washed me,
And we never got clean,
But we did shine like the underbelly of a seashell,
Kissed by sunlight for the first time,
As he warmed me,
Turned my insides back to butterflies,
Dancing in a festival of light spilling over that horizon,

His lips breathed back a slow stream of hope,
Twisting through the blood and bone,
Commanding that I move,
So my feet stumbled, and my muscles ached,
With the pain of underuse,

He brought me to an edge I'd been to,
But never peered over,
So when the sweet air touched my lips,
My eyes opened to the water crashing into my stiff body,
As I begged the breeze to push me deeper,

So if I get lost in you, sweet boy,
Guide me with the grip of that gentle voice,
That brought me to your lips,
Light show through Portland street lamps
We found for cover when we stayed behind,

And I'll make you a door frame while we travel, and
Our hands can build the walls with these poems for shelter,
One torn out notebook sheet at a time,
Words for artwork,
Sonnets for ceiling, and
Haikus, rengas, free verse for foundation,

So when we find each other again,
We can stand in the middle—
Holding each other as the sunlight peeks through,

Tellin' a story of two boys,
Who knew each other before they even met,
All vagabond fingertips and fishnet eyelids sayin'

Hey— let's take this house and put it on a cloud,
Somewhere between Kansas and Nebraska, and
Slingshot stanzas through the windows, so
When the dotted line on our tour maps collide,
We can write this poem one more time,
Pray that we can press rewind,
Knowin' that today is just a someday soon, and
Maybe someday I'll love you.
Maybe someday I'll love you.

Just Like Silicone Dicks on My Lips?

A text message:
I watched the sunrise on the way to Berkeley this morning,
My head resting on a drum case I imagined to be your chest.

I underestimated his cock,
Thought sex was just sex just like the opposite sex,
Just like silicon dicks on my lips,
But when he slid inside me,
I didn't forget I was once a woman,

Like I thought I would,
We smelled of free, post-show refreshments from a double bill,
I fucked him hard, just to see how much I could handle,

But in and out the moments,
My thoughts turned political,
Retraced identity politics during orgasms,
Never been with a man before,
So I tell him the truth—

I've never been with a man before
Never been with a man before,
Never been with a man before,
Never been with a man before.

Never sat on a dick on carpeted floors in a stranger's apartment,

Shit, this feels good,
Our bodies rocking together,
This feels good,
My hands on his muscular thighs,
This feels good,
The coarse chest hairs under my sweaty palms,

I put my arms around him and breathed in the weight of him,
A scent foreign, yet satisfying, like a secret I caught in the wind,
Pocketing the inhale before my memory released it,
But that moment, just like the dust and debris clinging to my hair in summer breeze,
I couldn't forget it.

How it felt to be wet with desire,
And fuck— straight up, fuck,
Trying to forget we just met,
Trying to forget this hole was mine,
Trying to forget his male privilege.

When I asked him what he wanted, he said,
sit on me
And I sat, and it hurt, and in that time between,
ow and ooh
The room stopped spinning,
And I got off him,
Almost falling over in hot queer dirty sex fatigue, and
I took his curls in my hands,
And had him suck my cock, until I came.

DANIEL ZAMPANELLI (CANADA, B. 1985)

Untitled
"I'm not gay, I'm from the future."—Christopher Nealon, *Plummet*
"Homos shoot photos of footlong schlongs."—Christian Bok, *EUNOIA*

/// You keep saying / you're from the future
but your BMW is a 95. // Used to
fuck in bathroom stalls
and now you do / it in your
600 square foot condo
before 9 pm because / the strata has been
concerned about
noise levels / and heteronormatizing. // The token
gay guy on
Big Brother,
never wins. // I'm sorry Ma'am your
Husband
has been / queer / eyed. // Have I
met you before / Dumbledore.

/// I've got
2 tickets to a 60 year
old heterosexual
woman telling
the story of
homosexual
cowboy love
in the 60's / gay sex isn't like that / no, not like that / there's
more spit than that / I tolerate the / popcorn // Capitalism is getting a stress
test, aliens hate homosexuality. / Buy it out
of your system. // Another Tom / Cruise Joke.

/// V neck your / chest for more
bust, the hair is / mascara and / masculinity is / on sale, it comes
with disappointment. // He was
clean as a whistle
or a rubber
orifice
sterilized // Help, // I fell
into the Gap // I'm sorry, I can't help you, I'm straight acting. // When
it came
to white pants, you
couldn't find
the right white pants,
they were eggshell, or off-white, or light grey,
and you couldn't find
the right white pants to match
your sailor outfit,
it was a
fashion / catastrophe / exclamation point // apostrophe / Rule
#46, if it exists

there is a porn
for it. / Torrent download / I borrowed it // A sex
toy story 5,
how will Woody get
out of this
sticky situation. Don't cock block, cock dock. / Every porn
is seeking
his father's validation.

/// I paid
for this
at the other
store. // I got this at
Boys Co, it
cost an
arm and a leg, but
thankfully it's
missing a sleeve // Smoothies
and a gym
pass,
and a tank top / tank top / tank top / tank top / tank top / and I only top. // Everyone's
wearing such amazing shirts, / where
did they find invisible
clothing? Sweat from drugs, sweat the drugs, hugs not drugs // Loathing loafers // I
bought
individuality
at the
shop on main, it
was a cute pack
of mints that
referenced
my homosexuality / in an ironic / tone. // Your
paycheque
is -315.24
after in-store
purchases.

/// Shots / Shots / Shots / Shots / Shots / Shots / Shots // My boyfriend's
underwear are
barely holding
themselves
together. Therapy
can't fix them,
they're too
far gone. Debrief me again? // Seriously? / fer seriously. // Bank with
TD? They
care. You can
tell by the
two stereotyped
gay males
on the side of
the bus, sitting
in a green chair, / smiling
like they
are considered
an equal during
pride week. // Did you / get a float in the / parade?

No, I'll just go
on the one for
Starbucks. It's half and half.

U.S.A.

1) Joel Allegretti, b. 1955

Joel Allegretti is the author of four collections, most recently, *Europa/Nippon/New York: Poems/Not-Poems* (Poets Wear Prada, 2012). His second book, *Father Silicon* (The Poet's Press), was selected by *The Kansas City Star* as one of 100 Noteworthy Books of 2006. His poetry has appeared in many national journals, including Smartish Pace, The New York Quarterly, Fulcrum and PANK. "The River Styx...." was first published in *MARGIE /The American Journal of Poetry*, Volume 6, 2007; "Bin Bin was first published in *The Más Tequila Review*, Issue #3, Summer 2011.

2) Chris August, b. 1976

Chris August is a special educator, writer and activist from Baltimore, Maryland. Since 2002, he has hosted Baltimore's only poetry slam series and represented Baltimore, Philadelphia and Washington, DC, at the National Poetry Slam and the Individual World Poetry Slam. In 2011, he was named the number one performance poet in the country at the Individual World Poetry Slam, held in Cleveland, Ohio. Since then, he has competed in Paris, France, representing the United States at the Poetry World Cup, ranking second in the world. His latest book, *A Life Called Special*, is a collection of poems dedicated to his time working at a private special needs high school in Baltimore. He currently performs and runs workshops at schools throughout Maryland as a teaching artist with Young Audiences of Maryland, a non-profit organization dedicated to arts education.

3) Samiya Bashir, b. 1970

Samiya Bashir's second book of poems, *Gospel*, was a finalist for both the Hurston/Wright Legacy Award and, along with her first collection, *Where the Apple Falls*, the Lambda Literary Award. Her poetry most recently appeared in *Poet Lore*, *Michigan Quarterly Review*, *Crab Orchard Review*, *Cura*, *The Rumpus*, and *Encyclopedia Vol. 2 F-K*, and has been honored of late by two Hopwood Awards from the University of Michigan and the Aquarius Press Legacy Award. An Ann Arbor, Michigan, native and recent NEA Writer-in-Residence at the Virginia Center for Creative Arts, Samiya teaches creative writing at Reed College. "Planck's Law" was originally published in *Crab Orchard Review, Vol. 17, No. 2, 2012*.

4) Ahimsa Timoteo Bodhran, b. 1974

Ahimsa Timoteo Bodhrán is the author of *Antes y después del Bronx: Lenapehoking* (New American Press) and editor of an international queer Indigenous issue of *Yellow Medicine Review: A Journal of Indigenous Literature, Art, and Thought*. His work appears in over a hundred fifty publications in Africa, the Américas, Asia, Australia, Europe, and the Pacific. Having completed a second poetry manuscript, *South Bronx Breathing Lessons*, Bodhrán is now finishing *Yerbabuena/ Mala yerba*, *All My Roots Need Rain: mixed-blood poetry & prose* and *Heart of the Nation: Indigenous Womanisms, Queer People of Color, and Native Sovereignties*.

5) Jericho Brown, b. 1976

Jericho Brown worked as the speechwriter for the Mayor of New Orleans before receiving his PhD in Creative Writing and Literature from the University of Houston. He also holds an MFA from the University of New Orleans and a BA from Dillard University. The recipient of the Whiting Writers Award and fellowships from the National Endowment for the Arts, the Radcliffe Institute at Harvard University, the Bread Loaf Writers' Conference, and the Krakow Poetry Seminar in Poland, Brown is an Assistant Professor at Emory University. His poems have appeared in journals and anthologies including *The American Poetry Review*, *The Believer*, *jubilat*, *Oxford American*, *Ploughshares*, *A Public Space*, *Tin House*, and *100 Best African American Poems*. His first book, *PLEASE* (New Issues), won the American Book Award.

6) J.T. Bullock, b. 1980

JT Bullock is poet, writer, and aspiring teller of stories who resides outside the District line (in Silver Spring, Maryland). His work has been published in several academic journals. He has competed in three National Poetry Slam competitions, most notably the 2006 Nationals in Austin where he ranked 19th in the nation. Currently, he is working on an autobiographical one-man show, which debuted as a work in progress at the Woolly Mammoth Theater through Artist Bloc.

7) Regie Cabico, b. 1970

Regie Cabico is one of the country's leading innovators and pioneers of the poetry slam having won 3 top prizes in the 1993, 1994 & 1997 National Poetry Slams and winning The Nuyorican Poets Cafe Grand Slam. *Bust Magazine* ranked him in the 100 Men We Love & *The Kenyon Review* called him the Lady Gaga of Poetry. He received 3 NY Innovative Theater Award nominations and won a 2006 Best Performance Art Production award for his work on *Too Much Light Makes The Baby Go Blind*. Other theater credits include the Hip Hop Theater Festival, The Humana Theater Festival & Dixon Place. He has appeared on two seasons of HBO's Def Poetry Jam and NPR's Snap Judgment. He is a former NYU Artist in Residence for Asian Pacific American Studies. He performs throughout the UK and North America & resides in Washington, DC.

8) James Caroline, b. ?

James Caroline has performed on three continents, competed in three National Poetry Slams, and represented the Cantab Lounge in the first ever Individual World Poetry Slam. He has been voted Best Local Author in a Boston Phoenix poll and won multiple Cambridge Poetry Awards for *Best Slam Poet, Male* and *Best Erotic Performance Poet*.

9) Ching-In Chen, b. 1978

Ching-In Chen is author of *The Heart's Traffic* (Arktoi Books/Red Hen Press) and co-editor of *The Revolution Starts at Home: Confronting Intimate Violence Within Activist Communities* (South End Press). They are a Kundiman, Lambda and Norman Mailer Poetry Fellow and a member of the Voices of Our Nations Arts Foundation and Macondo writing communities. A community organizer, they have worked in the Asian American communities of San Francisco, Oakland, Riverside and Boston. In Milwaukee, they are *Cream City Review's* editor-in-chief and involved in their union and the radical marching band, Milwaukee Molotov Marchers. They were born in 1978. www.chinginchen.com "Mutant" was first published at www.herkind.org; "Queer Poetry" was first published at http://www.metremaids.com/; "The True Tale of Xiaomei" was first published in *The Heart's Traffic*.

10) Franny Choi, b. 1989

Franny Choi has been a finalist at the National Poetry Slam, the Individual World Poetry Slam, and the Women of the World Poetry Slam. A Pushcart Prize nominee, her literary work has appeared in *Fringe, The Java Monkey Speaks Anthology, Issues*, and others. Her play *Mask Dances* was staged for the 2011 Writing is Live Festival. She co-coordinates ProvSlam Youth, a program for young writers in Providence, Rhode Island.

11) Elizabeth J. Colen, b. 1976

Elizabeth J. Colen is the author of Lambda Literary Award nominated prose poetry collection *Money for Sunsets* (Steel Toe Books, 2010), flash fiction collection *Dear Mother Monster, Dear Daughter Mistake* (Rose Metal Press, 2011), and poetry collection *Waiting Up for the End of the World: Conspiracies* (Jaded Ibis Press, 2012). Widely published, deeply flawed, four-time Pushcart Prize nominee, Elizabeth lives in Seattle. "January Window" was previously published in *Money for Sunsets*; "Erin Brokovich" is forthcoming in *What Weaponry*.

12) Jona Colson, b. 1979

Jona Colson's poems have appeared or are forthcoming in *Prairie Schooner, Subtropics*, and *Crab Orchard Review*. He teaches at American University and Montgomery College.

13) Jeffrey Conway, b. 1964

Jeffery Conway is the author of *The Album That Changed My Life* (Cold Calm Press, 2006), and two collaborations with David Trinidad and Lynn Crosbie, *Phoebe 2002: An Essay In Verse* (Turtle Point Press, 2003), and *Chain Chain Chain* (Ignition Press, 2000). His work is included in the anthology *Saints of Hysteria: A Half Century of Collaborative American Poetry* (Soft Skull Press, 2007). He is currently at work on "Descent of the Dolls," a Dante-esque collaborative epic about the 1967 film *Valley of the Dolls*, with poets Gillian McCain and David Trinidad. Poems from his newest manuscript "Showgirls: The Movie in Sestinas" appear in *Court Green, Vanitas, Clementine, Columbia Poetry Review*, and *Marco Polo*.

14) Guillermo Filice Castro, b. 1962

Born in Buenos Aires, Argentina, Guillermo Filice Castro is the author of two chapbooks, *Cry Me a Lorca* (Seven Kitchens Press, 2010) and *Toy Storm* (Big Fat Press, 1997). His work has appeared in *Assaracus, Barrow Street, Bellevue Literary Review, Brooklyn Rail, Court Green, Fogged Clarity, LaFovea.org, Quarterly West*, among others, as well as the anthologies *Divining Diva, My Diva, This Full Green Hour, Saints of Hysteria, This New Breed*, and more. His translations of Olga Orozco, in collaboration with Ron Drummond, are featured in *Guernica, Terra Incognita, U.S. Latino Review*, and *Visions*. Castro was a finalist for the Andrés Montoya Prize in 2012. "Argentine Music" was originally published in *Barrow Street*, 1999 ; "Ode to Lindsay Wagner as 'The Bionic Woman'" was originally published in *Court Green*, 2010 ; "You Wake Up" was originally published in *Otoliths*, 2010.

15) Theresa Davis, b. 1965

Theresa Davis is shiny. She uses her tongue for bounty and says shit you wish you did. She is the 2012 Mc Ever Chair for Poetry at Georgia Tech University and the Emerging Artist Grant recipient. In 2011, she held the title Women of the World Slam Champion and received a proclamation from the City of Atlanta making May 22nd Theresa Davis Day. "Because She Thinks She is Going to Hell" was first published in *After This We Go Dark* by Sibling Rivalry Press.

16) Meg Day, b. 1984

Meg Day is a three-time Pushcart-nominated poet, nationally awarded spoken word artist, & veteran arts educator who is currently a PhD fellow in Poetry & Disability Poetics at the University of Utah. Meg hails from San Diego by way of Oakland, where she taught young poets to hold their own at the mic with Youth Speaks & as a WritersCorps Teaching Artist in San Francisco. A 2010 Lambda Fellow, 2011 Hedgebrook Fellow, & 2012 Squaw Valley Fellow, Meg completed her MFA at Mills College & publishes the femme ally zine, *ON OUR KNEES*, out of Salt Lake City. A 2012 AWP Intro Award Winner & nominee for the Best New Poets of 2012, Meg's most recent work can be found in *Drunken Boat* & forthcoming from *Artful Dodge, This Assignment is So Gay: Poems from LGBTQ Teachers, Troubling the Line: An Anthology of Trans & Genderqueer Poetry & Poetics*, & in the chapbook, *When All You Have is a Hammer*, planned for publication in 2013 by Gertrude Press. www.megday.com

17) Ron Drummond, b. 1955

Ron Drummond, born in Amityville, New York, is the author of *Why I Kick At Night* (Portlandia Press, 2004). He has received writing fellowships from Ragdale Foundation, Virginia Center for the Creative Arts and Blue Mountain Center, and is a member of the Macondo Writers' Workshop. His poetry and translations have appeared in many literary journals and anthologies. "Why I Kick at Night" was previously published in 2004 by The Portlandia Group as a part of the collection *Why I Kick at Night*.

18) Julie Enszer, b. 1970

Julie R. Enszer is the author of *Handmade Love* (A Midsummer Night's Press, 2010) and *Sisterhood*, a chapbook (Seven Kitchens Press, 2010). She is the editor of *Milk and Honey: A Celebration of Jewish Lesbian Poetry* (A Midsummer Night's Press, 2011), which was a finalist for the Lambda Literary Award for Lesbian Poetry. Her second poetry collection, *Sisterhood*, is forthcoming in 2013 from Sibling Rivalry Press. She has her MFA from the University of Maryland and is a PhD candidate in Women's Studies at the University of Maryland. She is the co-editor of *Sinister Wisdom*, a journal of lesbian art and culture, and a regular book reviewer for the *Lambda Book Report* and *Calyx*. "In My Fantasy Single Life" and "Handmade Love" are From *Handmade Love* (New York: A Midsummer Night's Press, 2010.); "For Judith…" was first published in *Feminist Studies*.

19) Danielle Evennou, b. 1985

Danielle Evennou was banned from glitter in Girl Scouts and Sunday School. With her partner in poetic crimes, Regie Cabico, Evennou co-hosts Sparkle: a queer driven reading series for all at Busboys and Poets (5th & K) in the District of Columbia. She is the recipient of a Young Artist Grant, as well as the Larry Neal Writers' Award from the D.C. Commission on the Arts and Humanities. Her poems have appeared in literary journals, *Beltway Poetry Quarterly*, *Blue Collar Review*, *Xenith* and *Objet d'Art*, as well as the *Washington Post Express* and *DCist*.

20) Camongnhe Felix, b. 1992

A New York City-grown cupcake enthusiast and college sophomore with neurotic tendencies, Camonghne was featured on HBO's Brave New Voices as a member of the Urban Word 2010 team that became the 2010 National Brave New Voices Champions. She is a two-time New York Knicks Poetry Slam Finalist and the 1st Runner-Up of the 2010 NYC Youth Poet Laureate Program. In November of 2011, she was profiled in The Forward as a Young Jewish Philanthropic Hero. The fall of 2012 will feature her as a cast member of the upcoming HBO documentary Damn Wonderful, directed by Nelsan Ellis of True Blood. You can find her work in various publications, including *Pank Magazine*, *Kill Author Magazine* and *Specter Magazine*. She writes about the small things that happen when we've stopped looking.

21) Brittany Fonte, b. 1977

Brittany Fonte, co-editor, is the author of the prose poetry collection *Buddha in My Belly* (Hopewell Publications) and the Young Adult novel, *Fighting Gravity* (JMS Books, LLC.). She holds an MFA in Creative Writing and teaches writing at the university level. She co-hosts a monthly queer spoken word and poetry night in Annapolis, Md., called "The Walt and Gerty Show." Her work, both prose poetry and fiction, can be found in numerous literary journals.

22) Karen Garrabrant, b. 1970

Karen G is a slam master for the Art Amok Atl Slam Team, the team of odd winnings and champions, & she does bookings for poets in the SE. Host for 11 years of the alterna- voices, no-mic, Cliterati, she's rather famous for hugs & she's published in *Aim for the Head*, a zombie anthology with Write Bloody Press and Women Warriors; she's one of 35 leaders in the spoken word revolution. She's also received the 2011 Capturing Fire lifetime achievement award. The audio version of "West Louisiana into East Texas" was recorded in Pedestal Magazine, Issue 60, 2010.

23) John Giorno, b. 1936

John Giorno was born in New York and graduated from Columbia University in 1958. Four years later, he met Andy Warhol, who became an important influence for Giorno's developments on poetry, performance and recordings. He was the "star" of Warhol's film *Sleep*. He has collaborated with William Burroughs, John Ashbery, Ted Berrigan, Patti Smith, Laurie Anderson, Philip Glass, Robert Rauschenberg and Robert Mapplethorpe. He is the author of ten books, including *You Got to Burn to Shine, Cancer in my Left Ball, Grasping at Emptiness, Suicide Sutra*, and has produced 59 LPs, CDs, tapes cassettes, videopaks and DVDs for Giorno Poetry Systems. He founded the AIDS Treatment Project and has an important force in the development of Tibetan Buddhism in the West.

24) Brent Goodman, b. 1971

Brent Goodman was born in Milwaukee. He is the author of *Far From Sudden* (2012) and *The Brother Swimming Beneath Me* (2009) from Black Lawrence Press. His poems have appeared in *Pleiades, Diode, Sou'wester, Poetry, Pank, Court Green*, and elsewhere. Brent lives and works in Rhinelander, Wisconsin, with his partner and 3 cats. "Evaporation" was first published in *Linebreak*, 2008; "Closet High School Girlfriend" was first published in *Devil's Lake*, 2011.

25) Daphne Gottlieb, b. 1968

Daphne Gottlieb is the editor of *Dear Dawn: Aileen Wuornos in her Own Words* (correspondences from the "first female serial killer"). She is also the author of five books of poetry (most recently *15 Ways to Stay Alive*), a graphic novel (with illustrator Diane DiMassa), and editor of two multigenre anthologies: *Fucking Daphne: Mostly True Stories and Fictions*, and *Homewrecker: An Adultery Reader.*

26) Benjamin Grossberg, b. 1971

Benjamin S. Grossberg is an associate professor of English at The University of Hartford, where he teaches creative writing. His books are *Sweet Core Orchard* (University of Tampa, 2009), winner of the 2008 Tampa Review Prize and a Lambda Literary Award, and *Underwater Lengths in a Single Breath* (Ashland Poetry Press, 2007). His third collection, *Space Traveler*, is forthcoming from The University of Tampa Press in 2013. His poems have appeared in many journals, including in *New England Review*, *Southwest Review*, *Paris Review*, and *North American Review*, and in both the *Best American Poetry* and *Pushcart Prize* anthologies. "A Middle Class Consideration of Lust" was first published in *Underwater Lengths in a Single Breath* (Ashland Poetry Press, 2007); "Beetle Orgy" was first published in *Sweet Core Orchard* (University of Tampa Press, 2009); "Space Traveler" is forthcoming in *Space Traveler* (University of Tampa Press, 2013).

27) Carol Guess, b. 1968

Carol Guess is the author of ten books of poetry and prose, including *Switch*, *Tinderbox Lawn*, and *Doll Studies: Forensics*. She is Professor of English at Western Washington University, where she teaches Queer Studies and Creative Writing. "You sell everything you own…" was first published in Hayden's Ferry Review 2006-2007 and *Tinderbox Lawn*, 2008. "We watched a girl through her open window…" was first published in Bat City Review 2006 and *Tinderbox Lawn*, 2008. "In Nebraska" was first published in *Mid-American Review* and *Tinderbox Lawn*, 2008. "Revival of Rosemailing" was first published in *Sou'wester*, 2009 and *Darling Endangered*, 2011.

28) Adele Hampton, b. 1988

Adele Hampton is a storyteller, poet and visual journalist with roots planted in DC by way of upstate New York. She has performed at Busboys & Poets, Capturing Fire Spoken Word Festival and Mother Tongue. She is a third place finisher at the Beltway Poetry Slam Series and was one of four poets chosen to represent Washington, DC, in the Battle of the Beltway slam series.

29) Tara Hardy, b. ?

Tara Hardy is the working class queer femme poet who founded Bent, a writing institute for LGBTIQ people in Seattle, WA. She is the author of *Bring Down the Chandeliers*, published by Write Bloody Press in 2011, and is the current Writer-In-Residence at Richard Hugo House in Seattle. Tara is the 2011 recipient of the Washington Poets Association Burning Word Award, and was elected Seattle Poet Populist in 2002. Tara has performed on seven final stages during various National Poetry Slam competitions, and has been the Seattle Grand Slam Champion three times. Currently, Tara tours the U.S. as a poet, performer, keynote speaker, and teaching artist. A daughter of the United Auto Workers, and activist in anti-violence movements, Tara views art as a tool for social change. She holds an M.F.A. from Vermont College, and her work has appeared in numerous journals, two Seal Press anthologies and on various spoken word CDs. To contact Tara or arrange for a performance, email wordyfemme@hotmail.com or visit her webpage at www.tarahardy.net.

30) Trebor Healy, b. 1962

Healey was recipient of the 2004 Ferro-Grumley and Violet Quill awards for his first novel, *Through It Came Bright Colors* (Harrington Park Press). Trebor Healey is also the author of the novels, *A Horse Named Sorrow* (University of Wisconsin Press) and *Faun* (Lethe Press), released this fall; a collection of poems, *Sweet Son of Pan*, (Suspect Thoughts, 2006); and a short story collection, *A Perfect Scar & Other Stories* (Harrington Park Press, 2007). He co-edited (with Marci Blackman) *Beyond Definition: New Writing from Gay and Lesbian San Francisco* (Manic D Press, 1994) and co-edited (with Amie M. Evans*) Queer & Catholic* (Routledge, 2008). www.treborhealey.com. "These are the places where I am broken" was previously published in *Sweet Son of Pan* (Suspect Thoughts Press, 2006, and re-released by Rebel Satori Press, 2010). "Busboy Sutra" was previously published in *Sweet Son of Pan* (Suspect Thoughts Press, 2006, and re-released by Rebel Satori Press, 2010) and Ashe! (Vol 3, No. 2, 2003). "Shooting Star" was previously published in *Sweet Son of Pan* and *Lodestar Quarterly* (Issue 17, Spring 2006).

31) Scott Hightower, b. 1952

A native of central Texas, Scott is the author of four books and one bi-lingual collection. He teaches and translates. He lives in Manhattan and sojourns in Spain. "Idyll of the Seronegative" was first published in Tin Can Tourist, 2001. "Wilde and Genet Bequeathed" was first published in Self-Evident, 2012.

32) Joanna Hoffman, b. 1982

Joanna Hoffman is a poet from Silver Spring, Maryland, now living in Brooklyn. She has been on four Finals stages at national poetry slam competitions, and placed 4th in the world at the 2012 Women of the World Slam. She is the 2012 Champion of Capturing Fire and a workshop facilitator for queer youth. Her full-length poetry collection will be published by Sibling Rivalry Press in August, 2013. Find her at www.joannahoffman.com.

33) Natalie E. Illum, b. 1977

Natalie E. Illum is a performance poet and storyteller. Her work is included in several anthologies including *Word Warriors: 35 Women of the Spoken Word Revolution* and *Full Moon on K Street*. Her stories have also appeared on NPR's "Snap Judgment." She is a founding member of DC's mothertongue poetry organization, tours around the country and has been representing DC on the National Poetry Slam scene since 2008.

34) Karen Jaime, b. 1975

A New York-based spoken word/performance artist, cultural activist and writer, Karen Jaime served as the host/curator of the Friday Night Slam at the Nuyorican Poets Café from 2002-2005. Karen is currently a doctoral candidate in the Department of Performance Studies at New York University writing on spoken word, slam poetry, and hip-hop theatre.

35) David Keali'I, b. 1982

David Keali'i is a queer poet of mixed Kanaka Maoli descent born and raised in Western Massachusetts/Pocomtuc/ Nipmuc territory. In 2009 he represented Worcester, Massachusetts at the 2009 National Poetry Slam. His work also appears in *'Ōiwi: A Native Hawaiian Journal*, *Mauri Ola: Contemporary Polynesian Poetry in English (Whetu Moana, Volume II)*, *Assaracus*, and *Yellow Medicine Review*. His first collection of poems is forthcoming from Kuleana 'Ōiwi Press.

36) Collin Kelley, b. 1969

Collin Kelley is the author of the novels *Conquering Venus* and *Remain In Light*, which was a 2012 finalist for the Townsend Prize for Fiction. His poetry collections include *Better To Travel*, *Slow To Burn*, *After the Poison* and *Render*, forthcoming from Sibling Rivalry Press in April, 2013. His poetry, essays, interviews and reviews have appeared in journals and magazines around the world. www.collinkelley.com. "Siege" was first published in *In Motion Magazine*, 2004; "Fairytale eating disorder" was first published in *In Posse Review, 2007*.

37) Suty Komsonkeo, b. 1993

Laotian-American Suty Komsonkeo was born in 1993 and raised in Lowell, Massachusetts, but currently resides in Washington, D.C. where he is studying environmental engineering as a sophomore at The George Washington University. He has competed in the 2011 Brave New Voices competition with the Lowell Youth Slam Team and has featured at a variety of venues such as Sulu DC and Busboys and Poets. Alongside poetry, Suty has a strong passion for all styles of dancing and has also won first place at the 2012 RAS Nationals competition with the GW Raas team. When he is not writing poetry or dancing, he is coordinating events as one of two 2012-2013 Cultural Affairs Coordinators for the Philippine Cultural Society and works at the campus' LGBT Resource Center.

38) Bill Kushner, b. 1932

Bill Kushner is the author of 8 books of poetry, among them *Head* (United Artists), *In The Hairy Arms of Whitman* (Melville House), and *Walking After Midnight* (Spuyten Duyvil). His poetry has appeared in *Best American Poetry*, and *Out Of This World* (Crown) and *Up Late* (Codrescu). He has also been the recipient of 2 New York Foundation For The Arts grants.

39) Sam LaRoche, b. 1985

Sam LaRoche is a poet who performs and writes her poetry in many different styles. She performs Spoken Word poetry, but also hip-hop. She was born in CT, but now proudly lives in Brooklyn, NY, as a performance poet.

40) Dan Lau, b. 1985

Dan Lau is a recipient of a Kundiman Fellowship, a William Dickey Fellowship, an Archie D. and Bertha Walker Scholarship from the FAWC in Provincetown, and a Myna Brunton Hughes Award from the San Francisco Browning Society. He holds degrees from Hunter College of The City University of New York and San Francisco State University. His poems have appeared in *Generations*, *Cape Cod Review*, *CRATE*, *Gesture*, *RHINO*, *The Collagist*. He resides in San Francisco.

41) Joseph O. Legaspi, b. 1971

Joseph O. Legaspi is the author of *Imago* (CavanKerry Press) and the forthcoming chapbook, *Subways* (Thrush Press). He lives in Queens, NY, and works at Columbia University. Recent poems appeared in *American Life in Poetry, From the Fishouse, jubilat, World Literature Today, Smartish Pace, The Spoon River Poetry Review, The Normal School*, and the anthologies *Language for a New Century* (W.W. Norton) and *Collective Brightness* (Sibling Rivalry Press). He co-founded *Kundiman (www.kundiman.org)*, a non-profit organization serving Asian American poetry.

42) Eleanor Lerman, b. 1952

Eleanor Lerman is a lifelong New Yorker and unrepentant member of the Woodstock Nation. She is the author of five volumes of poetry, two collections of short stories, and a novel entitled *Janet Planet*, which is based on the life of Carlos Castaneda. She has a National Book Award nomination, was awarded the 2006 Lenore Marshall Prize, and more recently, has received both NEA and Guggenheim fellowships.

43) R. Zamora Linmark, b. 1968

Born in Manila and educated in Honolulu, R. Zamora Linmark is the author of two novels, *Leche* (Coffee House Press) and the best-seller *Rolling The R's* (Kaya Press), which he'd adapted for the stage and had its premiere in Hawaii in 2008. He also published three collections of poetry, *Prime Time Apparitions, The Evolution of a Sigh*, and *Drive-By Vigils*, all from Hanging Loose Press. He divides his writing life between Honolulu and Manila. Both poems in this anthology come from *Evolution of a Sigh*.

44) Paul Lisicky, b. 1959

Paul Lisicky is the author of *LAWNBOY, FAMOUS BUILDER, THE BURNING HOUSE*, and *UNBUILT PROJECTS*. His work has appeared in *THE AWL, FENCE, THE IOWA REVIEW, LO-BALL, PLOUGHSHARES, THE RUMPUS, TIN HOUSE*, and elsewhere. He is the New Voices Professor at Rutgers University and he teaches in the low residency MFA Program at Sierra Nevada College. A memoir, *THE NARROW DOOR*, is forthcoming from Graywolf Press in 2014. "Bulldog" was first published in *COBALT* in 2009; "Monster" was first published in *MEAD* in 2009.

45) Chip Livingston, b. 1967

Chip Livingston is the mixed-blood, two-spirit author of *Crow-Blue, Crow-Black* and *Museum of False Starts*. He grew up in northwest Florida, did grad schools in Colorado and Brooklyn, and wandered like Cain through North America before finding his paradise in Montevideo, Uruguay, where he now lives with his partner and puppy. "Nocturnal Admission" was first published in *Velvet Heat*, 2005; "To Sing a Man's Love to You" was first published in *Talking Stick*, 2009.

46) J. Mase III, b. 1984

J Mase III is a Black/Trans/Queer/Rowdy-as-Hell Poet with a capital [P] who will forever claim Philly. As a performer and teaching poet, J Mase III has rocked venues all across the country from San Diego to Boston, at colleges and radio stations to group homes and youth centers. An organ donor, J Mase is the author of *If I Should Die Under the Knife, Tell My Kidney I Was the Fiercest Poet Around* and creator of the annual performance event *Cupid Ain't @#$%!: An Anti-Valentine's Day Poetry Movement*. A bit of a public intellectual (not in the snotty way, though) J Mase can also be found contributing to publications such as the Vanderbilt African American Lectionary Online to talk about gay teens in the church and the anthology *Nina Arsenault: An Unreasonable Body of Work* to share insight about gender and genitalia. To find out what else J Mase is up to, stalk him online at, www.jmaseiii.com!

47) Lenelle Moïse, b. 1980

Lenelle Moïse (http://www.lenellemoise.com) creates jazz-infused, rhythmic performance texts about the intersection of race, class, gender, sexuality, memory and magic. Moïse is a current Huntington Theatre Company Playwriting Fellow and was a 2010 Hedgebrook Women Playwrights Festival Fellow. Her two-act comedy, *Merit*, won the 2012 Southern Rep Ruby Prize. She also wrote, composed and co-starred in the critically-acclaimed drama, *Expatriate*, which launched Off-Broadway at the Culture Project. Her other plays include *Matermorphosis* (commissioned by Serious Play Theatre Ensemble), *Little Griot* (commissioned by the Drama Studio), *Purple* (commissioned by the Kitchen Theatre Company), *Cornered in the Dark* and *The Many Faces of Nia*. Her solo performances, Womb-Words, Thirsting and Ache What Make (in development), have received standing ovations at theatres and colleges across the United States. Moïse was the fifth Poet Laureate of Northampton, Massachusetts, the 2012 Visiting Performing Artist in African & African Diaspora Studies at UT Austin and the 2011 Artist in Residence in Performance Studies at Northwestern University. She holds an MFA in Playwriting (2004) from Smith College. Her work has been published in several anthologies, including *Word Warriors: 35 Women Leaders in the Spoken Word Revolution*.

48) Gabe Moses, b. 1981

Gabe Moses is a transsexual Jewish man living with Asperger's Syndrome who began writing at a therapist's suggestion. His work encompasses these challenges, as well as his experiences overcoming poverty, abuse and addiction. Gabe has competed on three national poetry slam teams and at one individual world championship, has published poetry in several literary journals and anthologies, teaches writing workshops to youth and adults with developmental disabilities, and is writing a novel.

49) Sean Patrick Mulroy, b. 1983

A writer and an accomplished performer, Sean Patrick Mulroy (aka Sean Patrick Conlon) is a dedicated student of literature and a firm believer in the power of the oral tradition. Born and raised in Southern Virginia, the house where Sean Patrick Mulroy grew up was built in 1801 and was commandeered by the union army during the Civil War to serve as a makeshift hospital. As a boy, Sean loved to peel back the carpets to show where the blood from hasty surgeries on wounded soldiers had stained the wooden floorboards. Now he writes poems.

50) Eileen Myles, b. 1949

Eileen Myles was born in Cambridge, MA and moved to New York (where she still lives) in 1974 to be a poet. Her latest books are *Snowflake/different streets, Inferno (a poet's novel)* and *The Importance of Being Iceland* for which she received a Creative Capital/Warhol art writing grant. She's a 2012 Guggenheim fellow. "I always put my pussy" was first published in *Maxfield Parrish/early & new poems*, Black Sparrow Press: Santa Rosa, 1995; "Transportation" is from *Snowflake*, 2012; "Pencil Poems" from *in different streets*, 2012.

51) Julia Nance, b. 1978

Julia Nance loves you dearly and wants all your dreams to come true. She appreciates cats, sailboats, sunshine and words of all ilk. She lives by the four agreements in Sarasota, Florida, and looks forward to the downfall of civilization (as we know it). Her bra size is 32C....people try to tell her 34B is the "sister size" to that, but that size makes her boobs squish out the sides.

52) Letta Neely, b. 1971

Letta Neely was born in 1971 in Indpls, IN. Although, she didn't meet her first girlfriend until she was nine, she is sure she was a Black Dyke before she was emerged from her mother's birth canal.

53) Lesléa Newman, b. ?

Lesléa Newman is the author of 65 books for readers of all ages including the poetry collections, *OCTOBER MOURNING: A SONG FOR MATTHEW SHEPARD, NOBODY'S MOTHER, STILL LIFE WITH BUDDY, SWEET DARK PLACES* and *THE LITTLE BUTCH BOOK*. Her literary awards include poetry fellowships from the National Endowment for the Arts and the Massachusetts Artists Fellowship Foundation. From 2008 to 2010 she served as the poet laureate of Northampton, Massachusetts. She is a faculty member of Spalding University's brief-residency MFA in Writing program.

54) Dan Nowak, b. 1986

Dan Nowak is founder and editor of Imaginary Friend Press. His book, *Recycle Suburbia*, won the 2007 Quercus Review Poetry Series Award. He also has chapbooks out by RockSaw Press and Accents Publishing.

55) Jeffrey Oaks, b. 1964

Jeff Oaks' newest chapbook, *Mistakes with Strangers*, will be published by Seven Kitchens Press in 2012. He has published poems most recently in *Field, Bloom, Court Green,* and *Poemeleon*. His work was recently selected for inclusion in *Best New Poets 2012*, selected by Matthew Dickman. His essays have appeared in *My Diva: 65 Gay Men on the Women Who Inspire Them* and in *Creative Nonfiction*. He teaches writing at the University of Pittsburgh. "Little What" was published in Bloom, 2010; "Mistakes with Strangers" was published in Bloom 2005.

56) Dwight Okita, b. 1958

Dwight Okita was born in Chicago. His poetry book *Crossing with the Light* was published by Tia Chucha Press. His first novel *The Prospect of My Arrival* was a finalist in the Amazon Breakthrough Novel Awards and came out in 2011. He is presently finishing his second novel *The Hope Store*. In Chicago, Dwight does website design and also works with non-profits. Visit his website at: dwightland.homestead.com. Both poems in this anthology were previously published in *Crossing with the Light*, by Tia Chucha Press.

57) Alix Olson, b. 1975

Alix Olson is an internationally touring spoken word artist. She is the editor of *Word Warriors: 35 Women in the Spoken Word Revolution* (Seal Press), co-author of *Burning Down The House* (Soft Skull), self-published two books of poetry and two full-length spoken word albums, and co-produced the award-winning feature documentary *Left Lane*. Alix's work has been published in dozens of magazines and poetry anthologies, including cover articles in *Ms.* and *Curve Magazines*. Alix has been the recipient of a New York Foundation for the Arts Grant, a Barbara Deming Award, and OutMusic's award for OutActivist of the Year. Howard Zinn calls Alix "an ingenious poet, a brilliant performer, a funny person, a serious thinker. Quite simply, extraordinary." Alix is currently pursuing her PhD in Political Theory and Women and Gender Studies at the University of MA-Amherst.

58) Shailja Patel, b. ?

CNN calls Shailja Patel "the people-centered face of globalization." A Lambda Slam Champion and internationally acclaimed Kenyan poet, playwright and activist, her performances have received standing ovations on four continents. Her first book, *MIGRITUDE*, was an Amazon poetry bestseller and a *Seattle Times* Bestseller. 2011, the African Women's Development Fund named Patel one of Fifty Inspirational African Feminists. In 2012, she represented Kenya at the Cultural Olympiad in London. www.shailja.com @shailjapatel

59) Juliana Hu Pegues, b. 1969

Born in Taiwan and raised in Alaska, Juliana is a bisexual and biracial Asian American poet, playwright, and academic. She is published in numerous anthologies and journals, and is a former member of the women of color theater group, Mama Mosaic, and the Asian Pacific Islander American women and trans performance collective Mango Tribe. She currently lives with her family in Minneapolis, Minnesota, and teaches across the river at Macalester College in St. Paul.

60) Barruch Porras-Hernandez, b. 1981

Baruch Porras-Hernandez is a writer, organizer and actor who regularly performs in the San Francisco Bay Area and throughout North America. His work appears on *Aim for the Head* an anthology of Zombie Poetry –Write Bloody Publishing, *Divining Divas*: 100 poems by Gay Men on their Divas – Lethe Press *DanseMacabre* online literary magazine and has work forth coming in *Tamndem* anthology of the LitSlam Poetry Contest. His manuscript *The Trees, They Hate The Birds The Most*, was a finalist in the Write Bloody Publishing National poetry contest. He has been a resident artist in the Spoken Word Program 2011, at the Banff Center in Alberta, Canada and Air Space (Artists in Residence) part of the Garage All Stars in San Francisco, where he developed his first solo play, *Reasons to Stay on the Ground* which later premiered as part of the National Queer Arts Festival 2010. His other solo plays, *First Gentleman*, and *It Gets Gayer*, have previewed at The Mash Theatre, in 2011 and 2012. He was born in Toluca, Mexico, and grew up in Albany, California. He is currently the Head Organizer and Curator for The San Francisco Queer Open Mic, and lives in the Mission neighborhood of San Francisco.

61) Joseph Ross, b. 1958

Joseph Ross is a poet and teacher in Washington, D.C. He is the author of *Meeting Bone Man* (2012) and his poems have appeared in many journals and anthologies, including *Collective Brightness: LGBTIQ Poets on Spirituality, Religion and Faith* (Sibling Rivalry Press). He has been nominated twice for a Pushcart Prize and he writes regularly at www. JosephRoss.net. "The Silence of Lawrence King…" was first published in *Meeting Bone Man*.

62) Sam Sax, b. 1986

Sam Sax is the first ever Bay Area Unified Grand Slam Champion and Oakland's first two-time queer Grand Slam Champion. He curates 'the new sh!t show', a reading series in San Francisco, and is the poetry curator for The Modern Times Bookstore.

63) Nathan Say, b. 1983

Nathan Say is a Queer Disabled Performance Artist based out of Las Vegas, Nevada. He is a member of the International collective of performing artists with disabilities called the Krip-Hop Nation and has a Spoken Word CD titled "The Other Side of Rain." He was a coach of the 2012 Las Vegas Slam Team and was a competitor on their final stage. Nathan blends the intersections of disability and sexuality together like most people breath. In the process, he gives people an intimate look into one person's perception of disability, a world which is ignored by most, glossed over by some.

64) Jason Schneiderman, 1976, b. ?

Jason Schneiderman is the author of *Sublimation Point*, a Stahlecker Selection from Four Way Books, and *Striking Surface*, winner of the 2009 Richard Snyder Prize from Ashland Poetry Press. Jason moved to New York in 1999 to attend NYU, where found himself on the periphery of the Slam Scene at CBGBs and Bar 13. The second place winner of Urbana's Cute Boy Slam in 2000, and the youngest poet in *The Penguin Book of the Sonnet* in 2001, Jason was part of a generation that bridged community-based and institutionally-based poetics. He directs the Writing Center at the Borough of Manhattan Community College. He lives in Brooklyn with his poet/scholar husband, Michael Broder. "Moscow" was first published *Sublimation Point*, Four Way Books, 2004; "Pornography II" was originally published in *StoryQuarterly*; "Buffy Sestina" was originally published in *McSweeny's*.

65) Maureen Seaton, b. 1947

Maureen Seaton has authored sixteen poetry collections, both solo and collaborative—most recently: *Stealth*, with Samuel Ace (Chax Press, 2011); *Sinéad O'Connor and Her Coat of a Thousand Bluebirds*, with Neil de la Flor (Sentence Book Award, Firewheel Editions, 2011); and *Genetics* (Jackleg Press, 2012). Her "new and selected," *Fibonacci Batman*, is due out in early 2013 from Carnegie Mellon University Press. She has received numerous awards, including two Lambda Literary Awards (for lesbian poetry and lesbian memoir), the Iowa Poetry Prize, an NEA, and the Pushcart. She teaches poetry at the University of Miami, Florida, and writes about poets at "Glit Lit:" http://almostdorothy.wordpress.com/ category/themes/glit-lit/. You can also find her at www.maureenseaton.com "The White Balloon" was first published in *Outlook* and in *Fear of Subways*, The Eighth Mountain Press (1991). "When I was Straight" was published in *Green Mountains Review* (1995) and in *Little Ice Age*, Invisible Cities Press (2001). "Sex Talks with Girls" was first published in *The Gay & Lesbian Review Worldwide* (2006) and in *Genetics*, Jackleg Press (2012). "Sally Field" was firs published in *The Gay and Lesbian Review Worldwide* (2010) and in *Genetics*, Jackleg Press (2012).

66) Glenn Sheldon, b. 1957

Glenn Sheldon is a poet who grew up in Salem, Massachusetts, and has lived the majority of his life in the Midwest. Currently, he is the Honors Professor of Humanities at The University of Toledo. He is author of two full-length poetry collections and some chapbooks. "AIDS Arrives at its First Sweet Door" was first published in 1991 in *Hermosa Review*; "When Someone Cold Comes Home" was first published in 1995 in *Gerbil*.

67) Nathan Siegel, b. 1967

Nathaniel A. Siegel is a GAY poet in the tradition of homoSEXual writers, thinkers, and doers throughOUT time immemorial. His chapbook, *Tony*, is published by Portable Press at Yo-Yo Labs.

68) Danez Smith, b. 1989

Danez Smith is a Cave Canem Fellow from St. Paul, MN, now living in Madison, WI. He likes tattoos, piercings, reading good poems, and every once and a while, he writes one, too. He's been published or is going to be soon, in *PANK*, *Vinyl*, and other places. Danez is a regular contributor to his mother's fridge and awkward poems at family gatherings. He loves you.

69) Pamela Sneed, b?

Pamela Sneed is a New York-based poet and actress. She has been featured in *The New York Times Magazine*, *The New Yorker*, *BOMB magazine*, *Time Out* and on the cover of *New York Magazine*. She is author of *Imagine Being More Afraid of Freedom Than Slavery* published by Henry Holt and KONG and other works by Vintage Entity Press. She has performed at the Public Theater and Lincoln Center and in South Africa. She is a member of the theater faculty at Sarah Lawrence College and is published in the *100 Best African American Poems* by Nikki Giovanni.

70) Adam Stone, b. 1977

Adam Stone has been a member of the National Poetry Slam since 1998. He's represented the cities of Boston, MA; Worcester, MA; Burlington, VT; and the definitely not city of Cape Cod, where he also served as Spoken Word Poet Laureate from 2000-2006. He tends bar for The Cantab Lounge Open Mic and Slam, and runs The Thursday Night Writing But Mostly Drinking Group at The Crooked Treehouse in Cambridge, MA. He dislikes superfluous information.

71) Sonya Renee Taylor, b. 1976

Sonya Renee Taylor is the author of *A Little Truth on Your Shirt* (GirlChild Press, 2010). Her work has been included in several anthologies, including *Growing Up Girl* and *Spoken Word Revolution Redux*. She is a former National Poetry Slam Individual Champion.

72) Richard Tayson, b. 1962

Richard Tayson is the author of the poetry collections *The World Underneath* (2008) and *The Apprentice of Fever* (1998), winner of the Wick Poetry Prize, and the co-author of the memoir *Look Up for Yes* (1998). He has received a New York Foundation for the Arts Fellowship, a Chancellor's Fellowship from the City University of New York, *Prairie Schooner*'s Edward Stanley and Bernice Slote awards, a Pushcart Prize, and 2nd place in the 2011 DC Center for the LGBT Community's Smoking Words Poetry Competition. Tayson is a Part-Time Associate Professor at The New School and received his Ph.D. from the Graduate Center, CUNY in 2012. "Tracks" Reprinted from *Prairie Schooner* by permission of the University of Nebraska Press © 1998 University of Nebraska Press; "I Do" was first published in *Bloom* (Vol. 1, Issue 1, Winter 2004); "Sylvie's House" is section four of "Underneath the Leaves," and is from *The World Underneath* (2008).

73) Geoff Kagan Trenchard, b. 1978

Geoff Kagan Trenchard's poems have been published in numerous journals including *Word Riot*, *The Nervous Breakdown*, *The Worcester Review*, *SOFTBLOW* and *Pemmican*. He has received endowments from the National Performance Network, Dance Theater Workshop, The Zellerbach Family Foundation and the City of Oakland to produce original theatrical work. As a mentor for Urban Word NYC, he taught weekly poetry workshops in the foster care center at Bellevue as well as in Riker's Island with Columbia University's "Youth Voices on Lockdown" program. He is a recipient of a fellowship from the Riggio Writing and Democracy program at the New School and the first ever louderARTS Writing Fellowship. He has performed poetry on HBO's Def Poetry Jam, at universities throughout the United States, and in theaters internationally as a member of the performance poetry troupe The Suicide Kings. He lives in Brooklyn and can be found at kagantrenchard.com. "Another Matter Entirely" first appeared in the print journal *12th Street #2*; "The Hottest Places" was first published in *BreadCrumb Scabs #3*.

74) July Westhale, b. 1986

July Westhale is a fierce femme writer, activist, and radical archivist. She has been awarded fellowships from the Lambda Literary Foundation, Tin House, and the Dairy Hollow Writers Colony. Her poetry has most recently been published in *Generations Literary Journal*, *WordRiot*, *580 Split*, *Quarterly West*, *Muzzle* Magazine, *Barely South*, and *So to Speak: A Feminist Literary Journal*. She was nominated for the Best New Poets of 2012 anthology and for the 2013 AWP Intro Award. www.julywesthale.com

75) Bakar Wilson, b. 1977

Bakar Wilson is a fellow of Cave Canem, the prestigious organization nourishing vital new voices in African-American poetry. He has performed his work at the Bowery Poetry Club, Poetry Project, The Studio Museum of Harlem, and The Asian-American Writer's Workshop among others. His poetry has appeared in The Vanderbilt Review, three Cave Canem anthologies, The Lumberyard, Stretching Panties, and The Brooklyn Rail. A native of Tennessee, Bakar received his B.A. in English from Vanderbilt University and his M.A. in Creative Writing from The City College of New York.

76) Emanuel Xavier, b. 1971

Emanuel Xavier is author of the novel, *Christ Like*, and the poetry collection *If Jesus Were Gay & other poems, Pier Queen* and *Americano: Growing up Gay and Latino in the USA*. He has also edited the anthologies *Bullets & Butterflies: queer spoken word poetry, Mariposas: A Modern Anthology of Queer Latino Poetry*, and *Me No Habla With Acento: Contemporary Latino Poetry*. He appeared twice on HBO's *Russell Simmons presents Def Poetry* and performs regularly throughout the country and around the world as a spoken word artist. His spoken word/music collaboration album, *Legendary*, is available for download on iTunes.

77) Kit Yan, b. 1984

Kit Yan is a slam poet based in New York and originally from Hawaii. He has been on Boston's Lizard Lounge slam team, The Amazon Slam team, and a top 3 Capturing Fire finalist. Kit is a full-time touring artist who performs solo and has also toured with Sister Spit, The Tranny Roadshow, and Good Asian Drivers.

78) Lauren Zuniga, b. 1981

Lauren Zuniga is a nationally touring poet and teaching artist. She is one of the top 5 ranked female poets in the world, the 2012 Activist-In-Residence at the University of Oklahoma and the author of *The Smell of Good Mud* from Write Bloody Publishing. Most days, she identifies as granola/femme/queer/mama. Most days, she lives with her two kids in a house named Clementine. All her poems in this anthology were first published in *The Smell of Good Mud* by Write Bloody in 2012.

CANADA

1) Jo Bee, b. 1992

Jo Bee (AKA Olivia B.) is a queer, genderqueer, feminist, youth poet from Vancouver, BC. She has been on two Vancouver Youth Poetry Slam Teams, and was the Vancouver Poetry Slam Champion in 2011. She writes about everything from religion, libraries, and unconventional courtship rituals to Internet memes and highly-charged political issues like the liberation of potatoes. She is an activist and tap dancer.

2) David Bateman, b. 1956

David is an actor, spoken word poet, and performance artist presently based in Toronto. He has presented his work internationally and across the country over the past twenty years and also teaches drama, literature, and creative writing at a variety of Canadian post-secondary institutions. His fourth collection of poetry, *'tis pity*, was published by Frontenac House (Calgary) in the spring of 2012.

3) Bill Bissett, b. 1939

born on lunaria sum 4oo yeers ago approximatelee in lunarian time was sent 2 erth on first childrns shuttul from th at that time trubuld planet landid in halifax moovd 2 vancouvr at 17 moovd 2 london wher i was part uv luddites alternativ rock band thn toronto wher ium poet in residens at workman arts & recording with pete dako wanting alwayze 2 xploor words n sounds n image in th writing n painting showing paintings at th secret handshake art galleree Toronto "what brings abt th suddn quiet manfred," "speeking uv environmental issews," "sout refuge in an abandond car," and "nites undr th silvr pier" are from the upcoming 2013 novel *hungree throat*.

4) Tanya Davis, b. 1978

Tanya Davis was the 2011/12 Poet Laureate of Halifax, Nova Scotia. Her creative collaboration with Andrea Dorfman, the videopoem *How to be Alone*, has had 5 million views on youtube, garnering Tanya new fans and supporters from the world over. She regularly receives commissions to pen poems and speeches and has worked in this regard for such bodies as the Canada Winter Games, the PEI Advisory Council on the Status of Women, CBC Radio, and the National Film Board of Canada. She also works and performs as a songwriter and musician and has released 3 full length albums, picking up awards and nominations for each one. Her first book of poetry, *At first, lonely*, was published in 2011 by Acorn Press.

5) Allesandra Naccarato, b. 1984

Alessandra Naccarato is a spoken word poet, artist-educator and community organizer. A two-time finalist in the Canadian Festival of Spoken Word and the Canadian Individual Poetry Slam, she represented Toronto in the 2012 Women of the World Poetry Slam, and coached the Toronto Poetry Slam Team to a national bronze medal in 2012. She has studied and performed across Canada and the United States, in Ghana, Argentina, Brazil, and Italy, worked locally and internationally in gender advocacy and youth empowerment through the arts. The former Chair of Spoken Word Canada and Montreal Slam Master, she currently resides in Toronto with an all black cat. Like many Italians, her lucky number is thirteen.

6) Billeh Nickerson, b. 1972

Billeh Nickerson was born in Halifax, Nova Scotia, on Valentine's Day. He is the author of four books: the Publishing-Triangle-Award-nominated *The Asthmatic Glassblower*; *Let Me Kiss it Better: Elixirs for the Not So Straight and Narrow*; *McPoems*; and *Impact: The Titanic Poems*. He is also co-editor of *Seminal: The Anthology of Canada's Gay Male Poets*. He lives in Vancouver, BC, where he chairs the Creative Writing Department at Kwantlen Polytechnic University.

7) Andre Prefontaine, b. 1990

Andre is a slam poet based out of Calgary, Alberta Canada. At twenty-two, he's been crowned the Canadian Underground Slam Champion of 2012, been a finalist on the Canadian National slam stage 2012, three time team member, two time team captain for Calgary and former Haiku Death Match champion. He's got an unusual perspective on life and the world, which manifests upon the stage.

8) Lisa Slater, b. 1983

Lisa Slater is a queer spoken word artist living in Vancouver, BC, Canada. Feminist, survivor, and community builder, Slater's poems explore what it means to reclaim our bodies and identities from what broke us open and how we relearn love, sex, friendship and family in the process. A finalist at the 2012 Individual World Poetry Slam and a 2011 Vancouver Poetry Slam team member, Slater's work has been published in *The Moose & Pussy* and *Poetry is Dead*.

9) Anna Swanson, b. 1974

Anna Swanson has paid the rent by planning festivals, selling books, serving drinks, making maps, walking on stilts, writing press releases, and watching for forest fires. She studied Creative Writing and Women's Studies at the University of Victoria and the Memorial University of Newfoundland. Her first book of poetry, *The Nights Also*, won a Lambda Literary Award and the Gerald Lampert Award for best Canadian debut poetry collection. She currently lives in Vancouver, BC, and works as a librarian. All three poems were first published in *The Nights Also* (Tightrope Books, 2010).

10) Sheri-D Wilson, b. ?

@SheriDWilson has 8 collections of poetry, her most recent; *Goddess Gone Fishing for a Map of the Universe (1st book of poetry with interactive QR Codes)* launched in 2012. Her collection *Re:Zoom*, won the 2006 Stephan G. Stephansson Award for Poetry. In 2011 she edited, *The Spoken Word Workbook: inspiration from poets who teach*. She has 2 Spoken Word CDs and 4 award-winning VideoPoems and she is featured in the half hour documentary *Heart of a Poet* for Bravo!TV. In 2009 CBC called her one of the Top 10 Poets in Canada. In 2003 she won the USA Heavyweight title (Bumbershoot). In 2006 The National Slam (Can) awarded her Poet of Honour. In 1989 she attended Naropa (Jack Kerouac School of Disembodied Poetics) in Boulder, Colorado.

11) Daniel Zampanelli, b. 1985

Daniel Zomparelli is the editor of *Poetry Is Dead* magazine. His first book of poems, *Davie Street Translations*, was published in the Spring of 2012 from Talonbooks.

U.K.

1) Rachel Amey, b. 1970

Rachel is a writer and performer based in Edinburgh, Scotland. She is also many other things. She creates solo pieces for the stage, as well as poetry for spoken word performances, and has been published in anthologies and journals. She strives to make connections between our everyday lives and the other- working with politics, love, and laughter.

2) Jay Bernard, b. 1988

Jay Bernard was born in London and studied English at Oxford. She won the London Respect Slam (2004) and is the recipient of a Foyle Young Poets award (2005). Her first pamphlet *Your Sign is Cuckoo, Girl* (2008) was the Poetry Book Society's pamphlet choice for summer that year. She was the 2012 writer-in-residence at the Arts House and National University of Singapore. She has read at festivals such as Queer Up North, Homotopia and the National Gallery's queer "Iconic" season.

3) Dominic Berry, b. 1979

2012 has seen Dominic perform poetry on UK CBeebies 'Rhyme Rocket' and Channel 4's 'My Daughter The Teenage Nudist.' He is currently recording his poetry for use in a new BBC2 documentary about the NHS. He is winner of New York's infamous Nuyorican Poetry Cafe Slam (June 2011) and Manchester Literature Festival's Superheroes of Slam (Oct 2009).

4) Jackie Hagan, b. 1981

Jackie Hagan is a stand-up comic and performance poet who looks like an angry flea market. She delivers creativity-for-well-being projects for people with learning disabilities and mental health issues. When she was a child, her mother told her that her entire family was immortal because they'd be chosen specifically by a local magician... "The Little that Tells a Story" was first published in *The Wisdom of the Jumble Sale*, by Flapjack Press, 2010; "What We All Know" was first published in *Asylum Magazine*, 2012.

5) Rachel Jury, b. 1968

Rachel studied acting at East 15 Acting School, after which she has done a little less acting but a lot more writing, directing and producing. Rachel is in development with her first musical, *The Gates*, her second, *Miss Smith*, and her third, *Music of Strangers* premiered in October, 2012. She, also, is the Artistic Director for the cross-artform organisation conFAB. Rachel has performed her poetry at a variety of locations across Britain and Europe, from Brighton to Dundee to Dublin. Her poems and short stories have been published in: *Chameleon, Nomad, Cutting Teeth, Citizen 32, Poetry Scotland, The Gay Read, Hidden City, Mookychick* and her collection of poetry, *Laughin' Lesbians Vol 1*. In 2006 she received the Jackie Forster Memorial Award for Culture, Pride Awards, for outstanding contribution to culture in Scotland.

6) Adam Lowe, b. 1985

Adam Lowe is a writer, publisher and producer from Leeds, UK. His pamphlet *Precocious* was a reader nomination for the *Guardian* First Book Award. Adam was Yorkshire's Olympic poet in 2012, and as a result, he wrote a poem for display in the Olympic Park. His novella *Troglodyte Rose* was a finalist for a Lambda Literary Award. You can find him at adam-lowe.com.

7) Rosie Lugosi, b. 1960

Born in London to a runaway teenager, Rosie has always been a cuckoo in the nest. She is an eclectic writer and performer, ranging from singing in Gothband The March Violets to her alter-ego Rosie Lugosi, twisted cabaret chanteuse, electrifying performance poet and emcee. Rosie has five solo collections of poetry and her award-winning short stories, poems and essays have been widely anthologised. Her debut novel *The Palaceof Curiosities* is being published in March 2013 by Harper Collins. In 2009 she was diagnosed with throat cancer. The experience inspired the poems in her new collection, 'Everything Must Go' (Holland Park Press 2012). "Queer Thanksgiving" was first published in 'Things I Did While I was Dead', Flapjack Press, Manchester (UK), 2010; Dignity - published in 'Everything Must Go', Holland Park Press, London (UK), 2012.

8) Katherine McMahon, b. 1988

Katherine McMahon lives in Edinburgh, Scotland, where she performs widely, and helps to run Inky Fingers - a grassroots spoken word collective with an emphasis on creating a welcoming space for new voices. Her first pamphlet, which is paired with an album in
collaboration with musician/sound designer Fiona Keenan, is in print through Scottish performance poetry publishing collective Stewed Rhubarb. She also likes fighting heteronormativity, baking elaborate desserts, swimming in unlikely places, and growing things.

9) Colin McGuire, b. 1982

A thin 29 year old Glaswegian man, touch giddy in the head, sometimes poet of mangled form and dirty prose, sporadic drummer, drunk grammarian, waffler, painter using crayons, lover, hater, learner, teacher, pedestrian, provocateur, wanderer, confronter of shadows, irritating whine. He has read widely in Scotland and England. Produced a collection of poetry and short stories - *Riddle With Errors* - and is currently writing another for release by Red Squirrel Press in late 2013.

10) Steph Pike, b. 1967

Steph Pike is a performance poet and political activist. She has performed extensively across the UK and has been published in several anthologies. Her first collection of poetry, *Full of the Deep Bits*, was published in 2010. Her poetry is urgent, topical and eloquent and combines a militant mind with a penetrating eye for beauty.

11) Olumide Popoola, b. 1975

London-based Nigerian-German Olumide Popoola presents internationally as author, speaker and performer. Her publications include essays, poetry, short stories the novella *this is not about sadness*, the play *Also by Mail*, as well as recordings in collaboration with musicians. She is a PhD candidate in creative writing at the University of East London and the recipient of the May Ayim award (lyric). www.olumidepopoola.com

12) Gerry Potter, b. 1962

Gerry Potter is a poet of his history and futures. On a mission to write ten poetry books in ten years. book four is *Fifty*, which is a documentation of his HIV/HepC diagnosis. No stranger to controversy and the causes of controversy, Creator and destroyer of the gingham diva Chloe Poems. "The Soldiering of Soldiering On" was first published in *Flapjack*, 2010; "Cake" was first published in *Flapjack*, 2011; "Copse and Robbers" was first published in *Flapjack*, 2012.

13) Amir Rabiyah, b. 1978

Amir Rabiyah was born in London, England and currently lives in Oakland, California. His work has been featured in *Mizna, 580 Split, Left Turn Magazine, Gender Outlaws: The Next Generation, Collective Brightness: LGBTIQ Poets on Faith, Religion and Spirituality*, the Asian American Literary Review and more. He was a poetry finalist in the Enizagam 2012 Literary Award. He is currently working on a novel-in-poems, *The Disappeared*. "The Tightest Lines" was firs published in *580 Split*. www.amirrabiyah.com

14) Ian Iqbal Rashid, b. 1964

Ian Iqbal Rashid is an award-winning poet and filmmaker. Of Muslim Indian origin, he was born in Tanzania, grew up in Toronto and now lives in London. Poetry collections include "Black Markets, White Boyfriends (and Other Acts of Elision)" and "The Heat Yesterday." His cinema work includes the feature films *Touch of Pink* and *How She Move*. He has won many prizes for his work, including the Aga Khan Award for Excellence in the Arts and The Writers Guild of England Award for best writing for a television series (BBC's This Life). "Another Country" was first published in 1991 in Black Markets, White Boyfriends (and Other Acts of Elision), TSAR Press, Toronto.

15) Dorothea Smartt, b. 1963

'Brit-born-Bajan-international' is a respected poet, live artist, and literary activist. A recipient of an Arts Council England One-to-One award, and a former Attached Live Artist at London's Institute of Contemporary Art, she has held national and international residencies. She has two collections with Peepal Tree Press, *Connecting Medium* and *Ship Shape*, is currently co-director of their Inscribe Writer Development Programme, and Sable Litmag's Associate Poetry Editor. She was also guest co-editor of Sable's 2006 international LGBTQ issue, and is currently co-editing their 2014 LGBTQI issue. She has read on, chaired and convened several panels at academic conferences in the UK, Europe and the USA, and delivered the keynote address at the 2013 Frank Collymore Literary Endowment Award [Barbados]. "gambien sting" was first published in *Connecting Medium*, Peepal Tree Press, Leeds, 2001. "Eclipse Over Barbados" was first published in *Ship Shape*, Peepal Tree Press, Leeds, 2008.

16) Rod Tame, b. 1975

Rod Tame was born in the Garden of England that is Kent. Despite being both gay and a sci-fi geek, he somehow survived. He now lives in the urban jungle that is Manchester and his first collection *Strange World Odd Person* is coming out May 2013. "Renaissance Man" was previously published in The Ugly Tree #20/Vol. 7:2, 2009 and Best of Manchester Poets, Volume 1, 2010; "St. George is Cross" was first published in Best of Manchester Poets Volume 2, 2011.

17) Paula Varjack, b. 1978

Paula Varjack is a writer and performance artist. She has toured internationally for the last three years, in a variety of locations, from art galleries and cabaret nights to poetry slams. In 2009, her first solo show, *Kiss and Tell*, premiered at Hau Zwei as part of the Berlin 100 Degrees Theatre festival. In 2010, she was one of the nine artists in residence for the E.U. funded Poetry Slam Days project, creating a multilingual show, *Smoke and Mirrors*, which went on tour to over twenty European cities. She is currently developing her second solo show, *The Anti-Social Network*, exploring themes of socializing, social media, and the anxieties that can be present in both.

18) Sophia Walker, b. 1985

Sophia Walker is an Edinburgh-based slam poet and teaching artist. She won the 2012 Poetry Olympics, the 2012 Edinburgh International Book Festival Improv Slam and came in third at Capturing Fire. Her work has aired on radio stations in the UK, the US, Italy, Ireland, Singapore, Vietnam and India. In 2009, she represented Scotland at the UK Slam Championships. She is currently working on her first solo show, *Around the World in 18 Mistakes*, which will premiere at the 2013 Edinburgh Fringe. When not on tour across the UK and Europe, she works as a mental health worker in a psychiatric hospital.

19) Max Wallis, b. 1989

Max Wallis is a model @ Models 1. His debut pamphlet, *Modern Love*, has been shortlisted for the Polari First Book Prize 2012. It is available from Amazon and other retailers. Follow him @maxrobertwallis.